REVUE AFRICAINE DES SCIENCES JURIDIQUES

AFRICAN JOURNAL OF LAW

UNIVERSITÉ DE YAOUNDÉ II

SCIENTIA ARTES INGENIUM

THE UNIVERSITY OF YAOUNDÉ II

NUMÉRO SPÉCIAL/2015

UNE PUBLICATION DE L'UNIVERSITÉ DE YAOUNDÉ II

Faculté des Sciences Juridiques et Politiques

RASJ

L'Harmattan

UNIVERSITÉ DE YAOUNDÉ II

UNIVERSITY OF YAOUNDF II

FACULTÉ DES SCIENCES JURIDIQUES FT POLITIQUES

FACULTY OF LAWS AND POLITICAL SCIENCES

ORGANISATION DE LA REVUE AFRICAINE DE SCIENCES JURIDIQUES

5-7, rue de l'Ecole-Polytechnique, 75005 Paris

http://www.harmattan.fr
diffusion.harmattan@wanadoo.fr
harmattan1@wanadoo.fr

ISBN : 978-2-343-08332-2
EAN : 9782343083322

SOMMAIRE

ENHANCING THE EFFECTIVE AND SUSTAINABLE ENJOYMENT OF THE RIGHT TO WATER UNDER CAMEROONIAN LAW*

Christopher F. TAMASANG**

1. Introduction

1.1. Background and rationale

Generally speaking, water, which is one of the tangible natural resources the world over, features as the most indispensable. The well known adage, "water is life" confirms such a general conception. A global good in essence, 17 percent of humankind (1.5 billion people) has no access to clean water, 2.6 billion people do not enjoy sanitation facilities and 5000 children die every day contaminated by water.[1] The African continent, said to be rich in natural resources, water inclusive, do face the hydrological stress on a somewhat serious note. Statistics point to the fact that 25 percent of contemporary African population come under water stress while 69 percent live in relative abundance.[2] Unfortunately, this relative abundance does not take into consideration such other factors as portability, accessibility as well as quality for health. There have been considerable efforts at the international level between 1990 and 2000 to improve on this situation. This notwithstanding, only 62 percent of

---

* This article is a revised paper which the author presented during a workshop held in Geneva on water reforms organised by the International Environmental Law Research Centre in Geneva.

** Ph.D (Environmental Law), Senior Lecturer, Faculty of Laws and Political Science, University of Yaounde II - Soa, Cameroon, International consultant. Email : funwie2001@yahoo.fr **or** kittstamasangf@gmail.com

[1] See UNDP (2006), Human Development Report- Beyond scarcity : Power, Poverty and the Global Water Crisis, New York, p v.

[2] Vorosmarty,C.J. *et al* (2005), Geospatial indicators of emerging water stress : An application to Africa, Ambio,34(3), in ; Bates, B.C., Kunderzewicz,S. Wu and J. P. Palutikof (ed) (2008), Climate change and water, technical document no 7, IPCC, Geneva, p 94

African population, that of Cameroon not excluded, had access to better water conditions.[3] What is more? It is projected that by 2025 many more people will be subjected to the water stress.[4] One may want to add that the climate change phenomenon is likely to aggravate the water stress situation if a strong and promising global legal regime on the climate change saga is not adopted and put into immediate implementation. In fact, the above picture justifies the requirement for the right to water and explains why the right to water is increasingly recognized, albeit in a general, diverse and disjointed manner, at the global, regional and national level as a fundamental and inalienable right of the human person which states are called upon to recognize and enforce in their internal legal order with the cooperation of the international community.

Forming part of economic and social rights, the right to water means that everyone without discrimination, must have access to water in quality and quantity sufficient to meet his/her basic needs. The right to water consists in the provision of sufficient, physically accessible and at an affordable cost, clean and quality water acceptable for personal and domestic use of everyone.[5] The right to water has also been defined as the right of everyone regardless of his economic standard, to possess a minimum quantity of water of good quality which is sufficient for his life and health.[6] Consequently, rights linked to water are those rights enabling the use of a certain amount or quantity of water rather than rights of ownership of the resource itself. However, it is important to underscore at the outset of this debate that the right to water which is limited to personal and domestic uses exclude water for agricultural, industrial and commercial activities. Similarly, it does not concern additional water from rainfall for instance, which by its very nature has a

---

[3] OMS/UNICEF (2000), in ; Bates, B.C., Kunderzewicz, S. Wu and J.P.Palutikof (ed), *ibid.*

[4] Bates, B. C., Kunderzewicz, S. Wu and J. P. Palutikof, *ibid*, at p 96

[5] United Nations Committee on Economic, Social and Cultural Rights, The Right to Water, General Comment, No. 15 ; UN DOC. E/C.123/11, 29th Session, (2002).

[6] Smets, H. (2000), Le Droit à L'eau.www.academie-eau.org, p. 1.

low marginal utility.[7] In fact, water quantity for fundamental needs is a human right while additional quantity of water is hardly guaranteed and may not be accessible to marginalized people.[8] Finally, the right to water may not imply gratuitous provision of water or any quantity of it.

The right to water is also of capital importance in the ongoing battle against poverty.[9] In this regard, it relates more to the social categories of poor or vulnerable people in the rural areas but also those in the urban setting as well. Indeed, the poor are those most affected or essentially deprived of the right to portable water basically as a result of their economic and physical inaccessibility.[10]

In spite of the importance of the right to water enunciated at the national and international levels, a cross-section of the population continues to be deprived of such right in Cameroon. Within the territorial boundaries of a sovereign state, water is a *res communis* or *res nullius* at least as far as portable water is concerned. In fact, portable water is rare in Cameroon. Access to portable water remains a nightmare to the local population of the rural areas, indigenous people[11] as well as

---

[7] At this moment in the history of humankind where environmental challenges, air pollution in particular is increasing by the day, the quality of rain water is more and more questionable and its effect on the human system may be dangerous. Water from acid rain (an increasing environmental challenge) may even be more disastrous to human life.

[8] Smets, H., *op cit*, note 6, p 10

[9] See for example, FAO, World Food Day ; Water : Source of Food Security (2005). See also the Millennium Development Goals, in particular, Goal 1.

[10] *Ibid.*

[11] Indigenous peoples as a minority group have been identified across different regions of the world and have been clearly distinguished from local people and other minority groups not from a linguistic perspective but from cultural, social and other tenets. Indigenous people have generally been considered by art 1 (a) and (b) of Convention on Indigenous and Tribal Peoples, 1989, to be :

-Tribal people in independent countries whose social, cultural and economic conditions distinguish them from other sections of the national community and whose status is regulated wholly or partially by their own customs or traditions or by special laws or regulations ;

those urban and semi-urban populations in Cameroon with women and children bearing the grunts. Atemengue, J. N.[12] documents that of 11000 villages in Cameroon, only 5000 have access to more or less portable water and adds that of the 15 million people, only 3 million have direct access to more or less portable water. Today, three years after the above author's estimates, the situation is certainly more critical as census results[13] put Cameroon at 19.406.100 people, an increase of close to 4.5 million inhabitants not matched by a proportionate increase in the provision for portable water.

Cameroon is one African country with territorial pieces of legislation in general and water reform legislation in particular. This is explained by the fact that the country operates two systems of laws ; to wit, the Common Law and the Civil Law.[14] This bi-jural character of Cameroon

-Peoples in independent countries who are regarded as indigenous on account of their descent from the populations which inhabited the country, or a geographical region to which the country belongs, at the time of conquest or colonization or the establishment of present state boundaries and who, irrespective of their legal status, retain some or all of their own social, economic, cultural and political institutions. In Cameroon, they have been identified as the pygmies and the Mbororos. The current debate on their rights as a minority and marginalised people, has not excluded their right to water. A majority of municipal laws of countries of the world, Cameroon inclusive, have not clearly recognize the rights of indigenous people as a marginalised minority notwithstanding the UN Declaration of 2007 calling upon states to recognize the rights of indigenous people. For an exhaustive catalogue of the rights of indigenous people at the global level, see Convention 169 of the International Labour Organisation, which many African countries in general and Cameroon in particular, have signed but have not ratified.

[12] (2008), La Nature Juridique de l'eau, " Patrimoine Commun de la Nation", au Cameroun, Cahiers Juridiques et Politiques, Revue de la Faculté des Sciences Juridiques et Politique, Université de Ngaoundere,Vol 1, p 242.

[13] See Xinhua, available at http ://www.google.fr/search ?hl=fr&source=hp8q=INS-Cameroun8meta= visited on 25/09/2011

[14] It may be mentioned here that the administration of what is today Cameroon, began with the Germans (1896-1916). After having been defeated during the First World War by France and Britain, these two powers took over the territory from the Germans and partitioned the same between themselves. This was in the Treaty of Versailles in 1919. From then, Cameroon was under the Mandate System until 1945. Thereafter, the country became a Trust territory under the Trusteeship System of the United

is a result of two major world cultures inherited from Britain and France when the country came under the administration of these great powers. The bi-jural nature which m akes for the application of the Common Law in the English speaking Regions and the Civil Law[15] in the French speaking Regions of the country is gradually being mitigated since independence in 1961, by the harmonization of legal reforms across the country.[16] One of such harmonisation reforms in the area of environmental law is in water law,[17] although some writers[18] take the view that water issues as placed under land law, ought to assume a specific legal regime which should be reconstructed in Cameroon.

1.2. Theoretical/conceptual framework and methodology to the study

This paper is underpinned by the theory of rights. A good number of writers[19] have dealt with the question of rights distinguishing between natural/human rights, liberty rights, immunity, claimed rights, and

---

Nations. For more on this, see Tamasang, C. F. (2008), Sustainable Development : Some Reflections with regard to the new Constitutional dispensation in Cameroon, The African Law Review, vol 5, No 1, FSJP, University of Yaounde II- Soa, Cameroon, p 147

[15] For quite a long time after independence, that is, before the harmonization of water legislation, the Civil Code was applicable in Former East Cameroon. In particular, article 714 provides that " *il est des choses qui n'appartient a personne et dont l'usage est commun a tous. Des lois de police règlement la manière d'en jouir*". Understandly, reference is made to water. For a detailled development on the subject, see Cassin, R. et al (2003-2004), *Etudes et documents du Conseil d'Etat : L'eau et son droit, Conseil d'état, Paris*, p 52.

[16] There are many other areas where harmonisation of legal reforms has already taken place such as criminal law, land law, labour law, environmental law, business laws, criminal procedure, and investment law, just to name these few.

[17] Until fairly recently, water law was closely related to property or land law but because of its unique features (mobility, variation from season to season, location, simultaneously use by many users), it has become the province of modern environmental law.

[18]Notably, Atemengue, J.N. *op cit*, p 257

[19] See for instance, Follesdal A. & Maliks R. (2014) (Editors), Kantian Theory and Human Rights, Routledge, (210 pges) ;

power. This paper builds on the Hohfeldian[20] first order jural relations where a right which is normatively protected by the state must not be interfered with by whosoever. It equates such a right to a human right as posited by many leading legal philosophers such as Jeremy Bentham, H.L.A. Hart, Emmanuel Kant and others. There is therefore a correlative duty to ensure the enjoyment of such a right.

The methodology to this study consisted in the collection of data and in the treatment of such data. Secondary data was gathered through desk research and these included consulting existing literature on the subject. Primary data was gathered from field visits which elicited information on the number of people seeking connection to portable water and in the process, visited on several occasions, *Camerounaise des Eaux* billing and payment centres in the city of Yaounde ; from statutory instruments and also from court decisions. In treating these categories of data, we utilised the contents approach to critically analyse the information from the field visits, the statutory instruments, and court decisions to find out how they enhance the protection of human rights in the theories of rights as propounded by Bentham and Hohfeld and in relation to the protection afforded to the sustainable enjoyment of the right to water.

From the foregoing, it is therefore important to examine the sources of the right to water under Cameroonian law ; the nature of the right to water ; the contents of the right to water ; national mechanisms for enhancing and enforcing the right to water ; the hurdles or challenges, as well as some reform proposals to the effective and sustainable enjoyment of the right to water.

2. The Prescriptions on the Right to Water under Cameroonian law

The right to water has been recognized in international as well as in national legal instruments.

---

[20] See generally for exposition and analysis of Holfeldian Theory of Rights, for instance, Lazarev, N. (2005), Hohfeld's Analysis of Rights : An Essential Approach to a Conceptual and Practical Understanding of the Nature of Rights, Murdoch University Journal of Law, Murdoch.

2.1. International Legal Instruments

At the international level, two categories of legal instruments are discernible ; to wit : non-conventional and conventional instruments. It must be mentioned, however, that recognition of the right to water in these instruments is either explicit or implicit and in a general rather than a specific context.

2.1.1. Non-conventional or Non-binding Sources

The water crisis and its strategic importance have probably aroused the concern of the international community. In attempting to respond to the crisis, legal paradigms have been crafted at the international level in the direction of sustainably managing the *res publica* and to ensure that basic needs of the people of the world are met both of the present and future generations. In this regard therefore, one can decipher quite a litany of international legal instruments albeit non-binding in character, which provide for the right to water in a scattered and disjointed way as a fundamental right of the human person. The Universal Declaration of Human Rights[21] for instance, recognizes a wide range of social, economic and civil rights[22] which are today inextricably linked to the right to water.

The genesis of global interest to water as indispensable for human wellbeing attracted international concern in Stockholm with the Stockholm Declaration, 1972. The Declaration recognizes the fundamental right to 'an environmental of quality that permits a life of dignity and well-being.'[23] That global instrument adds that '[t]he natural

[21] The Universal Declaration of Human Rights was adapted by the General Assembly of the United Nations on 10th December 1948.

[22] Some of such rights include the right to life, the right to health, the right to work, the right to housing, the right to feeding, the right to adequate standard of living, just to mention these few.

[23] See Principle 1 of the Declaration which provides that," Man has the fundamental right to freedom, equality and adequate conditions of life, in an environment of quality... and he bears a solemn responsibility to protect and improve the environment.

resources of the earth including ...water...must be safeguarded for the benefit of the present and future generations...'[24]

By the mid-1970s, the UN began to take particular interest in water perhaps because of its increasing scarcity and degrading quality. In Mal del Plata in Argentina, a Declaration was made in 1977 sanctioning the end of the UN Conference on Water. In its preamble, firm commitments were taken to safeguard water resources and enhance the right to water by all human beings across the globe stating that all people have the right to water in quantities and of a quality equal to their basic needs.[25]

About one and a half decades after Mal del Plata, legal instruments relating to general environmental protection still under the auspices of the UN provided for the right to water within the context of the rights of the person. This was in the Agenda 21 Programme of Action[26] following the United Nations Conference on Environment and Development held in Rio de Janeiro in 1992. In the same year, a Declaration was adopted in Dublin at the end of the International Conference on Water and Development. That Declaration underscored the right to water as the cornerstone of development. The Dublin Statement which clearly adopts a holistic or comprehensive and multidisciplinary approach ranging from environmental, social, political and economic perspectives[27], states explicitly with regard to the human right to water that 'it is vital to recognize first the basic right of all human beings to have access to clean water and sanitation at an affordable price'[28]

---

[24] See Principle 2 which provides on its part that "... air, water, land, flora and fauna and especially representative samples of natural ecosystems must be safeguarded for the benefit of present and future generations through careful planning or management, as appropriate."

[25] See Report of the United Nations Water Conference, Preamble, Mar Del Plata, March 14-25, 1977. No E77II A 12, United Nations Publications, N .Y.

[26] Agenda 21 is a blueprint for the implementation of the Rio outcomes and for the enhancement of sustainable development. See with regard to water, paragraph 18.47.

[27] For a detailed exploration of the principles, see Fitzmaurice, M. (2007), The Human Right to Water, 18 Fordham Environmental Law Review 587 at p 546

[28] See Principle 4.

Again, from a general perspective, a Programme of Action[29] was adopted in the report of the International Conference on Population and Development held in Cairo in September 1994 which mentioned the right to water. Also within a general environmental context, the World Summit on Sustainable Development which held in Johannesburg in 2002[30] mentioned in the Johannesburg Declaration and Plan of Action that a pertinent crisis facing mankind today is the right of access to water and that governments from around the world should adopt appropriate measure of ensuring that this right is available to all citizens.

The most ambitious of the non-conventional instruments is undoubtedly the Millennium Declaration adopted by the General Assembly of the United Nations[31] after the Millennium Summit in New York. Their objectives are expressed in a number of chapters. The following commitment was taken :

> ...To reduce to half by 2015 the proportion of the world's population whose income is less than a dollar per day and that of people suffering from hunger, and to reduce to half within the same period, the proportion of people who have no access to portable water or who lack the means to procure it.[32]

Humanity is barely a year away from the D-year and the question for which one may be eager for an answer is whether such commitment is going to be met given that the proportion of people without access to portable water is on the rise or to say the least, is unlikely to be reduced to half by 2015 as there are more indicators that access to water is more and more difficult compounded by the impact of climate change.

It was also firmly promised in the same Declaration, to put an end to the irrational exploitation of water resources by formulating strategies at the regional, national and local levels to enable the guarantee of equitable

[29] See principle 2.
[30] See U.N.Doc. A/CONF.199/20
[31] See Resolution 55/22 of August 2002.
[32] See Chapter III on Development and Poverty Elimination.

access and adequate provision.[33] To date, how many African countries have mounted strategies to meet the MDG commitments with respect to access to portable water? Not many and prove is that the water stress is on the increase.

Cameroon has participated in most, if not all of the above international meetings and has appended her signature to the legal instruments translating the intentions of the government to ensure an effective and sustainable enjoyment of the right to water. It must be mentioned, however, that the instruments highlighted above generally have a non-binding legal status in international law.[34] States can therefore, hardly be obliged to comply with or enforced them even if they have signed them. They are usually referred to as soft law instruments. But we have argued that compliance with and enforcement of international legal instruments in general is much a matter of political will of the parties taking the commitment or expressing their wishes.[35] We used the Central African Sub-region as a barometer to test the veracity of this position and demonstrated that in the last ten years, the Central African leaders have relied heavily on soft law instruments (Declarations for instance) to protect the Congo Basin forest and other natural resources, water inclusive.[36]

---

[33] See Chapter IV entitled : Protecting our Common Environment.

[34] Hunter D., J. Salzman, and D. Zaelke, International Environmental Law, Foundation Press, New York, 1998, pp. 258-64.

[35] See Tamasang, C.F. (2011), Legislation for Sustainable Forest Management in the Central African Sub-Region : What Prospects for Effective Implementation ? in, Paddock, L. et al (editors), Compliance and Enforcement in Environmental Law : Towards a more Effective Implementation, IUCN Academy of Environmental Law series, Edward Elgar Publishing Inc, Cheltham, pp 501-519.

[36] *Ibid.* It is however believed by some people that the success in the effective implementation of the Yaounde Declaration is grounded on the Resolution of the General Assembly of United Nations (Resolution 54/314 of February 2000) supporting the adoption of the Yaounde Declaration and urging the international community to give it a wide recognition. But it must be noted that such a Resolution did not and cannot add any strength to the soft law instrument for it is itself a soft law instrument. If the General Assembly Resolution accounted in any way to the effective implementation of the Declaration, it was a moral booster.

Besides, the proliferation of these instruments at the regional and global level is the fact that the right to water is in a way a universally recognized right of the human person even if it fits itself into a large spectrum of matters falling within the ambit or province of the environment and related disciplines.

2.1.2. Conventional Legal Instruments

a) At the Global Level

At the international level, traditional sources (conventions, treaties, protocols, charters, Pacts, and covenants) of the right to water feature either explicitly or implicitly in the legal instruments. Firstly, express reference to the right to water has been made in the Convention on the Elimination of All Forms of Discrimination against Women (CEDAW).[37] It is therein provided that "State parties…shall ensure to women the right…to enjoy adequate living conditions, particularly in relation to housing, sanitation, electricity and water supply.[38]

Explicit reference to the right to water is equally made in the Convention on the Rights of the Child.[39] This Convention provides with regard to the right of the child to water that :

> State parties recognize the right of the child to the enjoyment of the highest attainable standard of health…and pursue full implementation of this right and shall take appropriate measure…through the provision of clean drinking water…[40]

The two Conventions just mentioned above appear discriminatory in addressing questions relating to the right to water as emphasis is made only on women and children. The reason may be simple. Women and children have generally been regarded as vulnerable social classes but also marginalised groups in decision making processes. This probably also

---

[37] The Convention on the Elimination of All Forms of Discrimination against Women was adopted by the General Assembly Resolution 34/180 of 8th December 1979.

[38] See Article 4(2) (h).

[39] The Convention on the Rights of the Child was adopted by General Assembly Resolution 44/25 of 20th November 1989.

[40] See Article 24(1), (2) (c).

explains why the international community has had to consider a separate legally binding instrument for them. Noting this with keen interest, the World Bank posits that women [and children][41] should be involved in decisions relating to water management as they are the managers of water in their domestic circles.[42] While we submit to such an authoritative view, we suggest that the involvement in decision making should not be limited to women but extended to children as they are the major collectors of water for domestic use in the developing countries, Cameroon inclusive.

Explicit reference to the right to water as a fundamental right of the human person had long been made but more so within the context of humanitarian law. The Geneva Convention of 1949[43] and its Additional Protocols II of 1977[44] on the treatment of prisoners of war, and on the protection of victims of non-international armed conflict, respectively, have clearly imposed on states the obligation to implement the right to water even during war situations.

In fact, there are several Conventional legal instruments at the global level alluding to the right to water but with differing weight of obligations on the state parties. The New York Convention of 1997, for instance, on the use of International Waters for purposes other than Navigation is contented with a simple invitation of states to be particularly diligent when it concerns the satisfaction of basic needs of their respective population.[45] This does not seem to impose succinct and concrete obligations on state parties. On the contrary, we find that the three Conventions and Protocols just discussed above actually provide for clear and firm obligations on the part of states as concerns the right to water. The question now is whether these legal obligations have been translated to practical realities on the ground by various countries.

---

[41] Emphasis is mine

[42] Banque Mondial (1993), Gestion des Ressources en Eau : Document de Politique Générale de la Banque Mondiale, Washington, D.C. p 17

[43] See Articles 20, 26, 29 and 46.

[44] See Articles 5 and 14.

[45] See Article 10, paragraph 2.

In the case of Cameroon, it may be important to note that she has signed and ratified the above Conventions.[46] It is debatable whether Cameroon operates a single or two-step procedure[47] in relation to the application of international legal instruments. As far as fundamental rights are concerned, it may be argued that the country is of the monist regime as matters relating to fundamental rights are set out in the Constitution which is applicable without necessarily domesticating the provisions of the international legal instrument by way of a legislative Act. But in other areas, notably natural resources, a legislative Act must be taken ; rendering the dualist argument for Cameroon a strong one. This implies that the right to water contained in these instruments is recognised in Cameroon if one were to go by its dualist character. But if the right to water is a related right to the right to life, to health etc, then of course, it is still recognized by reason of its monist conception. As to whether this right is enjoyed by the population is quite another question which shall be examined later in this paper. But a question which begs for answer at this juncture is whether the right must be explicit for it to impose obligations.

There are also implicit references to the right to water at the global level which impose implied obligations. The most important in this regard is the International Covenant on Economic, Social and Cultural Rights (ICESCR).[48] This Covenant recognises the economic and social rights of the human person to an adequate standard of living, to sufficient feeding and a right to health. The right to water is an integral

---

[46] Convention on the Elimination of All Forms of Discrimination against Women was ratified on 15th July 1988 by Law No. 88/11 ; Convention on the Rights of the Child ratified on 17th July 1991, by Law No. 91/006 and the Geneva Convention ratified on 16th September 1963 ; Protocol II of 1977 ratified on 16th March 1984.

[47] The two-step procedure as opposed to the single step procedure (the monist approach) is one where signature of an international legal instrument and ratification does not suffice for it to be applicable in the home or signatory country. Signature and ratification must be followed by domestication process within the internal legal order which then injects the legal instrument's provision into the internal legal order making it to become hard domestic law. It is usually referred to as the 'dualist approach'.

[48] Cameroon ratified the Covenant on Economic, Social and Cultural Rights on 24th June 1984

part of these rights universally recognised or which could be considered as indispensable components to the enjoyment of existing social and economic rights.

Within the framework of implementation of the Covenant, the UN Committee on Economic, Social and cultural Rights recognizes[49] that access to water is a fundamental right as contained in Article (11) (1) of the ICESCR. However, a more detailed coverage is afforded by the same Committee in its General Comment No. 15[50] on the right to water. It defines the right to water, delimits its boundaries and spells out the obligations which are expected from states in this regard. It should be noted that provisions of the Committee are not binding as the status of General Comment has been considered as soft law and hence non-binding on states.[51] However, there is no doubt that its provisions are insightful to the understanding and enforcement of the right to water.

Implicit reference to the right to water has also been made by the International Covenant on Civil and Political Rights.[52] The Covenant recognizes the right to life.[53] The right to life cannot be enjoyed without the right to water. The right to water is, therefore, a prerequisite for the enjoyment of the right to life. Although implicit, the right to life and hence the right to water are recognized in Cameroon by dint of the fact that the Covenant on Civil and Political Rights has been ratified[54] by Cameroon.

b) At the Regional Level :

The discussion here will be limited to the African continent for obvious reasons. Cameroon is in the African continent and is often referred to as Africa in miniature. Explicit reference to the right to water

---

[49] General Comment, No. 6

[50] See *Supra*, Note 5

[51] *Supra*, Note 33

[52] The International Covenant on Civil and Political Rights was adopted by the United Nations General Assembly Resolution 2200A (XXI) of 16th December 1966

[53] Article 6

[54] The Covenant on Civil and Political Rights was ratified on 12th June 1984.

in African continental instruments is found in the African Charter on the Rights and Welfare of the Child.[55] The Charter stipulates that "State parties to the present Charter...shall ensure the provision of adequate nutrition and safe drinking water..."[56] The fact that Cameroon has also signed and ratified[57] this charter implies that the right to water of the Cameroonian child is recognized under Cameroonian law as a matter of principle. One may want to know if such right of the African child is really enforced in the Cameroonian municipal law. Such a worry would be addressed subsequently.

Another legal instrument at the African continental level with explicit reference to the right to water is the revised African Convention on Conservation of Nature and Natural Resources now referred to as the Maputo Convention.[58] It is therein provided that state parties shall endeavour to guarantee to the population a sufficient and continuous flow of clean water.[59] Although this convention is not yet in force, we may applaud the initiative of having given a place to the right to water in the continent. In fact, given this reason together with the wide ambit of the Convention, we take the view that the Maputo Convention is a framework Convention for Africa although not labelled as such.[60]

---

[55] OAU DOC. CAB/LEG/24.9/49 (1990).

[56] See Article 14(1) (2) (c).

[57] Cameroon ratified the African Charter on the Rights and Welfare of the Child on December 17, 2004.

[58] Signed by 33 states in Maputo in 2003, this Convention has not yet entered into force. The original Convention was signed in Algiers in 1968. Unfortunately, it was short of a number of issues which were included in the revised version in 2003. These include a clear adherence to global multilateral environmental agreements (MEAs) ; modern approach to nature conservation ; clear reflection of African realities by way of cultural, traditional and indigenous concerns ; greater consideration to the poverty-environment nexus ; introduction of stronger institutional mechanisms in particular the COP for dialogue and cooperation, and financial mechanisms ; etc. Such additions not only make the Convention complete but also render it a modern Convention.

[59] See Article 7(2)

[60] Framework Convention because it generally touches on every aspect of contemporary African environment leaving it a challenge to the continent's legislators to eventually craft continental legislations by way of Protocols, Covenants, Pacts, and others to address in details specific domains of the environment gathering inspiration, of course,

We may also note implicit reference to the right to water in the African Continent in the African Charter on Human and Peoples Rights[61] which protects the right to health[62] and the right to a clean environment.[63] In fact, some writers[64] have argued that drastically changing environmental and social factors make the issue of water as a human right more significant. As already argued with regard to global implicit references, the implementations of these rights also imply the recognition and enforcement of the right to water in the continent, Cameroon belonging to it.

2.2. National Prescriptions on the Right to Water

2.2.1. The Constitution

The Constitution of the Republic of Cameroon[65] does not explicitly provide for the right to water. However, it has a number of preambular provisions relating to economic and social rights.[66] Since it is admitted above that the right to water is an integral part of economic and social rights,[67] it could, therefore, be submitted that the Constitution makes implicit reference to the right to water through its provisions for economic and social rights. As an integral part of environmental rights,[68]

---

from the framework Convention. Whether a convention is framework legislation or not does not really depend on its being labeled as such. Rather, it should be deciphered from its scope and content. It is for this reason that we also opine that the Convention on Biodiversity 1992, albeit not titled as a framework convention, is indeed one.

[61] This Charter on Human and Peoples Rights was signed in 1986.

[62] See Article 16.

[63] See Article 24.

[64] Scanlon, J., A. Casar, and N. Noemi (2004), Water as a Human Right ?, IUCN , Gland and Cambridge, p 15.

[65] Law No. 2008/001 of 14 April to amend and supplement some provisions of Law No. 96/06 of 18th January 1996 to amend the Constitution of 02 June 1972.

[66] For instance, see paragraphs 4, 12, 18, 21 and 22.

[67] The South African Constitution of 8th May 1996 provides for the right to water as part of the lengthy list of economic and social rights. For more, see Gowlland-Gualtieri, A. (2007), South Africa's Water Law and Policy Framework : Implications for the Right to Water, IELRC Working Paper No 3, International Environmental Law Research Centre, Geneva, p 1-2.

[68] See *Supra*, Note 17.

the right to water has a comfortable foundation in the Constitutional provisions. It is provided in the preamble that every person has a right to a healthy environment, that the protection of the environment shall be the duty of every Cameroonian, and that the state shall ensure the protection and improvement of the environment.[69] Therefore, in this light, and in relation to the other lengthy economic and social rights enshrined in the Constitution, we can safely state that there is, in principle, an implicit commitment to protect and improve on the right to water.

2.2.2. The Water Code[70]

Just like the Constitution, earlier pieces of legislation on the environment have not made any express provision on the right to water. However, probably inspired by the Constitutional provision on the right to a healthy environment and the other bundle of economic and social rights, the Cameroonian legislator passed the Water Code within the respect of environmental management principles and public health protection. In it, it is expressly provided that water is a public good or utility which the state ensures its protection and management and facilitates access to all.[71] From this provision, one can venture to state that the Cameroonian Water legislation is both supply and demand driven. This means that the legislator considers that it is incumbent on the state to ensure the supply of water to the population and that this is driven by the increasing demand for portable water by the population in seeking to enjoy their right to water.[72] We can equally aver, reading

---

[69]Preambular paragraph 21. See also TAMASANG, C.F. (2008), Sustainable Development : Some Reflections with regard to the New Constitutional Dispensation in Cameroon. The African Law Review, Vol. 5, No. 1, FSJP, University of Yaounde II-Soa, pp. 152-153.

[70] Law No. 98/005 of 14th April 1998 to lay down the Water Code and its Enabling Statutes.

[71] See Article 2.

[72] There are legislations in other African countries which have been demand driven rather than supply driven or both. A glaring example is the South African Water legislation. For more, see Movik, S. and De Jong, F. (2011), Licence to Control :

through the code, that the Cameroonian Water legislator has envisaged the application of the public trust doctrine.[73] In addition, measures of protection are clearly spelled out in the Code[74] and violators come under heavy criminal sanctions[75] without prejudice to civil claims. To ensure conservation, protection and sustainable utilization, the Code institutes a National Water Committee,[76] an institution placed under the Ministry in charge of water resources. With the above as the major sources of the right to water in Cameroon, a question that further springs to mind is what is the nature of the right to water?

3. The Nature of the Right to Water in Cameroon

A crucial question here is whether the right to water which is, under normal circumstances, a human right, considered a specific right or has been treated as relating to or intricately intertwined with other rights under existing legislation. In dealing with this question, some writers[77] take the view that issues touching on water in Cameroon require a specific legal regime rather than being tied to other traditional legal regimes like land law or [environmental law].[78] As we have noted above,

---

Implications of introducing Administrative Water Use Rights in South Africa, 7/2 Law, Environment and Development Journal, London, New Delhi, p 70.

[73] The public trust doctrine owes its origin to the ancient Roman Empire. At that time, the doctrine rested primarily on the principle that certain resources like the air, seas, forests and water are of such capital importance to the people that it would be wholly unjustified to make them a subject of private ownership. When the doctrine was received in England, it was first limited only to certain traditional uses such as navigation, commerce, and fishing. Today, its application has been extended to all natural resources for public use and enjoyment. In America, the Supreme Court of California has also manifested its interest in the application of the doctrine to American ecological important lands, water among others. For details, see Tamasang, C.F. (2008), Community forest Management Entities as Effective Tools for local Level participation under Cameroonian Law : A Case Study of *Kilum/Ijim* Mountain Forest, PhD thesis, Faculty of laws and Political Science, University of Yaounde II-Soa, p. 4

[74] See Articles 4-7

[75] See Articles 19-20

[76] Article 26(1)

[77] Notably Atemengue, J.N., *Supra*, note 12, p 257.

[78] Emphasis is mine

Cameroon like many other countries of the world has not expressly provided for the right to water in its Constitution. This may be explained by the fact that only one traditional international binding instrument in the field of human rights[79] has made express provisions to the right to water from which countries could easily be inspired or be obliged upon signature and/or ratification. But, there again, we notice that the provision is more in connection with access without discrimination than right *per se*. So the right to water had only been treated as a health-related right until the Water Code of 1998 explicitly recognised access by all to water. But is this to be taken to mean that access to water is a human right in Cameroon? By the wordings of Article 2(1) of the Water Code ; "*L'eau est un bien du patrimoine national dont l'état assure la protection et la gestion et en facilite l'accès à tous.*"

From the provisions of the sub-section above, the state ensures protection and management of water but only facilitates rather than ensures or guarantees access to it by all Cameroonians. This interpretation of the vaguely worded provision of the law may lead one to a conclusion that access to water is not a human right on which citizens can rely to bring an action where access is denied or not enjoyed by the individual(s).

This kind of ambiguous provisions in the law may justify the need for a global Convention for water[80] which would emphasize on the human right character of the right to water so as to better protect, develop and ensure access and enjoyment of it. We may also subscribe to the argument by some writers[81] that the right "to" water envisaged as a fundamental human right different from the right "of" water which refers to the sovereign right of states over their territorial waters, to justify

---

[79] See *Supra*, Note 37.

[80] See Bär, R. (2004), Why we need an International Water Convention, Alliance Sud, Berne p. 4. See also Water As Human Right, Chapter 1 at http ://www.who.int/water sanitation health/rtwrev.pdf accessed on May 21 2011.

[81] Notably, Dupuy, J.M. Le Droit à l'eau : Un Droit International, EUI Working Papers, Law No. 2006/06, Badia Fiesolana (2006), p. 3. See also Smets, H., Note 6, *Supra*

why access to water in Cameroon should have been treated explicitly as a human right and not as it appears from the law, a sovereign right. However, the weight of authority seems to swing in the direction of equating, 'facilitating access to water,' to the right to water. This is evident from the provisions of many international instruments and Constitutions[82] which have expressly recognised the right to water. However, a majority of the Constitutions across the globe allude to the right to a 'healthy', 'favourable', 'balanced', etc environment and therefore leaving it to subsequent legislative and regulatory instruments to define the nature of 'healthy', 'favourable', 'balanced' environment in each sphere of the environment[83] including the domain of water.

Having now understood the nature of the right to water in Cameroon, it is equally important to find out the components that may guarantee the effective and sustainable enjoyment of the right to water.

4. Contents of the Right to Water in Cameroon

Assuming that facilitating access to water by all is intended to mean the right to water, what criteria may be used to guarantee the enjoyment of or access to it? If access to water for domestic and personal use is to be sustainable, this must entail water, sufficient, safe, acceptable and accessible. The effective and sustainable enjoyment of the right also entails water which is affordable.

4.1. Access to Sufficient Quantity of Water

The right to water implies that everyone has access to water in sufficient quantity to enable satisfaction of his/her domestic and personal needs. The question has arisen as to what constitute domestic and personal use. Unfortunately, the Cameroonian water legislator does not

[82] The Constitutions of Ethiopia (Const, 90(1)) ; Gambia (Const, art 216(4)) ; Namibia (Const, 2001) ; South Africa (Const, sect 27) ; Zambia (Const, art 112), etc.

[83] For the constitutions of African countries referring to such wordings as explicitly encapsulating the right, we catalogued those of Benin (Const, art 27) ; Burkina Fasso (Const, art 31) ; Cape Verde (Const, art 70) ; Congo (Const, art 46) ; Eritrea (Const, art 10) ; Mali (Const, art 15) ; Togo (Const, art 41).

afford a clear definition of water supply for domestic purposes.[84] Nonetheless, water supply for domestic and personal use may be understood to mean water for household use which include drinking, preparation of food, bathing etc.[85] Of course, within the context of the right to water, water supply should be understood to mean a system of providing to a community for meeting its requirement for drinking and other domestic and personal uses.[86]

Access to sufficient quantity equally implies that availability of water should not only be sufficient but also must be continuous.[87] The question has been asked as to what amount of water is considered sufficient and in what context? In answering the first part of this question, reference must be made to the World Health Organisation (WHO) guidelines. By these guidelines, everyone must have at his/her disposal at least 20 litres of portable water per day.[88] With regard to context, it is estimated that normally in urban settings, sufficient access to water should be 50 litres per person per day and may even go up to

[84] Neither the Water Law nor its Enabling Statute brings out clearly the definition of domestic and personal use of water to which is hinged the right to water.

[85] Such definition excludes water supply for purposes of trade, business, fountains, swimming baths, public baths or tanks or any ornamental or mechanical purpose, for gardens or irrigation, for building, for animals where they are kept for sale or hire or for sale of their produce, for consumption and use at a restaurant or by inmates of a hotel, boarding house or residential club, for consumption and use by persons resorting to theatres and cinemas, for watering streets, or for washing vehicles where they are kept for sale or hire.

[86] It excludes supply for industry, recreation, and various public uses.

[87] It is important to note that although Cameroon is largely endowed with this natural resource, the geographical distribution is disproportionate. For instance, the extended Sudano-sahelian zone of Northern part of the country is largely less endowed with the hydraulic resource than the southern part. Consequently, it will be difficult to talk of sufficient and continuous supply of portable water especially in that part of the country. However, there exist resource potential which need to be developed and distributed and the major limitation here is appears to be the huge sums of money required for water development. But the fact that access to this resource for domestic and personal needs is indispensable militates in favour of the argument to prioritize access to portable water by all.

[88] *Supra*, Bär, R., note 76, p. 12.

100 litres.[89] It must be noted that some individuals and groups may require additional water due to health, climate and work conditions.[90] However, an African consumes on the average 30 litres of water a day.[91]

Cameroon generally adheres to the WHO guidelines on availability of drinking water but on the ground, it is difficult to find persons in urban areas in general and marginalised people in particular having access to 20 litres of water per day. How then can we talk of sufficient but also continuous supply of drinking water for the sake of enjoyment of the right to water when water disruptions even in urban areas are frequent?[92] The government argues that within its limited means, the present rate of portable water supply is all it can afford in the struggle to facilitate access to water by all Cameroonians within the meaning of Article 2(1) of the Water Code. Whether or not this argument is founded, is subject to debate. On the one hand, the state may really not possess adequate

---

[89] Smets, H. (2005), Le droit à l'eau dans les Législations Nationales, Académie de l'eau, AESN Nanterre, p 11.

[90] *Supra*, Note 9, p. 2.

[91] WHO/UNICEF Joint Monitoring Programme on Water Supply and Sanitation : Assessment Report (2000), p 7

[92] Such is the case in Yaounde, the political capital of the country, Douala, the economic capital, and Ngaoundere, the capital of Adamawa region. Garoua and Maroua, headquarters of the North and Far North regions respectively are not to be mentioned as they are permanently in very short supply of portable water. In fact, water disruptions have been so frequent and continuous especially in the nation's capital where some quarters-quartier Damas and others, for instance have gone without portable water for a period of three years such that the Head of State himself in 1999 had to summon the managers of the lone water provision company (Societe Nationale des Eaux – SNEC, now Camerounaise des Eaux – CDE, a Moroccan Consortium in charge of supplying portable water in the country) to take urgent measures to reestablish portable water having been interrupted for more two weeks.

In the East regional capital of Bertoua, the situation of non-connectedness to portable water and water disruptions have been acute and continuous that upon being interviewed by journalist, managers of the CDE were heard to say that they are unable to supply portable water to the growing population. They equally added that sometimes the water disruptions are deliberate because they have to ration the supply. This is really regrettable, yet 'water is live' ; this was the only time the populations of these regions could recall this adage.

resources to enforce the right to water but given that the right to water impacts seriously on health which no other thing can surpass, it ought to be a priority issue for the government such that more resources may be deployed from other sectors to enhance a more effective enjoyment of the right especially given that it is incumbent upon the government to do so.[93] On the other hand, it may actually be a question of lack of political will to comply with the right and the government relies on the provisions of Article 2 of the Covenant on Economic, Social and Cultural Right which states that, "states are obliged…to take steps…to the maximum of available resources with the view to achieving progressively the full realisation of the right…"

The enjoyment of the right to water means that people are entitled, besides sufficient and continuous availability of water, to adequately safe water. What this means is that drinking water for household uses must be of quality standard. To be acceptable, such water must be safe and therefore free from micro organisms, chemical substances, physical and radiological hazards that constitute a threat to people's health and sanitation. Acceptable standard of quality water must also consider colour, odour and taste. These quality standards are important because the death toll of people especially children ; from diarrhoea (2 million in 1998) resulting from poor water supply and sanitation[94] has continued to increase. To minimize this humanitarian scandal and safe succeeding generations, governments are required to adopt measures for developing

[93]Although public authorities enjoys certain rights in connection with the supply of portable water, their obligations in the direction of providing sufficient quantity of water for the purpose of enhancing the enjoyment of the right to water include *inter alia* the obligation to establish and protect priority for domestic uses ; ensure protection of water collection points and drinking water quality ; create a positive legal framework for investments and for operation of water services ; identity those who do not have access to water supply and sanitation and to take corrective measures ; ensure sustainable coverage of cost for water supply and sanitation ; ensure proper maintenance and renovations of installations and evaluate the quality of water supply and sanitation ; promote information for and participation of users ; and to ensure fulfillment of contracts with the private sector.

[94] *Supra*, note 89

and implementing drinking water quality set out in the "WHO Guidelines for Drinking Water Quality."

In Cameroon, one thing has remarkably caught the attention of the water legislator. Even if access to water in sufficient quantity has not been guaranteed, at least, in principle, a wide array of legal provisions have been envisaged for ensuring the quality standard of water for health. In fact, before judicial measures are resorted to, preventive measures[95] are envisaged in the Code. This perhaps explains why the Code has provided for water agents charged with inspection and control of water quality.[96] The Water Code has proscribed a number of acts[97] which may directly or indirectly impact on water quality. These are accompanied by heavy criminal sanctions.[98]

The importance in Cameroon, of the quality of water has been impressive with regard to criminal sanctions as it is provided in the law that such sanctions attract no mitigating circumstances.[99] All these are intended to protect the quality of water for domestic and personal use and ensure public health as provided in Article 7. In this regard, provisions have been inserted in the Code dealing with protection of the sources of water such that land within the perimeter of protection of sources of water is reserved for public use.[100] In fact, to reinforce the

---

[95] Of all the measures of protecting environmental resources, the preventive measure is most encouraged for the simple reason that most environmental damage may not be reparable by the award of damages. And in fact, in this context, lack of access to water in sufficient quantity and quality may cause irreparable damage to human beings like death or terminal illnesses arising therefrom.

[96] See Article 1(3) of Decree No. 2001/162/PM of 8th May 2001, Fixing the Modalities of Designation of Agents for Surveillance and Control of Water Quality.

[97] See Articles 4-9.

[98] Articles 15-18, see also S. 82(1) of Law No. 96-12 of August 1996 relating to Environmental Management and in particular, sanctions for non-compliance with provisions for quality of water, air and subsoil. See further, Law No. 65-LF-24 of 12th November 1965 and Law No. 67-LF-1 of 12th June 1967 instituting a Penal Code for the Republic of Cameroon, in particular S. 261 on infringement of Public Health.

[99] See in particular Article 18.

[100] See Article 7(2). Of course, this makes sense because what is public is, in principle managed by government for the interest of all.

guarantee for water quality and ensure public health, an enabling statute is in place in this connection.[101] Whether or not these measures are adequately implemented is quite another question to be examined subsequently in this paper.

4.3. Accessibility

This right to water may not be enjoyed simply because there is sufficient, safe and acceptable water for domestic and personal use. The right to water makes sense where water and water services are accessible to everyone within the jurisdiction of the state, Cameroon for instance. Salient ingredients of accessibility include physical, information accessibility and non-discrimination.

Physical accessibility in this context relates to water, its facilities and services being within safe reach of the population. It is also defined as "within the immediate vicinity of households, educational institutions and workplace."[102] Collection of water from distant sources imports both direct and indirect risk to health.[103] As already argued above, women and children are most affected in this sense because they are the major collectors of water for domestic and personal use.

In Cameroon, ensuring physical accessibility to water remains one of the legislator's major objectives. In the urban areas, although with intermittent frequent disruptions, this problem is not as acute as it is in the rural areas where the supply of portable water is almost non-existent.[104] However, there are continuous attempts by the government to facilitate physical access within the available financial resources.

---

[101] See Decree No. 2001/163/PM of 8th May 2001 regulating the Perimeter of Protection of the Sources of Water and Treatment of Water Stored for portable use.

[102] *Supra*, Note 5.

[103] *Supra*, Note 76, Chapter 2, p. 15.

[104] It may be important to note that the supply of portable water in the semi-urban and rural areas of the country is entirely the result of self-help initiatives of the village development committees or it is partly the initiative of international NGOs or governments of some western nations. In the Adamawa region, the North West and South west regions, and the Centre region for instance, one finds the commitment of international NGOs like HELVETAS, SCAN WATER, etc all from the Nordic

It is also necessary, in attempting to enforce the right to water, that the population should be able to seek, receive and impart information concerning water. The long and short of all these is the participation of the population in the various stages of decision-making and policy design, construction, implementation, monitoring and evaluation. Such is a fundamental right of the population especially regarding their right to water.[105] There is ample evidence that national legislations[106] across the world recognize the right of the population to participate in states affairs, water issues inclusive. The advantage of participation of the population is that the right to water and public health would be largely improved upon and implementation is unlikely to meet with many difficulties. Nevertheless where there are difficulties or blames, these would be shared between the state as the guarantor of the right to water and the population which seeks to enjoy and sustain the utilization of water and together they can conveniently and comfortably begin a search for viable solutions to improve on the right to water.

Unfortunately, this salient ingredient has been overlooked by the Cameroonian water legislator as no specific legal safeguards have been crafted to ensure compliance and implementation of such condition. The consequence is that the population is deprived of information concerning the provision and protection of the right to water. Meanwhile, participation of all stakeholders in the decision-making process and planning is crucial for an integrated water management for the purpose

---

countries, in the supply of portable water for the semi urban and rural populations with the aim of enhancing the enjoyment of the right to water.

[105] It is one of citizen's fundamental rights to water to be informed, consulted and to participate in the conception, construction and implementation of water projects and to initiate actions where these rights and others are violated by public authorities who have the responsibility to guarantee that the above rights and others are enjoyed by the citizens.

[106] For instance, the Water Service Act (119, 2001, S.16) in Finland, Loi N° 2002-276 du 27 Février 2002 relative à la démocratie de proximité en France ; Local Government Act of New Zealand, S.83-84 ; Utility Act 2000, N° 65, 2002, S.36 in Australia, Loi N° 10-95 sur l'eau, Article 101 in Morocco ; Loi N° 002-2001/AW du 8, Février 2001 portant loi d'orientation relative à la Gestion de l'eau au Burkina Faso.

of facilitating the enjoyment of the right to water.[107] The state is, therefore, failing to meet its obligation to respect, protect and fulfil the right to water under existing international law prescriptions.

Finally, the right to water is non-discriminatory. Both in law and in fact, the right of access to water should not be based on any of the prohibited grounds : race, colour, sex, religion, political or other opinions, national or social origin, birth and others. The law in Cameroon has not alluded to any of these grounds as inhibiting access to water. However, there are factual situations in Africa in general and Cameroon in particular where access to water has been discriminated upon.

After the fall of the Berlin Wall, the collapse of Communism and the end of the Cold War, the wind of change began blowing across Africa. Many dictators fought to remain in power through every means. They found ways of stifling their political opponents and their followers or supporters. One of such ways was discrimination on access to water. They suffered from prolonged interruption[108] for no just cause especially during the period of the state of emergency declared in the North West Region of the country in 1992 where the main opposition leader is based. It must however be emphasized that it was much a matter of fact than law anyway.

4.4. Affordability

To adequately enjoy the right to water, government must ensure that water is affordable by all. The right to water, therefore, does not imply that water is free of charge. The general principle is that everyone is obliged to contribute to the cost of supply and treatment of water although this contribution may vary depending on the capacity of individual users[109] and may be made directly or indirectly. But, for the

---

[107] See Global Water Partnership (2000), Integrated Water Resources Management, TAC background Papers, No 4, Stockholm, p 31

[108] This kind of prolonged interruption was possible as water privatization was not yet part of Government policy.

[109] *Supra*, note 79, p. 51.

right to water not to be illusory, the contribution must be made moderate and affordable, not exorbitant. Affordability must be taken to include rates payable to access water networks such as connecting water to homes or public taps, and the rates payable for consuming the water.[110]

Although, it is well settled a principle of law with respect to accessibility that there should be no discrimination, it must be admitted that certain circumstances may justify discrimination. When it relates to water charges, commonsense, logic and natural justice support discrimination which we may qualify as positive discrimination. This implies that the less privileged, marginalised, deprived population and those incapacitated should benefit from preferential rates than other segment of the population without these characteristics. This would ensure that the right to water is respected, protected and fulfilled. For this to happen, government will generally need to monitor the water and take appropriate action to ensure that all can access a minimum service through such mechanisms as pricing policy and tariff regulation.[111]

In Cameroon, a cross-section of the population does not enjoy access to water either because the cost to connect the water and/or the cost per metre cube is too high (the cost per metre cube has risen from 339 francs CFA/m3 to 470 francs CFA/m2 – about one US dollar/m3). Given the general financial situation of the people, such amount is too high and this partly explains why water cuts for failure to pay or delays to pay are significantly many. Access to portable water in Cameroon is equally not guaranteed because of unnecessary and prolonged delays by the water enterprise to connect numerous applicants to portable water even where

---

[110] *Ibid*, p 29.

[111] In fact, it is one of the duties of public authorities to set up water prices taking into account user's capacity to pay ; cut of supply of water to those who are able to pay but choose not to do so ; to subsidize service operators and water utilities companies where there is privatization in the proper sense of the word so that such companies and service providers can charge lower rates to marginalized and vulnerable population without running out of service.

they have fulfilled the tedious conditions.[112] From the foregoing, one may safely conclude that the enjoyment of the right to water in the country under study is not only hinged on the inability to meet the financial requirements in connection to access but on unnecessary, unexplained and prolonged delays in connecting the demanding population to portable water as well.

5. Mechanisms for the Guarantee of Implementation or Enforcement of the Right to Water under Cameroonian Law

For quite a long time now, the problem in Africa in general and in Cameroon in particular is to translate theoretical legal issues or principles into realities on the ground.[113] In most areas, the environment in particular, there are a chunk of legal instruments regulating its management. But these instruments hardly find themselves into implementation. If laws cannot find their ways into implementation, it would be the same like having a right without a remedy which, as it is often said, 'is a vain thing.' And the question may be asked whether it is consequential upon the absence of enforcement mechanisms or the fact that such enforcement mechanisms do exist but are perhaps weak or again the lack of procedural rights (right to information, public participation, just administrative action, right to justice, etc) necessary complements to a substantive human right to water? In most cases, the problem is that the enforcement mechanisms are weak. It is thus important to dissect and diagnose the mechanisms in Cameroon for the enforcement of the right to water. Legal and policy, administrative institutional and judicial frameworks are some of the mechanisms in

---

[112] Of 30 persons randomly chosen out of about 52 queued up in the CDE (former SNEC) office in Melen quarter in Yaounde, 18 told us that they came in respect of repeated appointments given them by the water enterprise to connect them to portable water. 12 of them indicated that they had been chasing their application files for many months. In a similar study carried out in Nkol-Ndongo quarter in Yaounde, of 22 persons out of about 40 randomly interviewed, 13 of them equally stated that they came to check the evolution of their application files for water connection which had kept several months in spite of the fact that they had paid the fabulous connecting charges. Interviews conducted in July 2011.

[113] See UNEP (2006), *Africa Environment Outlook* 2, Nairobi, p. 126.

place to enforce the right to water. It is thus noteworthy that Cameroon manifested her willingness to respect international commitments whether of the so-called hard law or soft law portfolio in keeping with the *pacta sunt servanda* principle to which she equally adheres.[114]

5.1. Legal and Policy Frameworks

From our discussion above, there is no doubt that there are attempts to lay down a framework that recognises and guarantee the right to water and its enforcement. The texts of laws are implemented more easily when there is a clear policy. In this connection, there are enabling instruments[115] detailing the manner of enforcement of the right to water. The problem with these is that some are usually in contradiction with the law itself, in contradiction with other related enabling statutes, are obscure and having ambiguous provisions or again are full of vacuums. All these render the enforcement of the law difficult hence making it a weak regulatory tool.

5.2. Administrative Institutional Framework :

The major institution in charge of overseeing the implementation of the right to water is the Ministry of Water and Energy. This is the government's eye on issues relating to water. Technical expertise on water issues is offered by this Ministerial Department. In fact, it is this Department and decentralised administrative institutions[116] that facilitate the understanding and practical implementation of the right to water to the population. Ministerial Departments and other institutions, whose activities relate to or have implications on the right to water,[117] liaise with the Minister of Water and Energy. This may explain why the Water

[114] See generally, MINFOF & MINEP (2001), *Rapport Nationale du Cameroun sur l'Environnement et le Developpement Durable, Rio + 10*, 88 pages.

[115] See *Supra*, note 93 and 98 for instance.

[116] See Article 2(2) of the Water Code.

[117] For instance, the Ministries of Finance, Health, Environment and Protection of Nature, Forestry and Wildlife, Territorial Administration and Decentralization, Lands and Housing, Urban Affairs, Regional Development, Agriculture, Industry, Mines and Technological Development, Concessional Services for Water and Energy Supplies and Mayors.

Code institutes a National Water Committee[118] bringing together representatives from every Ministerial Department whose activities directly or indirectly relate to water resources management. The competence, organisation and functioning of the National Water Committee is dictated by a Prime Ministerial Decree.[119]

Collaborative institutions which enhance the enjoyment of the right to water are concessionaires of water supply and treatment. They enter into contracts with the Ministry of Water Resources and Energy. Where they do not meet their concession agreements notably the regularity and quality of water according to "WHO Guidelines" the Minister can propose the withdrawal of authorisation to operate in the water sector. To date, the Ministry of Water and Energy has done no more than made serious warnings to the lone company supplying drinking water (CDE).[120]

In its mission, the Ministry of Water also plays the role of an arbitrator.[121] Out of Court arrangements or compoundment can be made by the Minister with the author of an offence relating to the right to water. So therefore, the Ministry is an arbitration centre. This may partly explain why court cases on the right to water are difficult to come by.

5.3. The Human Rights Commission

Considering that the right to water is a human right, it may therefore, be protected by human rights institutions. In Cameroon, the human rights institution is the National Commission on Human Rights and Freedoms (NCHRF).[122] The Commission was created to protect and promote human rights of Cameroonians, the right to water forming an

---

[118] See *Supra* Article 26(1).

[119] See Decree No. 2001/161/PM of 8th May 2001, fixing the Competence, Organisation and Functioning of the National Water Committee.

[120] This is information which we gathered from the Sub-Director in charge of water for domestic and personal use in the Ministry in charge of water and energy in an interview he granted us.

[121] See Articles 22 and 23 of the Water Code.

[122] This Commission was created by Law No. 2004/016 of 22nd July 2004. this law relates to Creation, Organisation and Functioning of the Commission.

integral part of these rights. Unfortunately, the Commission is tilted towards the protection and promotion of civil and political rights thereby paying little or no attention to economic, social and cultural rights, the right to water being a crucial component.

Even in the enforcement of Civil and Political rights, their interpretation does not consider that the right to life being a civil and political right includes the right to water for life. Consequently, first aid measures in respect to the effective and sustainable enjoyment of the right to water which ought to have been provided by the Commission are not available to the population suffering from abuses relating thereto. The only option in the phase of such a disappointment is resort to the courts.

5.4. The Role of the Judiciary Power

The role of the judiciary is crucial in the enforcement of the right to water. It is the reference of last resort providing a basis for enforcement and redress in the case of abuse. Some jurisdiction in Africa[123] have long recognised in their national constitutions and legislative instruments, and enforced in the courts, the right to water as a specific and not a related right. In Asia,[124] some jurisdictions upheld the right to water not as a specific and separate right but as a right under the right to life.

Unfortunately, there is paucity in Cameroon, of judicial decisions on the enforcement of the right to water whether as a right *per se* or a right in relation to the right to health, to life, or to a healthy environment. The question is what accounts for this situation. One may argue that for a considerably long time in Cameroon, the right to water was not explicitly recognised but was only tied to other rights like the right to life. Even so, the right to life was a preambular provision[125] and as

---

[123] In South Africa, for instance, in the case of *Residents of Bon Vista Mansions v. Southern Metropolitan Local Council*, High Court (Witwaterrand Local Division), Case No. 12312(2001).

[124] In India, for instance, in the case of *Attakoya Thangal v. Union of India*, High Court (Kerala), 1990.

[125] See *Supra*, Preambular paragraph 17 of the 1996 Constitution as amended on April 14, 2008.

generally acknowledged, preambular provisions are non-justiciable. However, fairly recently, the legal value of the preamble was recognised in the new Constitutional dispensation of 1996 as amended on April 14, 2008.[126] The preamble is now part and parcel of the Constitution.[127] But then, since 1996, what has been the trend? Many human rights like the right to water, for instance, needs to be more specifically set out in legislative texts so as to spur litigation for purposes of enforcing the enjoyment of such a right. With regard to the right to water, legislative recognition came in 1998 but the Enabling Instruments were passed only in 2001. Such a state of affairs probably explains reluctance to litigate on the right to water. This notwithstanding, the Court of Appeal of Yaounde[128] did not hesitate to uphold the decision of the High Court of Mfoundi which in a summary trial requested the appellant Water Corporation – SNEC (as it then was) to proceed with an immediate effect to reconnect water to the benefit of a certain Mr SENDE Jean Victor who brought an action against the Water Corporation for having disrupted water flow for reasons of fraud on his part. The Court of Appeal held that even in cases of fraud to access water, the corporation could address same in another way but not by disrupting water supply to the defendant given that the right to water is a human right. The court emphasized the summary nature of the trial stating that access to portable water is a vital and fundamental need for human beings that no one has to temper with.

The decision in this case could be praised for at least two reasons. That in the Cameroonian context, whether there is local legislation on the issue or not[129], the judges consider the right to water as a fundamental human right, the breach of which may not be tolerated. In the second place, that the courts are willing to uphold the right either as

---

[126] See Law No 2008/001 Of 14 April to amend supplement some provisions of Law 96/06 of 18 January 1996 to amend the Constitution of 1972.

[127] *Ibid*, see Article 65.

[128] See C.A. Arrêt N° 390/Civ du 28 juillet 2000, *Affaire la Société Nationale des Eaux du Cameroun (SNEC) c/ SENDE Jean Victor.*

[129] Note should be taken of the fact that at the time the decision was handed down the enabling instrument to the Water Code had not come into force.

a right *per se* or a right closely related to the right to life, to health, to a healthy environment, to food, housing enumerated in the preamble of the Constitution. But that notwithstanding, our submission here is that in addition to ordering immediate reconnection of the water, the court could also award damages for damage or inconvenience suffered in the meantime. In spite of this, it must also be acknowledged that a vast majority of Cameroonians are generally reluctant to seek redress for the abuse of their human rights especially economic, social and cultural rights as the promotion and protection of this class of rights are near peripheral issues in the Cameroonian context.

6. Hurdles or Challenges to the Effective and Sustainable Enjoyment of the Right to Water under Cameroonian law

The effective enjoyment of the right to water in Cameroon is hampered by a number of factors including interruptions of supplies, imprecise legal protection, human resources problem among others.

6.1. Interruption of Water Supplies

A major problem affecting the right of the population to water in Cameroon is frequent interruption of water supplies. Interruption here may take two dimensions. Firstly, interruptions may be for some sections of the communities and could last for several months.[130] Some questions frequently asked are whether it is load shedding or a collapse of the distribution system? Unfortunately, these questions usually do not receive appropriate answers as no one is usually informed either in advance or during the interruptions of water of what is happening. Consequently, the population is deprived of water for basic human needs.

Secondly, interruptions may also be for non-payment or delays in paying water bills. It happens in the vast majority of cases of interruptions that the persons affected have not paid their bills. We have argued earlier that although the right to water does not mean free water, it does not however, imply that failure to pay should automatically result

[130] See supra, the examples in note 108.

to interruption of supply without investigation of the cause of such comportment. Although such argument may sound lame because interruption is grounded on failure to respect the clauses of the water contract[131] (express or implied) with the company in charge of supplying water, it however impinges on a basic and fundamental right – the right not only to water but to a continuous supply of it or sustainable enjoyment. The interruption for non-payment or delays is also explained by the exorbitant rates[132] charged per metre cube of water. Worse still, delay in paying bills attracts 'penalty' usually higher than the amount of the bill itself.[133] If a household has been unable to secure an amount of a water bill less than such penalty, how would one reasonably expect such a household to afford an amount more than the bill by way of a penalty in addition to the amount of the bill? In our humble opinion, such a fine is tantamount to implicitly denying the enjoyment of the right to water and should be reduced drastically. This seems to prioritize and treat water as an economic commodity or good than a basic need for the human survival. This state of affairs constitutes a hurdle to the sustainable enjoyment of water.

6.2. Imprecise Legal Protection

The effective implementation of the right to water under Cameroonian law is also hampered by imprecision in the recognition of the right. The Water Code has failed to spell out succinctly that access to water is a human right. Moreover, by that law, the state only facilitates access to water but this does not in any way and can hardly impose clear obligations on the state to provide water to all. A litigant cannot, therefore, rely exclusively on the provision of the Code but must invoke his right to water as arising from the ratification of international legal instrument relating to the right to water as a human right. In fact, there

---

[131] The contract is usually a standard form contract. The individual or family seeking water supply does not negotiate the terms. It is a "take it or leave it" contract with all what this entails for the weaker party, the individual or the family.

[132] See *Supra*, discussions on affordability.

[133] The fine for delay is a fixed amount of four thousand five hundred francs (4500) FCFA, the equivalence of about 10 US dollars.

is ambiguity in the Code which makes the human right character to water a doubtful one. Squaring this dilemma is crucial for the sustainable utilisation of water for domestic and personal needs.

6.3. Human Resource Capacity

Human resource capacity is a huge problem militating against the effective and sustainable enforcement of the right to water. The law provides that the surveillance and control of water quality is ensured by Water Inspectors and their Assistants.[134] It is provided that such officials must be appointed by the Minister of Water to control the quality of water, research and establish offenders and should institute proceedings acting as Judicial Police Officers against the said persons.[135] Although these inspectors have a crucial role to play for the purpose of protecting the right to water and its sustainability, they are not only few but also many of them are not specialists in water matters. What is more? Regrettably, some of them facilitate the Commission of water offences or fraternise with the offenders for their personal gains. The quality of water is compromised and the right to water jeopardized.

7. Conclusion and Recommendations

From the foregoing, it is clear that the right to water is a fundamental human right recognised explicitly and implicitly in many global non binding and regional legal instruments of binding and non binding character in response to the well founded legal theories on human and natural rights enunciated above albeit not specifically on the right to water. It is also clear that the reception and implementation of such right remain country specific. In Cameroon, the right to water is recognised in the Constitution as a related right to other human rights but legislative instruments on which we rely heavily to clearly set out the right as a specific right with emphasis on the human rights character, has failed to do so. Besides, the implementation of the right as provided in the Water Code meets many challenges.

---

[134] See Article 19 of the Water Code.

[135] See *Supra*, Note 51.

However, at the national level, we recommend that to surmount the hurdles to the effective and sustainable enforcement of the right to water and guarantee its sustainable enjoyment, governments should subsidise heavily the sector where the provision of water for domestic and personal uses has been privatised. This way, the rates will be reduced and the affordability ingredient of the right would be guaranteed[136]. This is not asking too much from the government. It is not a farfetched matter if the government is truly committed to build a strong and healthy leadership and a just and sustainable society. Alternatively, it could shy away from privatisation and provide water for domestic and personal needs simply by prioritising the sector for obvious reasons. This way, water is not an economic good but the basic need for human survival. Finally, effective realisation of the quality of water so well emphasised in the Code and its Enabling Statutes can only be adequately guaranteed by building capacity of those in charge of surveillance and control and also sufficiently motivating them to avoid them getting involved in corrupt practices. The population and civil society organisations should be involved in the process of decision-making relating to the right to water.

The generalisation, diversity, and segregated style with which the global and regional community, legal systems and even countries address the issue of the right to water may equally lead us to ground the argument in favour of the need, at the global level, of a legal framework (charter, convention, or treaty, Pact, etc), encapsulating all the provisions on the right to water in all domains and to all the social categories. In this regard therefore, we recommend a revolting and aggressive lobby for a globally binding human right framework on the right to water. Of course, this does not exclude the possibility of crafting an African

[136] In some advance countries, Britain for instance, the British Utilities have learnt that privatization cannot mean they are free to conduct their business as they wish. Because water supply is a natural local monopoly and privatization requires a strong and permanent public regulator. In a sense, privatization is a misnomer. The water remains under government control ; tariffs and services remain tightly regulated ; and even if assets and sewers are transferred to a private company, their use is circumscribed, and the companies are licensed to operate only for 25 years. For details on this, see Fitzmaurice, M. *supra*, note, 25.

regional legal instrument on the right to water given the peculiarities of the continent in many regards including the water stress. This way, there would be accent on the human right character of the right to water and countries, Cameroon inclusive, will be enjoined to elaborate more comprehensive and specific legislations that guarantee the effective and sustainable enjoyment of the right to water, guided of course, by the global or regional agreement on the subject.

LES RÈGLES DE ROTTERDAM OU LA MARCHE ARRIÈRE DU DROIT DES TRANSPORTS MARITIMES INTERNATIONAUX DES MARCHANDISES

Victor-Emmanuel BOKALLI

Agrégé des Facultés de Droit
Professeur Titulaire à l'Université de Yaoundé II

C'est un truisme qu'il règne aujourd'hui une véritable insécurité juridique dans le secteur des transports internationaux des marchandises par mer, du fait notamment d'une mosaïque de conventions imposant chacune un régime juridique différent de l'autre, mais toutes susceptibles de s'appliquer. Or, la sécurité juridique recherchée dans le commerce maritime, comme du reste dans tous les autres domaines[1], suppose une harmonie internationale des solutions et la prévisibilité du droit applicable. Cette dernière, obtenue par le biais du droit uniforme, se trouve liée à l'accessibilité, la stabilité, la simplification et la certitude des règles de droit qui en résultent. L'unification du droit est aussi un élément de simplification dans la mesure où elle facilite la recherche du droit applicable en évitant très souvent de fâcheux conflits de conventions. En l'état actuel du droit positif des transports maritimes internationaux de marchandises, cette unification se trouve compromise par une « *superposition désuniformisante* »[2] des conventions internationales, véritable source d'insécurité et de désordre. Et pourtant, ce ne sont pas les occasions d'œuvrer pour cette uniformisation qui ont manqué[3]. Mais la cause doit certainement être recherchée du côté de

---

[1] Voir Pougoué (P-G) : « Les figures de la sécurité juridique », RASJ, vol. 4, n° 1, 2007, pp. 1-8.

[2] Selon l'heureuse expression de VIALARD (A) : « Sisyphe et l'uniformisation internationale du droit maritime », in *Revue le Droit Maritime Français* (DMF), 1999, p. 213 et spéc. 216.

[3] Voir BERLINGIERI (F) : « Uniformité de la loi sur le transport maritime : perspectives de succès », in Mélanges Pierre BONASSIES, Ed. Moreux 2001, p. 57.

l'exacerbation des égoïsmes partisans qui plombe toute volonté de changement. L'on vient encore de le vérifier au regard du contenu de la dernière convention en la matière.

L'Assemblée générale des Nations unies a en effet adopté le 11 décembre 2008 « La Convention sur le contrat de transport international de marchandises effectué entièrement ou partiellement par mer », plus connue, selon la recommandation de ses auteurs[4], sous la dénomination de « Règles de Rotterdam », du nom de cette ville des Pays-Bas où s'est tenue le 23 novembre 2009 la cérémonie d'ouverture à la signature. Ambitionnant d'unifier les règles de droit des transports internationaux des marchandises, les Règles de Rotterdam sont destinées à remplacer non seulement la convention internationale pour l'unification de certaines règles en matière de connaissement signée à Bruxelles (Belgique) en 1924 avec ses divers protocoles modificatifs de 1968 et 1979, mais également la Convention des Nations unies sur le transport des marchandises par mer conclue à Hambourg (Allemagne) le 31 mars 1978 et plus connue, selon la volonté de ses auteurs, sous l'appellation de « Règles de Hambourg »[5]. L'adoption de cette convention est diversement accueillie : avec enthousiasme par les transporteurs et regrets par les chargeurs. Ces regrets s'expliquent par le fait que cette convention recule considérablement, au détriment des chargeurs, dans la quête permanente de l'équilibre entre les différents intérêts en présence, ceux des transporteurs et ceux des chargeurs[6].

---

[4] Voir l'avant-dernier paragraphe du texte de la Résolution adoptée par l'Assemblée générale lors de sa 67e séance tenue le 11 décembre 2008.

[5] Voir BOKALLI (V.-E.) : « Le nouveau droit des contrats de transports maritimes internationaux des marchandises : les Règles de Hambourg », in *Revue Africaine de Droit International et Comparé* (RADIC), tome 9 n° 4, 1997, p. 836 et s.

[6] Voir BOKALLI (V.-E.) : « Les chargeurs et les Règles de Rotterdam », in *Revue Africaine des Sciences Juridiques* (RASJ), vol. 8, n° 1, 2011, p. 1 ; voir également ma communication sur les « Incidences de l'entrée en vigueur des Règles de Rotterdam pour les pays africains (avantages et inconvénients pour les pays africains) » présentée à la journée nationale de réflexion sur les Règles de Rotterdam organisée à Douala le 16 novembre 2010 par le Conseil national des chargeurs du Cameroun (CNCC).

L'histoire des règles des transports maritimes internationaux apparaît en effet comme une lutte permanente que livrent les chargeurs pour la défense de leurs intérêts. Sans rentrer dans les profondeurs de l'histoire, l'on peut remarquer que le régime en vigueur avant la convention de Bruxelles de 1924 favorisait exclusivement les transporteurs. Bien qu'en théorie responsables de droit des dommages causés aux marchandises à eux confiées, les transporteurs se protégeaient par de multiples clauses d'irresponsabilité. Malgré l'illicéité ou l'immoralité dont certains auteurs[7] les accusaient, la jurisprudence d'une manière générale, validait ces clauses. Cette présence abusive des clauses d'irresponsabilité, plus connues sous l'appellation de « *negligence clauses* », faisait des connaissements des « chiffons de papier »[8], car ils permettaient des transports par mer sans aucune garantie. « Les armateurs, comme le relève un auteur, étaient libres de remettre la marchandise quand ils voulaient et dans n'importe quel état »[9].

Le premier pays à réagir pour protéger les chargeurs fut les États-Unis d'Amérique, alors pays chargeur à cette époque. Leur Cour suprême frappait en effet de nullité les clauses d'exonération de responsabilité du transporteur. Le *Harter Act* adopté le 13 février 1893 par le Congrès américain consacra cette décision. Ce texte joua un rôle décisif dans l'évolution mondiale du droit des transports maritimes ; en effet, il inspira notamment les rédacteurs de la Convention de Bruxelles de 1924.

Cette convention de Bruxelles, en posant le principe du caractère d'ordre public des règles légales sur la responsabilité du transporteur, représentait pour les chargeurs une importante victoire dans leur lutte contre les abus des transporteurs. Désormais, les transporteurs ne pouvaient plus en particulier invoquer ces fameuses clauses de non-responsabilité. Pareillement, la Convention leur rappelait leurs obligations fondamentales : procéder de façon appropriée et soigneuse au

---

7 Voir BONNECASE : *Traité de Droit Maritime*, n° 511, cité par RODIERE (R) : *Traité Général de Droit Maritime*, T. 2, Affrètement et Transports, n° 576.

8 Selon l'heureuse expression de LIGONIE (J.A.M) : *Le connaissement et la lettre de voiture maritime*, LGDJ 1968, p. 11.

9 *Idem.*

chargement, à la manutention, à l'arrimage, au transport de la marchandise, à leur livraison, et exercer la plus extrême diligence pour assurer la navigabilité nautique et commerciale de leur navire... La convention de Bruxelles de 1924 apparaissait ainsi à cette époque comme un texte réellement révolutionnaire. Le chargeur y paraissait relativement bien protégé.

Mais tout n'y était pas en faveur du chargeur. Certaines dispositions traduisaient encore la survivance de la prépondérance des intérêts des armateurs. C'est le cas, au niveau de la responsabilité du transporteur, de la multitude des cas exceptés ou causes exonératoires de cette responsabilité et notamment de la faute du capitaine dans la navigation ou l'administration du navire – plus connue sous la dénomination de faute nautique -, faute paradoxalement exonératoire de la responsabilité de son auteur. D'autres, réellement favorables aux chargeurs au moment de l'adoption de la Convention, avaient entre-temps perdu de leur dimension protectrice. Ainsi en est-il du montant de la limitation de responsabilité, fixé par colis à 100 livres-or. Cette somme, probablement équitable en 1924, est très vite devenue dérisoire ; d'abord à cause de l'érosion monétaire, ensuite, parce fixé par colis, ce montant était nettement inférieur au préjudice subi, les sacs et les caisses de 1924 étant de plus en plus remplacés par des conteneurs capables de renfermer plusieurs marchandises représentant d'importantes valeurs. Dès lors, une réforme devenait nécessaire, car avec cette conteneurisation croissante, il a fallu déterminer quel était le colis de référence lorsque les colis de marchandises étaient groupés dans un grand colis, conteneur ou autre engin équivalent : chaque colis inclus ou alors le conteneur tout entier lui-même ?

La réforme souhaitée intervint en 1968 sous la forme d'un protocole modificatif de la convention de 1924. Élaboré par le Comité maritime international[10], à l'époque seule expression des milieux maritimes

---

[10] Voir ROHART (J-S) : « Le CMI aujourd'hui », DMF 2004, n° 652, p. 789 ; voir également LEFEBVRE CHALAIN (H) : « L'Organisation maritime internationale (OMI) : soixante ans d'évolution » in *Revue de Droit des Transports*, n° 6, juin 2009, p. 17.

internationaux, ce protocole n'améliora d'une manière générale cette convention que sur le mode de calcul, le taux de limitation de responsabilité et sur la précision de la notion de colis[11]. Il ne put par conséquent combler toutes les attentes et sauver la convention de Bruxelles.

Aussi de nouvelles institutions mises en place entre-temps par les Nations unies, en l'occurrence la Conférence des Nations unies sur le commerce et le développement (CNUCED) et la Commission des Nations unies sur le droit commercial international (CNUDCI), allaient-elles s'emparer de la maîtrise du droit maritime international et travailler à l'élaboration d'un texte entièrement neuf. Et, parce que fortement majoritaires dans ces organismes, les pays en voie de développement, chargeurs pour l'essentiel, qui s'estimaient jusque-là injustement traités par le droit maritime international dont les règles et les institutions favorisaient dans l'ensemble les besoins des nations occidentales, transporteurs en général, trouvaient là l'occasion sinon de renverser la tendance, du moins de rétablir enfin un véritable équilibre[12]. Aussi vont-ils peser de tout leur poids numérique dans l'élaboration d'une nouvelle convention[13]. Celle-ci, adoptée le 31 mars 1978 à Hambourg (Allemagne) lors de la conférence des Nations unies sur le transport par mer, apparaissait comme « un produit direct de l'effort délibéré entrepris pour ajuster les mécanismes juridiques internationaux aux exigences nées du désir de fortifier la position commerciale des pays en voie de développement »[14].

---

[11] Voir BONASSIES (P) et SCAPEL (C) : *Traité de Droit Maritime*, LGDJ, 2006, n° 1109.

[12] Voir CHAUVEAU (P) : « La convention sur les connaissements mise en accusation », ADMA, 1974.7.

[13] Voir ZEH ONDOUA (J) : « Les pays du tiers monde et la réglementation internationale des transports maritimes entre Etats. De l'OMI à l'OMC : Contribution à l'étude de l'évolution du processus d'élaboration des normes internationales », thèse de droit, Lille II, 1997 ; LOPUSKI (J) : « Les principales lignes d'évolution du droit maritime privé : l'influence exercée par la pression des pays en développement » in DMF 1987.217.

[14] Voir BERTHOUD (P) : « Les transports maritimes dans le dialogue Nord-Sud ». Contribution au colloque du Mans sur le thème « Aspects actuels du droit international

D'une manière générale, les Règles de Hambourg consacrent un renforcement de la responsabilité du transporteur[15]. Tout en maintenant le principe de la responsabilité objective ou de plein droit du transporteur maritime, cette convention fait perdre au transporteur le bénéfice de nombreux cas, excepté dix-sept qui allégeaient considérablement sa responsabilité dans la convention de Bruxelles, et, notamment, de la très controversée exonération pour faute nautique. N'ont été conservés que les cas exceptés d'incendie (art. 5 § 4), d'assistance (art. 5 § 6) et un cas excepté de formulation générale inspirée directement de l'article 20 de l'ancienne convention de Varsovie du 12 octobre 1929 sur le transport aérien international. De même, cette convention augmente la limite monétaire de la réparation. Elle accroît par ailleurs, de façon indirecte, mais certaine, la charge du transporteur : élargissement de son champ d'application par l'intégration dans son giron non seulement des phases terrestres *ante* et *post* transport maritime, mais aussi du transport des animaux vivants et surtout, des transports en pontée, sanction du retard dans la livraison de la marchandise, allongement du délai de prise des réserves par le destinataire de la marchandise à quinze jours et ouverture à l'ayant droit à la marchandise d'un éventail de juridictions compétentes pouvant connaître de l'action en responsabilité contre le transporteur…

Bien que ces dispositions soient réellement favorables aux chargeurs[16] – n'en déplaise à quelques voix curieusement discordantes[17]- et que les

---

des transports » », tenu en mai 1980 et dont les Actes ont été publiés aux Éditions Pédone, p. 44 et spécialement p. 47. Dans le même sens, PHILIP (C) : « Souveraineté, Intérêts économiques et Coopération dans le droit international des transports », *idem,* p. 3.

[15] Voir SCAPEL (C) : « Les réformes apportées par les Règles de Hambourg à la responsabilité du transporteur maritime » et BONNAUD (J) : « Les réformes apportées par les Règles de Hambourg aux exonérations de responsabilité et limitations de réparation du transporteur maritime », in Actes du colloque du 25 novembre 1992 sur la Convention des Nations unies sur le transport des marchandises par mer, IMTM 1992, p. 51 et 73 ; *Revue Scapel* 1992, p. 98 et 124.

[16] Voir BOKALLI (V-E) : « La protection des chargeurs à travers les Règles de Hambourg » in DMF, 1997, 237 ; MAKOUTA (M) : « La protection des chargeurs à travers la Convention du 25 août 1924 et le Règles de Hambourg », in *Journal de la*

pays en voie de développement représentés dans ces institutions des Nations unies par le Groupe dit des soixante-dix-sept y étaient fortement favorables, il aura paradoxalement fallu attendre treize ans pour réunir les vingt signatures nécessaires à sa mise en application, laquelle n'est survenue que le 1er novembre 1992. La raison de ce retard tient à plusieurs facteurs. D'une part, il y a le fait que de nombreux pays en voie développement, pays chargeurs pour l'essentiel, qui avaient soutenu et même pris une part active à l'élaboration et à l'adoption de cette convention, sont devenus entre-temps des transporteurs avec la création de leurs propres armements nationaux[18]. Et avec un régime de responsabilité du transporteur assez strict et par conséquent peu attractif pour les compagnies de transport, l'engouement pour la ratification de cette convention s'est émoussé chez ses principaux promoteurs. D'autre part, les pays occidentaux, transporteurs pour la plupart, qui n'appréciaient guère cette convention, ont mené pendant tout ce temps contre elle une véritable campagne de boycottage. D'où finalement son succès mitigé, avec seulement un peu plus d'une trentaine d'adhésions à ce jour.

Conscient du faible rayonnement des Règles de Hambourg, le Comité maritime international (CMI) a, dès 1996, engagé une réflexion sur les lacunes de la convention de Bruxelles en vue de l'élaboration d'une nouvelle convention. Et s'étant rapproché de la Commission des Nations unies pour le droit commercial international (CNUDCI) pour en réalité

Marine Marchande (JMM) du 31 mars 1988, p. 821 ; BONASSIES (P) : « Les Règles de Hambourg : une avancée certaine, mais modeste »in JMM du 19 mai 1988 p. 1341.

[17] Voir KHALIL DIALLO (I) : « Les Règles de Hambourg : un leurre pour les chargeurs ? (Le point de vue d'un juriste africain) », in *Etudes et Documents de l'Association sénégalaise du Droit Maritime*, février 1993, p. 471.

[18] Voir NDENDE (M) : « Les armements d'Etat et leur participation au transport maritime », thèse de Doctorat en Droit, Brest 1990. Selon les statistiques données par cet auteur à cette époque, en Afrique par exemple, les armements d'État représentaient 97 % des flottes en activité, et en Amérique latine, plus de 60 %.

rechercher juste le sceau de cette organisation internationale, il sortira de cette concertation, en 2008, les Règles de Rotterdam[19].

Ces Règles de Rotterdam, si elles préservent certains acquis traditionnels dans le domaine des transports maritimes internationaux des marchandises, réalisent aussi incontestablement des avancées certaines, notamment dans le sens de la modernisation de ce droit. Nous pouvons en relever ici quelques exemples significatifs.

Tout d'abord, prenant en effet en compte l'évolution technologique, les Règles de Rotterdam reconnaissent les documents électroniques de transport qui peuvent être émis sous forme négociable (art. 8). À la différence des Règles de Hambourg qui sont peu prolixes à l'égard des documents de transport autres que le connaissement et qui admettent simplement la signature électronique (art. 14-3), les documents électroniques sont effet expressément admis désormais comme support du contrat de transport par les Règles de Rotterdam. Il s'agit là en réalité de la consécration par le législateur international d'une pratique expérimentée depuis longtemps pour explorer toutes les possibilités offertes par les moyens modernes d'appréhension et de transmission des informations que constituent la télématique et l'informatique[20], notamment pour juguler les inconvénients découlant du formalisme du connaissement, comme la fraude maritime documentaire[21]. Mais il faut

[19] Voir BAILLEUL (O) : « La Convention sur le contrat de transport international de marchandises effectué entièrement ou partiellement par mer : les Règles de Rotterdam », Thèse professionnelle Euromed Management 2009 ; DELEBECQUE (P) : « La Convention sur les contrats internationaux de transport de marchandises effectué entièrement ou partiellement par mer : *a civil law perspective* » in DMF 2009, spécial CMI Athènes, p. 335 ; NGUENE NTEPPE (J) : « La nouvelle Convention des Nations Unies dite « Règles de Rotterdam » et le défi de la construction d'un nouvel ordre maritime international » in *Revue Africaine des Affaires Maritimes et des Transports*, n° 3 de janvier 2011, p. 33.

[20] Voir DU PONTAVICE (E) : «Le connaissement et l'informatique » in *Annales* IMTM 1985, 240 ; DMF 1983, 381 ; KNUT HELGE REINSKOU : « *Bills of lading and automatic data processing : description of a computerized system for carriage of goods by sea* », étude publiée par la CEE, réf. Trade/WP.4/RC 159 du 12 novembre 1981.

[21] Voir BOKALLI (V-E) : « La fraude maritime documentaire », Mémoire de DESS droit maritime et droit des transports, Aix-Marseille III, 1986.

pour cela que le transporteur et le chargeur aient donné leur consentement.

L'on peut ensuite saluer la reconnaissance par les rédacteurs des Règles de Rotterdam d'un droit de contrôle. Ce droit, connu jusqu'à présent seulement dans les transports aériens et terrestres sous le nom de droit de disposition, est accordé à la partie contrôlante, c'est-à-dire le chargeur, son ayant droit cessionnaire, le chargeur documentaire ou le tiers porteur du document négociable. Il lui permet de donner au transporteur de nouvelles instructions concernant les marchandises et même, de modifier les conditions initiales du contrat de transport, par exemple en remplaçant le destinataire (art. 50).

Enfin, les règles de Rotterdam étendent considérablement leur domaine d'application sur le plan géographique et cherchent à couvrir l'intégralité de l'opération de transport. L'on se souvient que la convention de Bruxelles de 1924 régissait le transport des marchandises depuis leur chargement à bord du navire jusqu'à leur déchargement du navire, c'est-à-dire en réalité, la seule phase purement maritime. Elle excluait ainsi de son champ d'application les phases terrestres qui sont pourtant des préalables et des suites nécessaires au transport maritime.

Avec le développement considérable du transport des marchandises dans des conteneurs, cette convention est apparue déphasée par rapport aux exigences de ce transport conteneurisé. Malheureusement, les Règles de Hambourg, qui se veulent modernes et comprennent la nécessité d'étendre le domaine du droit des transports maritimes, ne sont pas allées jusqu'au bout de leurs ambitions. Elles n'ont fait qu'intégrer dans leur giron ces phases terrestres du transport maritime, oubliant tout l'aspect multimodal qui avait pourtant déjà pris une envergure considérable au moment de leur adoption[22]. Leur article 4-1 dispose en effet que « la responsabilité du transporteur en ce qui concerne les marchandises

[22] Voir BOKALLI V-E) : « Conteneurisation et transport multimodal international des marchandises », Thèse de doctorat en droit, Aix-Marseille III, 1989 ; encore de moi : « Le droit du transport multimodal des marchandises des pays de l'Afrique centrale » in RASJ, vol. 1, n° 3, 2003, p. 1 ; BONASSIES (P) : « Le transport multimodal transmaritime : approche juridique » in *Annales* IMTM 1988, 93.

couvre la période pendant laquelle les marchandises sont sous sa garde au port de chargement, durant le transport et au port de déchargement ». Et le paragraphe 2 du même article précise que les marchandises sont réputées être sous la garde du transporteur à partir du moment où celui-ci les prend en charge jusqu'au moment où il en effectue la livraison. Certes, lorsque l'on sait qu'en fait le transporteur prend souvent la marchandise en charge avant le chargement et la délivre au destinataire bien après le déchargement et dans un lieu généralement éloigné du quai, l'on mesure parfaitement l'ampleur de l'extension du domaine couvert par les Règles de Hambourg. Mais, ce n'est pas suffisant.

Les Règles de Rotterdam, fort heureusement, vont plus loin et cherchent à couvrir l'intégralité de l'opération de transport. En effet, si le titre de la convention met en avant le segment maritime, elle se veut partiellement multimodale ou, plus exactement, elle organise le transport « *maritime plus* », c'est-à-dire le transport maritime international éventuellement précédé ou suivi des segments routiers, ferroviaires ou même aériens. Les Règles de Rotterdam, en définissant le contrat de transport maritime, précisent qu'il « peut prévoir, en outre, le transport par d'autres modes ». Dès lors, si les parties le souhaitent, les Règles de Rotterdam couvrent la chaîne de transport dans sa totalité, de bout en bout, « *door to door* »[23].

Les Règles de Rotterdam s'appliquent ainsi en principe aux voyages maritimes, mais rien ne s'oppose à ce que le transporteur maritime propose à son client d'assumer les trajets terrestres ou aériens qui précèdent ces voyages ou qui les suivent. Si le client accepte cette formule, l'intégralité du transport sera couverte par les Règles de Rotterdam : la couverture juridique est donc étendue. Mais ces Règles de Rotterdam peuvent entrer en conflit avec d'autres conventions susceptibles de s'appliquer pendant les périodes pré ou post acheminement. Les rédacteurs des Règles de Rotterdam ont pensé à ce risque et ont prévu en conséquence deux garde-fous. L'article 82,

[23] Voir BERLINGIERI (F) : « Aspects multimodaux des Règles de Rotterdam » DMF 2009.867.

d'abord, prend le soin de réserver l'application des conventions multimodales existantes. L'article 26, ensuite, précise que les Règles de Rotterdam doivent céder le pas à la convention de droit matériel et impérative applicable lorsqu'une perte, une avarie ou un retard survient pendant la période de pré ou post acheminement ; en d'autres termes, les Règles de Rotterdam retiennent ici le système dit de réseau (*network system*) pour régler les questions de responsabilité qui peuvent se poser.

De manière générale, l'on doit pouvoir reconnaître que les avancées réalisées par les Règles de Rotterdam dans le sens de la modernisation du droit des transports maritimes internationaux des marchandises sont réelles. Mais la visibilité de ces avancées se trouve malheureusement brouillée par des remises en cause d'importants progrès effectués dans ce domaine par les conventions internationales antérieures. En effet, dans des domaines hautement sensibles, les Règles de Rotterdam font « machine arrière toutes » et confirment tout le poids de la tradition maritime[24]. Ainsi, avec la réinstauration de la liberté contractuelle qui irradie la future convention, l'on semble revenir à un régime de droit des transports maritimes, supplétif que toutes les réglementations précédentes avaient cru abolir en instaurant un régime de droit des transports maritimes impératif à l'abri des manipulations des contractants, notamment de la part du transporteur considéré comme la partie la plus forte (I) ; bien plus, «l' exhumation » de la presque totalité des cas exceptés des régimes en vigueur avant les Règles de Hambourg témoigne d'une volonté à peine déguisée de faire resurgir comme par le passé le régime d'irresponsabilité du transporteur maritime (II).

I – Le retour à la liberté contractuelle.

Les Règles de Rotterdam consacrent la liberté contractuelle des parties au contrat de transport maritime international des marchandises. Jadis apanage des contrats d'affrètement pour lesquels les dispositions légales

---

[24] Selon l'heureuse expression de FEDI (L) : « Présentation de la Convention des Nations Unies sur le contrat de transport international de marchandises effectué entièrement ou partiellement par mer » in *Revue de Droit des Transports*, n° 7-8 de juillet/août 2009, p. 20.

sont par nature supplétives, la liberté contractuelle fait curieusement aujourd'hui son retour dans le domaine du contrat de transport maritime international des marchandises pourtant caractérisé depuis la Convention de Bruxelles de 1924 par un cadre rigide et impératif[25].

Depuis le *Harter Act* américain du 13 février 1893 qui symbolise la première réaction contre les abus des armateurs, le caractère impératif des dispositions légales constitue le moyen de protection par excellence de la partie la plus faible dans la relation contractuelle de transport. L'on se souvient en effet qu'avant ce texte, le régime en vigueur fondé sur la liberté contractuelle favorisait exclusivement les transporteurs qui, parce qu'étant en situation de force, inséraient dans les contrats de transport des clauses abusives d'irresponsabilité.

Le caractère impératif des dispositions légales qui interdisent aux transporteurs d'invoquer ces fameuses clauses d'irresponsabilité, parce que jamais remis en cause par les différents textes nationaux ou internationaux relatifs au contrat des transports maritimes des marchandises élaborés depuis lors, apparaissait comme une protection définitivement acquise aux chargeurs. Aussi comprend-on difficilement que les Règles de Rotterdam qui, tout en donnant l'impression de rester dans cette lignée parce que se déclarant aussi impératives, consacrent paradoxalement dans le même temps la liberté contractuelle[26]. En effet, si les clauses élusives de responsabilité sont par principe interdites (art 79), le transporteur se voit néanmoins reconnaître la possibilité, soit en agissant, de déroger à telle ou telle disposition de la convention (A), soit

---

[25] Voir DELEBECQUE (P) : « La Convention des Nations Unies sur le contrat de transport international de marchandises entièrement ou partiellement par mer et la liberté contractuelle » in *Annuaire de droit maritime et océanique*, 2008, p. 485 et s. ; Von ZIEGLER (A) : « *The Rotterdam Rules and the freedom of contract : redrag or rule of the game of commercial law ?* » ; ZUNARELLI (S) : « Les Règles de Rotterdam : Règles impératives ou Règles supplétives », communication au colloque de l'IMTM des 20 et 21 mai 2010 sur le thème « Les Règles de Rotterdam : le droit des transports maritimes du XXIe siècle » et dont la synthèse des travaux se trouve rapportée à la *Revue de Droit des Transports*, 2010, 11 et s.
[26] *Idem.*

en s'abstenant d'agir, de se mettre à l'abri d'une éventuelle responsabilité en cas de retard à la livraison (B).

A- Le recours explicite à la liberté contractuelle.

La liberté contractuelle, c'est connu, profite au contractant le plus fort au détriment du contractant considéré comme le plus faible. Dans la relation contractuelle de transport, notamment maritime, le transporteur est de loin le contractant le plus fort. La loi lui accorde la possibilité de faire sortir les rapports contractuels du cadre légal supposé impératif pour les placer dans un régime des règles librement négociées. On peut effectivement s'en rendre compte dans l'examen du régime des obligations traditionnelles du transporteur (1), mais aussi et surtout de celui du contrat de volume (2).

1 – Le régime des obligations traditionnelles du transporteur maritime

Il est traditionnellement admis qu'il incombe au transporteur, dans l'exécution du contrat de transport, certaines obligations évidentes : la manutention de la marchandise, son chargement dans l'engin de transport, son arrimage et son déchargement à destination. Cette exigence tient non seulement à la nature des choses, mais participe également des mesures de sécurité. En effet, c'est le transporteur qui est mieux placé pour s'assurer, à travers la qualité du chargement et surtout de l'arrimage, de l'équilibre et de la stabilité de l'engin de transport, donc finalement de sa sécurité. Certes, dans le régime de liberté contractuelle en vigueur avant que le législateur ne s'empare de la réglementation du contrat de transport maritime, les transporteurs, par certaines clauses dites sous palan, faisaient peser ces obligations sur les chargeurs. La convention de Bruxelles y a mis un terme. Elle dispose en effet dans son article 3-2 que « le transporteur … procédera de façon appropriée et soigneuse au chargement, à la manutention, à l'arrimage, … et au déchargement des marchandises transportées ».

Les Règles de Rotterdam reviennent curieusement sur cette importante avancée. En effet, après avoir pourtant rappelé dans son article 13 (1) que le transporteur maritime assume des obligations dites

« particulières », consistant à prendre réception, charger, manutentionner, arrimer, garder, soigner, décharger, la future convention autorise, dans l'alinéa 2 de cet article, le transporteur maritime, par une clause spéciale du contrat, à transférer au chargeur ou au destinataire la responsabilité du chargement, de la manutention, de l'arrimage et du déchargement. Les contrats de transport constituant généralement des contrats d'adhésion, le risque est très élevé que tous les connaissements contiennent cette clause spéciale refilant ces obligations à l'ayant droit à la marchandise.

C'est le retour des clauses sous palan et la consécration sur le plan juridique des clauses FI/FO « *free in/free out* » (qui signifie « bord/bord », c'est-à-dire que le taux de fret maritime ne comprend pas les frais de chargement et de déchargement) et FIOS « *free in and out stowed* » (qui signifie bord et arrimé, c'est-à-dire que le taux de fret ne comprend pas les frais de chargement, d'arrimage, de désarrimage et de déchargement).

2 – Le régime du contrat de volume

La liberté contractuelle se trouve davantage affirmée dans les contrats dits de volume. Aux termes de l'article 1er (2) des Règles de Rotterdam, le contrat de volume « désigne le contrat de transport qui prévoit le déplacement d'une quantité déterminée de marchandises en plusieurs expéditions pendant une durée convenue. La quantité, précise cet alinéa *in fine*, peut être exprimée sous la forme d'un minimum, d'un maximum ou d'une fourchette ». Et l'article 80 de la convention détermine le régime de ces contrats de volume. D'une manière générale, pour ce type d'accord spécifique, les parties pourront déroger aux droits, obligations et responsabilités dans un sens plus ou moins favorable que celui prévu par la convention internationale.

Certes, ce recours aux contrats de volume paraît suffisamment encadré par l'exigence de certaines conditions de fond et de forme. Ainsi, le contrat de volume doit énoncer de manière apparente qu'il déroge aux dispositions de la convention internationale ; il doit avoir fait l'objet d'une négociation individuelle ; il doit indiquer lesquelles de ses clauses contiennent les dérogations ; le chargeur doit être mis en mesure de conclure un contrat de transport conformément aux dispositions du texte international sans aucune dérogation et il doit être informé de cette possibilité ; enfin, la dérogation ne doit être ni incorporée par référence ni contenue dans un contrat d'adhésion non soumis à négociation.

Toutefois, en dépit de ces précautions qui d'ailleurs satisfont plus la théorie, plusieurs imprécisions relatives à la notion même de contrat de volume subsistent qui peuvent légitimement laisser craindre que les transporteurs ne retournent la situation à leur profit. Que faut-il en effet entendre par « *quantité déterminée* » ? Deux conteneurs, trois ou davantage ? Et que dire de l'expression « *plusieurs expéditions* » ? Deux, trois, quatre ou davantage ? Et la « *durée convenue* » alors ? Elle renvoie à combien de mois, 3, 6 ou 12 ? Avec une notion aussi vague qu'imprécise, les transporteurs, généralement assez futés, peuvent abuser de cette liberté contractuelle au détriment des petits chargeurs de faible volume d'expédition très souvent inexpérimentés.

Le moins que l'on puisse dire est que la liberté contractuelle telle que consacrée ne va pas profiter aux chargeurs malgré tout l'intérêt éventuel de ce principe. En effet, la définition du contrat de volume est tellement large qu'elle peut englober la majorité des contrats de transports maritimes aujourd'hui et l'engagement sur un taux de fret attractif pourra permettre aux transporteurs d'imposer le contrat de volume. Les prétendus garde-fous de la Convention internationale s'avèrent illusoires. D'autant plus qu'il apparaît clairement que les Règles de Rotterdam ont voulu par ces conditions de forme qui tiennent lieu de garde-fous assurer la protection des chargeurs par l'information. Mais si l'information permet effectivement à une personne de s'engager en connaissance de cause, il est permis de douter qu'elle assure automatiquement la protection de la partie faible dans une relation contractuelle.

En somme, l'on est en droit de se demander jusqu'où irait cette liberté contractuelle sachant qu'elle favoriserait l'insertion dans le contrat de transport des clauses désavantageuses à l'une ou l'autre partie selon le rapport de force existant – mais sans doute plus au détriment des chargeurs. Ce souci n'est pas illusoire lorsque l'on sait que dans la pratique quotidienne, les conditions de transport se trouvent généralement déjà pré rédigées sur les connaissements présentés par les transporteurs, les chargeurs, qui n'ont pas le réflexe de se faire toujours assister d'un conseil juridique lors de la signature de tout engagement, devant seulement les signer pour marquer leur adhésion à ces contrats. Par conséquent, l'on voit mal les transporteurs, qui ne nous ont pas beaucoup habitués à un esprit d'abnégation et d'altruisme, insérer dans ces contrats des clauses qui leur soient un tant soit peu défavorables. Le risque est très grand que les acquis des précédents instruments juridiques et de la jurisprudence en faveur des chargeurs ne soient conventionnellement anéantis dans la mesure où cette liberté contractuelle permet non seulement d'accroître la responsabilité du chargeur, mais surtout de réduire corrélativement celle du transporteur.

B – Le recours implicite à la liberté contractuelle

Il se manifeste dans le traitement du retard. Dans un sens général, le retard apparaît comme le fait d'arriver trop tard, de se manifester, de se produire après le moment fixé, attendu. Le retard ainsi défini prend une résonance particulière en droit des transports. L'expéditeur escompte que la marchandise soit acheminée le plus rapidement possible. De même, le destinataire attend que cette marchandise lui parvienne dans les meilleurs délais. La rapidité du transport comble les attentes tant de l'expéditeur que du destinataire. Le retard, à l'inverse, risque d'engendrer pour eux un préjudice. En outre, tout transport encourt le risque potentiel d'un retard. Comme le dit si bien un auteur[27], « le risque de retard est en effet consubstantiel au transport en général [et] il n'est donc pas étonnant que le retard soit pris en compte par des textes spécifiques du droit des transports ».

À l'instar des autres modes de transport, le droit maritime lui aussi est concerné par le retard. Mais à l'observation, et contrairement au sort réservé aux transporteurs dans les autres modes de transport, le régime juridique de la responsabilité du transporteur maritime pour retard à la livraison des marchandises repose sur une indulgence manifeste envers le

---

[27] RACINE (J-B) : « Le retard dans le transport maritime des marchandises », RTDCom 2003, p. 224.

transporteur maritime. D'ailleurs, aucune disposition de la convention de Bruxelles ni dans sa version initiale de 1924 ni dans sa rédaction issue du protocole de Visby de 1968 n'est consacrée au retard dans l'acheminement des marchandises[28]. Cette indulgence dont bénéficie le transporteur maritime s'expliquerait par le caractère aléatoire de ce mode de transport. Au regard de ce caractère aléatoire en effet, le retard à la livraison est traité plutôt avec bienveillance. Ainsi, une juridiction a pu déclarer qu'« on ne peut exiger d'un navire soumis aux aléas de la navigation qu'il ait la précision d'un transport ferroviaire ou routier »[29]. La doctrine classique va dans le même sens : le doyen Ripert lui-même relevait qu'« on ne peut, dans le transport maritime, arriver à la régularité du transport terrestre ; les opérations sont plus longues, les départs moins nombreux, les risques plus grands, la durée du transport plus longue »[30].

S'il est vrai que le transport maritime reste encore aujourd'hui le mode de transport le plus aléatoire, la mer étant un élément naturel difficile à domestiquer même avec les moyens techniques contemporains, l'on ne saurait occulter les énormes progrès réalisés dans ce domaine et qui invitent à s'interroger sur la légitimité d'une telle indulgence envers le transporteur maritime. Plusieurs raisons militent d'ailleurs en faveur d'une sévérité plus accrue du régime de responsabilité du transporteur maritime en cas de retard[31].

Tout d'abord, et cela a déjà été relevé, la navigation maritime a bénéficié de progrès techniques immenses. Les transports maritimes ont considérablement évolué et sont devenus de plus en plus sûrs et rapides. Le caractère aléatoire de la navigation s'est donc considérablement atténué. Aussi un auteur[32], bon observateur de cette évolution, a-t-il pu

---

[28] Voir ACHARD (R) : « La responsabilité résultant du retard dans le transport international des marchandises par mer » in DMF 1990, pp. 668 et s. ; LAAZIZI (M) : « Le retard à la livraison et la responsabilité du transporteur international de marchandises par mer », A.D.M.A., 1993, pp. 325 et s. ; TINAYRE (A) : « Réflexions sur le retard », Mélanges Pierre BONASSIES, éd. Moreux, Paris 2001, p. 387 et s.

[29] T.C. de Paris, 19 janvier 1982, DMF 1982. 686.

[30] RIPERT (G) : Droit maritime, n° 1529, p. 438.

[31] Voir RACINE (J-B), *op. cit.*, n° 14.

[32] SERIAUX (A) : *La faute du transporteur*, Ed. Economica, 2e éd. 1998, n° 19, p. 16

affirmer que « de nos jours, les routes maritimes sont parfaitement connues et éprouvées ; la navigation maritime, quoique parfois soumise à des aléas naturels, offre plus de sécurité et de stabilité. Il apparaît alors normal, conclut-il, de faire peser sur le transporteur par mer une certaine obligation de célérité ».

Ensuite, le retard dans la livraison de marchandises est très préjudiciable dans une économie concurrentielle. Le temps, aujourd'hui, représente une valeur économique. « *Time is money* », disent les Anglais, opérateurs économiques par excellence. Le destinataire a généralement un besoin immédiat des marchandises transportées pour satisfaire sa propre clientèle. Parmi les points communs à tous les contrats de transport, un auteur[33] a relevé l'importance que revêt le temps en écrivant que « pressé par sa clientèle de tenir ses délais, le transporteur vit contre la montre ; le contentieux du contrat de transport atteste mieux combien notre société est pressée ».

Compte tenu de la pertinence de ces arguments, le transport maritime ne devrait pas faire exception à la règle[34]. De manière générale, il est traditionnellement enseigné que la rapidité est de l'essence du commerce. Le droit commercial prend en compte cette donnée. Pourquoi le droit maritime n'irait-il pas dans ce sens ? Et comme le dit si bien une fois de plus cet auteur[35], « l'indulgence envers le retard – antithèse de la rapidité – ne se justifie certainement plus à l'heure actuelle ».

Les rédacteurs des Règles de Hambourg avaient compris la leçon et ont bien pris la mesure des progrès réalisés en ce domaine. Aussi ont-ils prévu des dispositions permettant d'appréhender spécifiquement le retard. Aux termes de l'article 5-2 de cette convention, la responsabilité du transporteur se trouve ainsi engagée non seulement « lorsque les marchandises n'ont pas été livrées au port de déchargement prévu par le contrat de transport par mer, dans le délai expressément prévu », mais

---

33 REMOND-GOUILLOUD (M) : *Le contrat de transport*, coll. Connaissance du droit, 1993, p. 11.

34 Voir dans ce sens, DELEBECQUE (P) : « Le particularisme des contrats maritimes » in Mélanges Pierre BONASSIES, éd. Moreux, 2001, p. 127, spéc. p. 151.

35 RACINE (J-B), op. cit. n° 14 *in fine*.

aussi, « à défaut d'un tel accord, dans le délai qu'il serait raisonnable d'exiger d'un transporteur diligent compte tenu des circonstances de fait », précise *in fine* cet article. C'est dire qu'il appartient aux parties contractantes de fixer librement le délai d'acheminement des marchandises au-delà duquel le transporteur verrait sa responsabilité engagée. Et dans l'hypothèse où les parties n'auraient pas pris la précaution d'en fixer un, les Règles de Hambourg, de manière supplétive, sanctionnent le retard lorsque celui-ci apparaît déraisonnable, c'est-à-dire en fait, anormalement long. Autrement dit, un certain retard est toléré à la condition qu'il ne dépasse pas ce qui est raisonnable. Le critère du raisonnable est un standard du droit, une norme souple et adaptable[36].

C'est ce régime que remettent en cause aujourd'hui les Règles de Rotterdam. Dominées en effet par le principe de la liberté contractuelle, elles ne sanctionnent le retard que dans la seule hypothèse où la livraison des marchandises est faite après le délai expressément convenu par les parties contractantes. Aux termes de leur article 21 en effet, « il y a retard lorsque les marchandises ne sont pas livrées au lieu de destination prévu dans le contrat de transport dans le délai convenu ». Elles ont supprimé le délai légal supplétif auquel on devrait se référer dans l'hypothèse où les parties contractantes n'auraient pas convenu d'un délai pour effectuer la livraison des marchandises à destination. Ce qui, en dépit de l'intention louable d'indemniser le retard, a pour conséquence que le principe de l'acceptation du délai par le transporteur rend cette indemnisation virtuelle, d'autant qu'il n'est pas d'usage de définir des délais de livraison précis, que les *transit time* ne sont communiqués qu'à titre indicatif. En abandonnant à la liberté contractuelle cette importante question de l'indemnisation pour cause de retard, c'est-à-dire en conditionnant cette indemnisation au non-respect du seul délai librement prévu par les parties, les règles de Rotterdam, sachant qu'il ne sera jamais facile de faire accepter à un transporteur maritime un délai contraignant de livraison, consacrent subtilement de manière particulière son irresponsabilité en ce

[36] Voir KAIRALLAH (G) : « Le raisonnable en droit privé, développements récents », in RTDCiv. 1984. 439 ; FORTIER (V) : « Le contrat du commerce international à l'aune du raisonnable » in JDI 1996. 315.

domaine, comme du reste, d'une manière générale, dans le régime de sa responsabilité.

II – Le retour à un régime de quasi-irresponsabilité du transporteur maritime

La volonté des rédacteurs des Règles de Rotterdam de retourner à un régime de quasi-irresponsabilité du transporteur maritime tel qu'il était en vigueur par le passé se manifeste à travers non seulement le régime des délais des réserves à la livraison des marchandises qui conditionne le succès de l'action en responsabilité de leur ayant droit contre le transporteur (A), mais aussi le régime de la responsabilité même du transporteur (B).

A – Du fait des délais impartis pour des réserves à la livraison des marchandises

Les réserves jouent un rôle important dans le régime de la responsabilité du transporteur des marchandises. Tenu en effet à l'obligation de résultat, le transporteur, sur qui pèse cette lourde responsabilité, doit être rapidement fixé sur le fait de savoir, une fois la livraison de la marchandise effectuée, s'il a parfaitement accompli son obligation ou non. Aussi a-t-il toujours été admis que le destinataire, pour agir en responsabilité contre le transporteur, devait d'abord prouver qu'il a fait des réserves à la livraison de la marchandise ou, à tout le moins, dans le délai à lui imparti. Le destinataire qui ne les avait pas faites était déchu de tout droit d'action. C'était une fin de non-recevoir. C'est ce régime que l'on retrouve consacré dans le code de commerce qui, en son article 105, édicte pour les transports terrestres une fin de non-recevoir en l'absence des réserves[37]. Au niveau international, à l'image de la convention de Varsovie de 1929 (art. 26-4), la convention de Montréal de 1999 sur le transport aérien international conserve

[37] Voir AKAM AKAM (A) : « La conservation de l'action en réparation contre les transporteurs terrestres de marchandises : les exigences de l'article 105 du Code de Commerce » in Revue *Lex Lata,* n° 18 et 19 de septembre/octobre 1995, p. 10 ; CHAO (A) : « L'article 105 du Code de Commerce : un texte redoutable et dépassé », in B.T. 1987, 553.

également ce régime ; aux termes de son article 31 (4) en effet, « à défaut de protestation dans les délais prévus, toutes actions contre le transporteur sont irrecevables, sauf le cas de fraude de celui-ci ».

Affirmant très tôt son particularisme, le droit maritime s'est de tout temps éloigné de cette rigueur du droit classique des transports. Au système de la fin de non-recevoir qui a un caractère absolu, la Convention de Bruxelles de 1924 avait substitué le principe de la présomption de livraison conforme. Si les réserves ne sont pas faites dans les délais, l'on présume que les marchandises ont été réceptionnées par le destinataire telles qu'elles se trouvent décrites au connaissement. Cette présomption n'entraîne nullement pour l'ayant droit à la marchandise déchéance du droit d'agir contre le transporteur ; mais elle emporte tout simplement renversement de la charge de la preuve. Les Règles de Hambourg sont restées fidèles à cette démarcation, tout comme aujourd'hui, les Règles de Rotterdam qui disposent en leur article 23 (2) que « l'absence d'avis n'a pas d'incidence sur le droit de demander réparation en cas de perte ou de dommage subi par les marchandises... ».

Mais, tout en maintenant le principe de la présomption de livraison conforme hérité de la convention de Bruxelles, les rédacteurs des Règles de Hambourg, conscients du fait qu'avec le gigantisme des navires actuels permettant de transporter en même temps plusieurs milliers des conteneurs, il peut être livré au même moment à un destinataire plusieurs d'entre eux, ont rallongé à juste titre les délais impartis pour faire des réserves en cas de dommages survenus aux marchandises pendant le transport. Ainsi, en cas de dommages apparents, c'est-à-dire des dommages que le réceptionnaire peut constater par un examen rapide, mais diligent à l'aide des sens dont chacun dispose, les Règles de Hambourg prévoient que les réserves pourront être faites non seulement le jour de la livraison de la marchandise, mais également le premier jour ouvrable suivant ce jour (art. 19). Les Règles de Hambourg corrigent ainsi la convention de Bruxelles qui, en pareille hypothèse, exigeait du destinataire qu'il adresse des réserves écrites au transporteur ou à son représentant au port au plus tard au moment de la livraison seulement. Faisant une fois encore marche arrière, les Règles de Rotterdam font fi de cette avancée et reviennent systématiquement aux dispositions de la Convention de Bruxelles. Aux termes de leur article 23-1, elles disposent en effet que « le transporteur est présumé, en l'absence de preuve contraire, avoir livré les marchandises telles que celles-ci sont décrites dans les données du contrat, à moins qu'un avis de perte ou de dommage subi par les marchandises indiquant la nature générale de la perte ou du dommage n'ait été donné au transporteur ou à la partie exécutante qui les a livrées, *avant (!) ou au moment de la livraison…* ».

À la lecture de ce texte, l'on ne peut manquer de relever la manifestation de la légèreté dans la rédaction de cette convention internationale. Peut-on imaginer en effet que le destinataire à qui incombe en réalité la charge de faire des réserves relativement à la qualité ou à la quantité des marchandises reçues ou de leurs emballages le fasse *avant la livraison ;* par quelle alchimie a-t-il pu inspecter les marchandises avant même qu'elles ne lui soient présentées au point d'encourir une sanction si jamais il ne faisait pas des réserves sur des marchandises que, par hypothèse, il n'a même pas encore vues ?

Dans le même sens, en cas de dommages non apparents, le délai de trois jours qui incluait du reste les jours fériés, imposé par la convention de Bruxelles a été porté à quinze jours par les Règles de Hambourg. Les rédacteurs des Règles de Rotterdam, sans gêne, l'ont tout bonnement ramené à sept jours ouvrables (art. 23-1 *in fine*). Ce qui est pour le moins incompréhensible quand on sait par exemple que dans le transport aérien où les quantités de marchandises transportées sont de loin très inférieures à celles du transport maritime, la convention de Montréal accorde néanmoins au destinataire un délai de quatorze jours à dater de la réception des marchandises pour adresser sa protestation en cas d'avarie (art. 31-2).

Au regard de ce régime des délais des réserves à la livraison des marchandises, l'on comprend aisément l'état d'esprit des rédacteurs des Règles de Rotterdam, lequel dissimule de manière très imparfaite leur nostalgie d'un droit des transports maritimes originel que l'on croyait à jamais révolu et où le transporteur se trouve pratiquement à l'abri de toute responsabilité, quelle que soit la qualité de l'exécution de ses obligations. Pour preuve de cette volonté, si besoin est, le régime général de la responsabilité par trop favorable au transporteur.

B – Du fait du régime de la responsabilité adopté

L'on se souvient qu'aux transporteurs qui avaient pris l'habitude de truffer les connaissements des *negligence clauses* tendant à faire peser l'intégralité du risque du transport maritime sur les chargeurs, à l'instar des clauses exonératoires ou limitatives de responsabilité, la convention de Bruxelles de 1924, s'inspirant du *Harter Act* américain, avait imposé de nouvelles règles en matière de responsabilité. Et bien qu'elle ait été considérée en son temps comme améliorant le sort des chargeurs par rapport à la situation qui prévalait à cette époque, cette convention a fait l'objet, plus tard de virulentes critiques, notamment par les pays en voie de développement, pour la plupart pays chargeurs. Le principal reproche fait à cette convention était que le transporteur y apparaissait en fin de compte comme bénéficiant d'un régime de responsabilité somme toute très favorable. En effet, bien que pesant sur lui une présomption de responsabilité, celle-ci se trouvait vidée de son contenu par une impressionnante longue liste des cas exceptés.

Et c'est en réaction à cet état de choses que, sous l'impulsion des pays en voie de développement, sont adoptées en 1978 les Règles de Hambourg. Cette convention, tout en reconduisant contre le transporteur maritime une présomption de responsabilité, a supprimé la presque totalité des cas exceptés comme causes exonératoires contenues dans la convention de Bruxelles. Seuls deux cas exceptés ont été maintenus. Le premier est celui de l'incendie. Aux termes de l'article 5 (4) des Règles de Hambourg, le transporteur est responsable des dommages causés aux marchandises par l'incendie, mais seulement dans le cas où le demandeur fait la preuve, soit que l'incendie résulte d'une faute ou négligence du transporteur ou de l'un de ses préposés, soit qu'une faute du même ordre a été commise en ce qui concerne les mesures qui peuvent être raisonnablement exigées pour éteindre l'incendie et éviter ou atténuer ses conséquences. Pareillement, et c'est le second cas maintenu, le transporteur est déchargé de la responsabilité pour les dommages résultant des mesures prises pour sauver des vies en mer ou, s'il s'agit d'assistance aux biens, des mesures raisonnablement prises à cet effet. Les raisons humanitaires justifient le maintien de ce cas excepté. Comme le relève effectivement un auteur, « si l'on veut que la solidarité en mer ne reste pas un vain mot, le transporteur qui se déroute et dépense ses soins pour tenter de sauver des personnes ou des biens ne doit pas être pénalisé »[38].

Hormis ces deux cas exceptés, tous les autres ont été abandonnés. Un auteur pouvait dès lors constater à juste titre qu'« aux yeux de la plupart des pays en développement… la disparition des exonérations de responsabilité accordées au transporteur est leur victoire »[39]. L'équilibre des intérêts en présence, ceux du transporteur, mais aussi ceux des chargeurs ou ayants droit à la marchandise, paraît assuré.

Malheureusement, c'est cet important acquis auquel tenaient particulièrement les chargeurs que viennent remettre en cause les Règles de Rotterdam. En effet, tout en maintenant le principe de la présomption de responsabilité du transporteur, les Règles de Rotterdam, faisant brutalement contre toute attente « marche arrière », ont reconduit la presque totalité des cas exceptés de la convention de Bruxelles. Aux termes de l'article 17 (3) des Règles de Rotterdam en effet, « le transporteur est aussi déchargé de tout ou partie de sa responsabilité (…) si (…) il prouve qu'un ou plusieurs des évènements ou circonstances ci-après ont causé la perte, le dommage ou le retard ou y ont contribué :

a) « Actes de Dieu » ;

b) Périls, dangers ou accidents de la mer ou d'autres eaux navigables ;

c) Guerre, hostilités, conflit armé, piraterie, terrorisme, émeutes et troubles civils ;

d) Restriction de quarantaine, intervention ou obstacle de la part des États, d'autorités publiques, de dirigeants ou du peuple, y compris une

---

[38] REMOND-GOUILLOUD (M) : Droit maritime, op. cit. n° 591.

[39] LEGENDRE (C) : « La Convention des Nations Unies sur le transport des marchandises par mer » in DMF 1978, 387.

immobilisation, un arrêt ou une saisie non imputable au transporteur ou à l'une quelconque des personnes mentionnées à l'article 18[40] ;

e) Grèves, lock-out, arrêts ou entraves apportés au travail ;

f) Incendie à bord du navire ;

g) Vices cachés échappant à une diligence raisonnable ;

h) Acte ou omission du chargeur, du chargeur documentaire, de la partie contrôlante ou de toute autre personne dont les actes engagent la responsabilité du chargeur ou du chargeur documentaire en vertu de l'article 33 ou 34 ;

i) Chargement, manutention, arrimage ou déchargement des marchandises réalisé en vertu d'une convention conclue conformément au paragraphe 2 de l'article 13, sauf si le transporteur ou une partie exécutante réalise cette opération au nom du chargeur, du chargeur documentaire ou du destinataire ;

j) Freinte en volume ou en poids ou tout autre dommage ou perte résultant d'un vice caché, de la nature spéciale ou d'un vice propre des marchandises ;

k) Insuffisance ou défectuosité de l'emballage ou du marquage non réalisé par le transporteur ou en son nom ;

l) Sauvetage ou tentative de sauvetage des vies en mer ;

m) Mesures raisonnables visant à sauver ou tenter de sauver des biens en mer ;

n) Mesures raisonnables visant à éviter ou tenter d'éviter un dommage à l'environnement ;

---

[40] Aux termes de l'article 18 qui traite de la responsabilité du transporteur pour fait d'autrui, le transporteur répond du manquement aux obligations qui lui incombent... résultant des actes ou omissions d'une partie exécutante, du capitaine ou de l'équipage du navire, de ses propres préposés ou de ceux d'une partie exécutante ou de toute personne qui s'acquitte ou s'engage à s'acquitter de l'une quelconque des obligations incombant au transporteur en vertu du contrat de transport, dans la mesure où elle agit, directement ou indirectement, à la demande de ce dernier ou sous son contrôle.

o) Actes accomplis par le transporteur dans l'exercice des pouvoirs conférés par les articles 15[41] et 16[42] ».

« L'exhumation » de tous ces cas exceptés surprend. S'ils pouvaient se justifier au début du XXe siècle où la navigation maritime était encore relativement aléatoire, bon nombre de ces cas exceptés n'ont plus leur raison d'être de nos jours au regard des progrès techniques réalisés dans ce domaine et ayant rendu les transports maritimes plus sûrs. Bien plus, leur caractère « fourre-tout » est de nature à permettre au transporteur maritime d'y trouver une cause pouvant l'exonérer pour n'importe quelle faute commise dans l'exécution de ses obligations contractuelles.

Certainement pour des raisons de décence, cette « exhumation » n'a épargné que le fameux cas excepté de faute dans la navigation et l'administration du navire, plus connu sous la dénomination de faute nautique. Devenu célèbre par l'importance du contentieux qu'il avait suscité[43], ce cas excepté défiait tout bon sens. Quelque voix avait du reste déjà entonné son requiem[44]. L'évocation constante de ce cas excepté paraissait véritablement indécente, d'autant plus que non seulement les progrès techniques avaient rendu moins aléatoire, donc plus sûre, la

---

[41] Aux termes de l'article 15, le transporteur ou une partie exécutante peut refuser de recevoir ou de charger les marchandises et peut prendre toute autre mesure raisonnable, notamment les décharger, les détruire ou les neutraliser, si celles-ci présentent, ou risquent selon toute vraisemblance raisonnable de présenter, pendant la durée de la responsabilité du transporteur, un danger réel pour les personnes, les biens ou l'environnement.

[42] Aux termes de l'article 16, « le transporteur ou une partie exécutante peut sacrifier des marchandises en mer lorsque cette décision est prise de manière raisonnable pour le salut commun ou pour préserver d'un péril la vie humaine ou d'autres biens engagés dans l'aventure commune ». Ce sacrifice est connu dans le jargon maritimiste d'avarie commune ; pour plus de détails sur cette pratique, voir BOKALLI (V-E) : « L'avarie commune : réflexion critique sur une institution traditionnelle du droit maritime » in DMF 1996, 355 et s.

[43] Voir RODIERE (R) : « Faute nautique et faute commerciale devant la jurisprudence française », DMF 1961, 451 ; LAFAGE (G.H.) : « La notion de faute nautique en droit maritime français », *Rev. Jurisp. Com.*, 1961, 103.

[44] MOLFESSIS (N) : « Requiem pour la faute nautique », in *Mélanges Pierre Bonassies*, *op. cit.*, p. 207 et s.

manœuvre d'un navire, mais en plus, ainsi que le relève un auteur[45], « la jurisprudence [sur la faute nautique] semble en quelque sorte récompenser les fautes les plus évidentes et les négligences les plus grossières ... du transporteur ». Aussi le Professeur Bonassies, dans un style aimablement ferme qu'on lui connaît, pouvait-il écrire, au lendemain de l'adoption des Règles de Hambourg, que « quelque regret que l'on ait de voir disparaître l'un des traits les plus originaux du droit des transports ... la disparition de la cause d'irresponsabilité que constitue la faute nautique, était conforme à l'évolution de notre droit. Aussi attaché que l'on soit au particularisme du droit maritime, reconnaît-il, l'irresponsabilité pour faute demeure choquante »[46].

Concluons. Le droit des transports maritimes internationaux des marchandises baigne dans un véritable désordre compte tenu de la diversité des textes applicables. En effet, le transport international des marchandises par mer est aujourd'hui régi, selon les cas, non seulement par la convention de Bruxelles relative à l'unification de certaines règles en matière de connaissement de 1924, soit dans sa version initiale pour les États qui n'ont pas ratifié l'un ou l'autre des protocoles modificatifs de 1968 et 1979, soit dans l'une de ces versions modifiées, mais aussi par la convention des Nations unies sur le transport de marchandises par mer de 1978 dite Règles de Hambourg. Cette mosaïque de textes institue autant de régimes subtilement différents les uns des autres. Cette coexistence est source de sérieux problèmes de conflits de conventions

---

[45] *Idem*, p. 236.

[46] BONASSIES (P) : « Règles de la Haye, Règles de Hambourg, Règles de Marseille » in *Annales* IMTM 1989, p. 116. Mais aussi curieux que cela puisse paraître, certains nostalgiques en sont encore à déplorer aujourd'hui le fait que le cas excepté de faute nautique n'ait pas été reconduit par les rédacteurs des Règles de Rotterdam : c'est le cas, à en croire les indiscrétions de certains membres de la commission d'élaboration de la nouvelle convention, de la délégation grecque qui plaidait pour la reconduction de ce cas excepté ; c'est également le cas, à en croire monsieur le professeur IN HYEON KIM de l'université de droit de Séoul, des armateurs coréens qui s'opposent à la ratification des Règles de Rotterdam, en particulier en raison de la disparition de la faute nautique (voir le compte rendu de sa communication intitulée « *The Rotterdam Rules from Korean Perspective* » au colloque de l'IMTM précité et synthétisé par FEDI (L), p. 16.

dans ce domaine et d'énormes difficultés dans la détermination du droit applicable au contrat de transport[47].

Devant cette situation inconfortable, tout le monde semble s'accorder sur la nécessité d'avoir une législation unique qui, tout en préservant autant que faire se peut les intérêts de toutes les parties en présence, assure la sécurité juridique dans ce domaine. Comme le dit fort à propos un auteur[48], « le droit a horreur du multiple. Sa vocation, c'est l'ordre unifié et hiérarchisé, unifié parce que hiérarchisé ». D'autres auteurs [49]de préciser, dans le même sens, que « l'une des tâches principales qui incombent au juriste soucieux de faciliter les rapports internationaux est de mettre fin à cette anarchie ; dans un monde où les rapports internationaux ont pris une si grande importance, il convient de donner une assise sûre à ces rapports. Une entente doit être réalisée entre les divers pays, pour que partout soit appliqué, à un rapport donné, le même droit. Les États doivent élaborer et accepter, en la matière, des solutions uniformes. Des conventions internationales doivent être conclues, et en dehors même de telles conventions, la jurisprudence, lorsqu'elle établit une règle de conflit, doit, dans chaque pays, être encouragée à prendre en considération la manière dont le problème qui se pose à elle a d'ores et déjà été résolu par la loi ou la jurisprudence dans d'autres pays ».

---

[47] Voir NGUENE NTEPPE (J) : « Les conflits de conventions internationales de droit privé, le cas de la Convention de Bruxelles de 1924 et des Règles de Hambourg de 1978 sur le droit des transports maritimes internationaux de marchandises », Thèse de doctorat en droit, Nantes, 1997 ; KHALIL DIALLO (I) : « Les conflits de lois en matière de transport international des marchandises par mer », Thèse de droit, Paris II, 1987 ; DELEBECQUE (P) : « Le droit international des transports maritimes », Académie de droit international de la Haye, Centre d'Etude et de Recherche de Droit International et de Relations Internationales, 1999, M. NJIHOFF Publishers, 2001, P13 ; NICOLAS (P-Y) : « Les conflits de conventions internationales », *Mélanges Pierre Bonassies*, op.cit. p. 265 ; BERGEL J-L) : « Méthodes de coordination des textes et droit des transports », *Revue Scapel*, 1994, p. 13.

[48] DELMAS-MARTY (M) : Trois défis pour un droit mondial, Seuil, essais, Paris 1998, p. 104.

[49] DAVID (R) et JAUFFRET-SPINOSI (C) : *Les grands systèmes de droit contemporains*, 10 e éd. Dalloz, Paris 1992, pp. 7-8, n° 7.

C'est ici le lieu de dénoncer cette attitude des rédacteurs des Règles de Rotterdam qui ont fait montre d'un parti pris inacceptable en faveur des transporteurs. La convention de Bruxelles de 1924 avait été élaborée par le Comité maritime international (CMI), organisation non gouvernementale rassemblant essentiellement juristes et professionnels des grandes puissances maritimes, à une époque où la plupart des pays en voie de développement, tous principalement pays de chargeurs, n'existaient pas en tant qu'États souverains et n'avaient donc pas pris part à sa rédaction. Aussi est-il aisé de comprendre que cette convention ait fait la part belle aux transporteurs. D'ailleurs, presque personne ne l'a jamais nié.

Les Règles de Hambourg, produits de la CNUCED et de la CNUDCI, structures des Nations unies où ces pays en voie de développement, regroupés à cette époque au sein du Groupe dit des 77, sont majoritaires, ont voulu corriger ce déséquilibre. S'il est incontestable que la responsabilité du transporteur s'en trouve renforcée, l'on ne saurait prétendre qu'elles aient versé dans l'excès inverse. Et quand bien même cela aurait été le cas, les Règles de Rotterdam donnaient ainsi l'occasion d'élaborer enfin un véritable texte de compromis entre les intérêts des partisans de la convention de Bruxelles et ceux des partisans des Règles de Hambourg. Mais au lieu de cela, les rédacteurs des Règles de Rotterdam, ignorant superbement les intérêts des chargeurs, ont tout simplement recopié, dans les questions pourtant bien connues comme étant très sensibles, les dispositions de la convention de Bruxelles, comme si les reproches adressés à ce texte étaient sans fondement.

Cette démarche peu constructive et empreinte de nostalgie n'est pas de nature à ramener en cette matière la sécurité juridique tant recherchée par les parties à la relation de transport international des marchandises par mer. Bien au contraire, en s'inscrivant comme une convention de plus, voire de trop, les Règles de Rotterdam rajoutent au désordre tant décrié déjà dans la mesure où il est en effet facile de deviner que cette nouvelle convention, dont on ne doute nullement de l'entrée en vigueur un jour compte tenu non seulement de la puissance des pays développés qui ont joué un rôle moteur dans son élaboration – bien qu'eux-mêmes curieusement ne se hâtent pas à la ratifier[50] —, mais aussi et surtout de la forte pression qu'ils exercent sur certains pays en développement pour les amener à la ratification[51], sera vraisemblablement rejetée par bon nombre de ceux-ci. Finalement, l'avènement d'une accalmie de la mer tant souhaitée se trouve renvoyé aux calendes grecques…

---

[50] Voir BONASSIES (P) et DELEBECQUE (P) qui ont « du mal à comprendre la réticence, en la matière, des Etats de l'Union Européenne », in DMF hors série, n° 18 de juin 2014, n° 69 *in fine*, p. 67.

[51]Sans que ses motivations aient été explicitées, « le législateur » de la Communauté Economique et Monétaire de l'Afrique Centrale (CEMAC) regroupant le Cameroun, le Congo, le Gabon, le Tchad et la Guinée Equatoriale, s'est empressé d'intégrer purement et simplement ces Règles de Rotterdam dans le Code de la Marine marchandise de cette communauté [voir Kenguep (E) : « Les Règles de Rotterdam : dérive et servitude du législateur maritime de la CEMAC », in *Revue Juridis Périodique*, n° 97] alors même que les pays européens, sous la pression de leurs associations des chargeurs, hésitent à adhérer à ce texte.

SOCIAL LICENSING AND ITS BEARING IN CAMEROON

Dashaco John TAMBUTOH*

Bande Gulbert MBAH TARH**

* (Associate Professor), The University of Bamenda
** University of Yaounde II

SUMMARY

This Article examines the nature and attributes of Social License to Operate (SLO) and its growing significance as a critical success factor for sustainable development and it is intended to enhance its contextualization. Thus, the policy implications is that even though local conditions, needs and customs vary considerably and are often opaque, they have a significant impact on the likelihood of success of the various approaches in building social capital and trust. In this light, the governments could facilitate the necessary stakeholder mapping for which they are responsible and provide a regulatory framework that sets companies on the right path for engagement with the communities and stakeholders. Also, it stresses that the growing reliance on social media tools by stakeholders and proponents alike, and the risks associated with disclosure through them, may lead to an increased need for the development of guiding ethical and technical codes of conduct or other standards. These voluntary measures to corporate responsibility frameworks can contribute in achieving SLO, particularly through enhancing a company's reputation and strengthening its capacity for effective communication, engagement, and collaboration. Since the process of acquiring social license to operate demands early and ongoing investment of effort to develop and maintain social capital within the context of trust-based relationship with indigenous communities and other interested groups, this is often intangible and informal, and is realized through a robust suite of actions centered on the timely and effective communication, meaningful dialogue, and ethical and responsible behaviour. Hence, the evolving policy and regulatory context within which social license exists in Cameroon. The implications of the convergence between the social media platforms and technologies in building trust and social capital, which are key determinants of social license, are also explored. Finally, the paper concludes by highlighting the trends of SLO in Cameroon by recommending the need for a viable social responsibility legislation and institutional framework.

INTRODUCTION

The search for *social justice* in, and *equitable distribution* of, resources and development opportunities in Cameroon and elsewhere appear central to the concept of benefit sharing and the energy and mining sectors are not an exception[1]. It still has to be determined, however, whether in the circumstances the firm or project promoter considers benefits-sharing as an instrument of local development? In other words, does local development entail the forfeiture of financial performance or put at bay the hitherto well established economic rationale concept of the company? The management of social risks should therefore be well understood by the stakeholders, that is administrative authorities, financiers of large projects, the civil society and the communities concerned since social risks emanate essentially from the dissatisfaction of the latter groups of persons[2] and can jeopardize the social license to operate.

---

[1] International Energy Agency (2000), *Hydropower and the Environment : Present Context and Guidelines for Future Action*, IEA Technical Report, Annex III-Volume I : Summary and Recommendations, Paris, France ; World Commission on Dams (2000), *Dams and Development : A new framework for decision-making*, The Report of the World Commission on Dams, Earthscan, London.

[2] Engineers Against Poverty (EAP) (2008)., *A systematic approach to project social risk & opportunity management*, Briefing Note, Institution of Civil Engineers, London.

The term social license to operate (SLO) emerged in the mining sector as a response to social risk in the mid-1990s[3] and is today widely used by mining companies[4], civil society and non-governmental organizations[5], research institutions[6], governments[7], and consultants.[8] Social license to operate has also been adapted by a range of other industries, including pulp and paper manufacturing[9], alternative energy generation[10], and agriculture[11]. However, what constitutes a social license and the underlying processes to obtain one are less well-understood. Additionally, limited research to date has been conducted to explore what factors contribute to and/or undermine acceptance of mining

---

[3] Boutilier, R., Thomson, I. (2011*), Modeling and Measuring the Social License to Operate : Fruits of a Dialogue Between Theory and Practice,* International Mine Management, Queensland, Australia.

[4] BHPB, (2011), *Our future : Sustainability report 2011.* BHPB, Melbourne, Australia ; Kurlander, L.T., (2001), *Newmont mining : the social license to operate.* Proceedings of the Global Executive Forum, University of Colorado Denver.http ://www.ucdenver.edu/academics/InternationalPrograms/CIBER/GlobalForumReports/Documents/Newmont_Minin_Social_License.pdf

[5] Slack, K. (2009), Mining Conflicts in Peru : Condition critical Oxfam America, Boston.

[6] CSIRO. (2013), *Social licence to Operate, Minerals Down Under CSIRO*, Brisbane, Australia.) ; McNab,K., Onate, B., Brereton, D., Horberry, T., Lynas, D., Franks, D.M. (2013)., Exploring the Social Dimensions of Autonomous and Remote Operation Mining : Applying Social Licence in Design CSIRO, Brisbane, Australia.

[7] Australian Government. (2009)., Community Engagement and Development : Leading Practice Sustainable Development Program for the Mining Industry Australian Government, Canberra, Australia.

[8] Black, L., (2013)., The social licence as a framework for managing cumulative impacts : A case study of the Upper Hunter mining dialogue. In : Proceedings of the International Association of Impact Assessment Conference, Calgary, Canada.

[9] Gunningham, N., Kagan, R.A., Thornton, D. (2004)., Social license and environmental protection : why business go beyond compliance Law Soc. Inq., 29, pp. 307–341

[10] Hall, N., Ashworth, P., Devine-Wright, P. (2013)., Societal acceptance of wind farms : analysis of four common themes across Australian case studies Energy Policy, 58, pp. 200–208. http ://dx.doi.org/10.1016/j.enpol.2013.03.009

[11] Williams, J., Martin, P. (2011)., Defending the Social Licence of Farming : Issues, Challenges and New Directions for Agriculture, CSIRO Publishing, Collingwood, VIC, Australia.

developments by host communities. From these studies, SLO has been described as intangible and unwritten[12], and difficult if not impossible to measure[13]. It has also been represented as a set of meaningful relationships between operational stakeholders based on mutual trust[14], and as a set of demands and expectations for how a business will operate by local stakeholders and broader civil society[15]. Most studies of social license are descriptive in nature and seek to provide companies with guidance for securing a social license. For instance, strategies such as ongoing communication with affected operational stakeholders, transparent disclosure of information to host communities, and strengthening community development agreements have been recommended as practical ways for obtaining a social license with local communities.[16]

In their influential theoretical work on the SLO construct, *Thomson and Boutilier*'s cumulative pyramid model of social license identified three central components : legitimacy, credibility and trust.[17] They suggested that as a mining operation develops legitimacy and then credibility with its local stakeholders, acceptance and then approval of the operation will follow. As this relationship develops into full trust, the

---

[12] Franks, D.M., McNab, K., Brereton, D., Cohen, T., Weldegiorgis, F., Horberry, T., Lynas, D., Garcia-Vasquez, M., Santibáñez, B.O., Barnes, R., McLellan, B., (2013)., Designing mining technology for social outcomes : Final Report of the Technology Futures Project.

[13] Parsons, R., Lacey, J., (201).,. Maintaining discursive legitimacy of a contested practice : how the Australian minerals industry understands its SLO. In : Proceedings of the 5th Australasian Caucus of the Standing Conference on Organisational Symbolism, Melbourne, Australia.

[14] Warhurst, A. (2001)., Corporate citizenship and corporate social investment : drivers of tri-sector partnership, J. Corp. Citizsh., 1, p. 57.

[15] Gunningham et al., (2004)., *op cit.*

[16] Nelsen, J.L. (2006)., Social license to operate, Int. J. Min., Reclam. Environ., 20, pp. 161–162 ; Owen, J.R. ; Kemp, D. (2012)., Social licence and mining : a critical perspective, Resources Policy, 38, pp. 29–35 ; Wilburn, K.M., Wilburn, R. (2011)., Achieving social licence to operate using stakeholder theory, J. Int. Bus. Ethics, 4, pp. 3–16

[17] Boutilier and Thomson, (2011)., *op cit.*

local community would be expected to begin to co-identify with the mining company and actively support its interests. However, the authors' own attempts to empirically validate these hypothesized cumulative relationships have been unsuccessful to date.[18] Indeed, to fill this gap in the literature, we shall critically elaborate on the elements of social license. Specifically, we propose that community trust in a mining company is central in this model of social license and a strong predictor of community acceptance of its operation. Apparently, while it is universally accepted that legal permits or license is required from the relevant government agencies, project proponents are also acknowledging the importance of obtaining a SLO.

As earlier noted, the concept of SLO is to address the demands and expectations that emerge from neighbourhoods, environmental groups and community members, and other elements of the surrounding civil society. Failure to properly understand these expectations can generate a diversity of risks, that is, reputational damage, project delays or abandonment, security problems, etc. Thus, the term "social license," or "social license to operate," generally refers to a local community's acceptance or approval of a project or a company's ongoing presence. It is usually informal and intangible, and is granted by a community based on the opinions and views of stakeholders, including local populations, indigenous committee, and other interested parties.[19] In fact, due to this intangibility, it can be difficult to determine when social license has been achieved for a project. Social license may manifest in a variety of ways, ranging from absence of opposition to vocal support or even advocacy, and these various levels of social license may occur at the same time among different interested parties social license is dynamic, generally taking time to achieve and effort to maintain, and can be lost or degraded in response to events and behaviours exhibited by a company or its agents. Thus, while the notion of social license is consistent with

---

[18] *Ibid*

[19] Yates, B.F and Horvath, C.L. (2013)., Social License to Operate : How to Get It, and How to Keep It, All Summit Working Papers. Available for download at http ://www.nbr.org.

the norms and legal frameworks of many countries and jurisdictions, it is distinct from regulatory or legal license, which can typically only be conferred by governments. Legal license comprises formal authorization related to specific legislative and regulatory requirements and procedural conditions, and must be obtained before a regulated project or activity can proceed. In this light, legal license is usually clearly defined in scope and issued for a specific time, by a recognized government authority. Social license, in contrast, is informal and has no basis in law. Nevertheless, social license shares certain attributes with legal license. In particular, social license is often conditional and not mandatory as the legal license is, but it is increasingly regarded as a practical necessity before a project or activity that is regulated or not can proceed. In short, legal license does not obviate the need for and value of social license in most circumstances. Indeed, many energy, mining, and other resource-based firms are finding that attention to social license is beneficial for their long-term prospects in a region. The lessons of some notable failures in the regulatory approval process can be linked to broader issues of social license and community engagement, and many firms are now striving to learn from the cautionary tales of failed projects. We shall consider the conceptual framework of SLO before looking at its orientation in Cameroon.

I. SOCIAL LICENSE- THE CONCEPTUAL FRAMEWORK

Social license can be earned through a combination of activities and behaviours, centered on timely and effective communication, meaningful dialogue, and ethical and responsible environmental and social behaviour, all of which contribute to building trust and credibility : effectively communicating projects and activities, including providing timely and complete information ; undertaking community engagement in a respectful manner ; listening to the concern of the local community and using community input to improve upon projects and activities ; providing support for and building capacity in local communities by using a range of tools ; undertaking projects and activities in an environmentally, fiscally, and socially responsible manner - including but not necessarily limited to regulatory compliance ; striving to ensure that local communities benefit from or are not unfairly affected by projects and activities. In particular, the development of social license is increasingly viewed as an essential aspect of a company's long-term ability to develop and manage its endeavours and as a factor in maintaining the goodwill of regulators and the value of a company's brand. In addition, social license is important to companies because it provides the legitimacy for their presence and actions from a local community's perspective ; provides regulators with a level of comfort that a proponent is acting responsibly ; minimizes the risk of costly delays in regulatory approvals due to opposition ; assures shareholders and investors that a company is managing social and other risks associated with its projects and activities ; enhances trust by demonstrating to regulators and other stakeholders that the company is genuinely striving for good performance ; and protects a company's reputation in times of crisis. Social license is therefore dynamic, generally taking time to achieve and effort to maintain, and can be lost or degraded in response to events and behaviours exhibited by a company or its agents. We shall now consider the underlining principles of the approaches and tools, the understanding of situational diversity, and other key considerations for achieving social license.

A. EARNING A SOCIAL LICENSE

Earning a social license presupposes that the proponent indulges in a number of activities or make use of certain tools or adopt approaches well established in the domain of social corporate responsibility. These activities, approaches or tools include, but are not limited to direct, one-on-one consultation and engagement ; community information sessions, open houses, and workshops ; community investment programs ; local employment and procurement programs ; disclosure and reporting ; and the establishment of accessible communication channels and options, such as liaison officers, toll-free telephone numbers, websites, and social media platforms. The approaches and tools used must be appropriate for local conditions, needs, and customs. For example, in Australia, some aboriginal groups have traditional protocols for communication, and violation of these protocols can seriously harm the long-term relationship with the group. In other instances, particularly in remote communities, as is the case in some areas in Cameroon, stakeholders may not have ready access to the Internet or other media and thus must be engaged through other means. Other challenges include complex systems of representation, governance, and decision-making within local communities and groups that may warrant special engagement methods. These local conditions, needs, and customs are often opaque to outsiders but enable the development and implementation of an effective strategy to build and maintain social license. Thus, social media is transforming the very nature of dialogue and communication between and among proponents and stakeholders. Viewed initially as an optional or even peripheral medium, and still regarded by many as a potentially risky venue, social media is quickly emerging as the communication medium of choice for many stakeholders.

1. The Management of Diversity

The activities of a company in any given place or in relation to a project can affect its ability to achieve social license. For example, a company that has a reputation for meaningful and constructive dialogue with local communities, compliance, and proactive environmental management and responsiveness to crises will likely have it easier to gain social license for an undertaking in a new region. In contrast, a company that has a poor compliance and performance record and a reputation for disregarding community concerns will face a much greater challenge in building the trust and social capital necessary to gain SLO. Indeed, social license is often spatially diverse. It may be achieved for one kind of activity or project but not for another, and in one region but not another. This variation partly stems from the difference in risk associated with different kinds of projects and activities, the company's experience in effectively managing those risks, and the differing interests and concerns of stakeholders at different times and places. With respect to the latter social license does not generally reflect a consensus view held broadly by a single, homogenous community, but rather it is a patchwork of divergent views on the level of social license achieved by a company and held by a diverse array of stakeholders with various political agendas and perceptions. These stakeholders can range from indigenous peoples with ancient claims to traditional use and occupation of the land to outside environmental groups who are interested in the project because of conservation goals established outside the project region. Consequently, acquiring social license often demands a flexible approach that is responsive to the diverse needs and interests of a range of stakeholders and interested parties. A successful strategy will be grounded in early and careful characterization of the stakeholder landscape ; this may be aided by engaging members of the local community as liaison officers who can identify and navigate local customs and issues. In fact, the local government services may also be helpful in this regard, because they are likely to be aware of the spectrum of stakeholders and issues in the region for which they are responsible. Thus, a distinction must also be made between broad and abstract matters of general public opinion, often reflected in and influenced by media coverage, and specific interests of local stakeholders, usually expressed through direct engagement. Proponents typically have greater capacity to establish relationships with local stakeholders and address specific issues than to shift public opinion directly. However, as local, specific social license increases in strength, particularly if that license manifests at the highest possible level of advocacy and partnership, there often is a favorable shift in paradigm on the part of the public.

2. The Key Considerations of Social License

The grant of social license vary, depending on the needs and priorities of those potentially affected by or interested in a project, but it generally relates to the conduct of company and how consistent it is in its messages and actions. These factors include, *inter alia* whether the company says what it will do and does what it says in a consistent manner, whether the company respect its commitments and promises, including those made in regulatory proceedings and community engagement? Whether the company voluntarily involves the community in the identification of issues to be resolved? Whether local customs are respected? Whether the company creates opportunities for the local community to benefit from the project or activity? Whether fair wages are paid and fair compensation made where necessary? Whether the company responds appropriately and promptly to any crisis situation or does it abdicate its responsibility when something goes wrong?

Positive performance in these areas takes a company closer to obtaining social license. However, when evaluating company action and behaviour, stakeholders often draw not only from present evidence but then also draw from information about past performance that may be contained in regulatory proceedings, media coverage, and the company's own communications. In fact, this list of factors illustrates the complexity of social license. The ease of achieving social license is typically inversely related to the complexity and potential severity of impacts that may arise from a project and the diversity of needs and priorities of stakeholders and interested parties. Thus, it depends on a timely, sustained, and adequate effort to understand the potential impacts and opportunities presented by a project and to build and maintain trust with stakeholders predicated on common interests. It is therefore easier to know when social license has not been granted than when it has been. But indicators of the former include the reduction or absence of vocal opposition to development, continued and increasing constructive participation in community and stakeholder dialogue, advocacy and expression of support for development, cooperation in community-based activities and enhancement measures, and willingness of key stakeholders to enter into partnerships or other forms of agreement. Although not a reliable indicator of social license as such, favorable and balanced media coverage may reflect growing social capital. Therefore, proponents should avoid making assumptions about social license and rely instead on stakeholders to articulate their own level of satisfaction.

It is important to note, however, that not all projects are eligible for social license. Examples are projects that do not serve the interests of local communities. Also, efforts to secure social license cannot overcome fundamental weaknesses in a project design or planning. The concept of social license is accordingly indicative of a departure from an era when regulatory license alone was adequate to advance a project or undertake an activity. Today, the primacy of the proponent in particular is diminished in relation to the ascendant influence of external stakeholders. In the context of social license, it is important to recognize that stakeholders will identify and define their own objectives and criteria for granting social license. The above notwithstanding, the influence exerted by stakeholders are not necessarily the same. While this reality makes achieving, confirming, and documenting social license more difficult, it also points to the need for the proponent to understand the scope of social license and determine who holds the key for its success.

3. The Cost-Benefit analysis of Social License

This is enclosed from the perspective of the communities, proponents, and the country. Thus, in hydropower projects, for example, the Local communities of the project areas during construction or operation phases usually face a number of risks. Their legitimate claim is not to become worse-off as a consequence of the new project and the mitigation and compensation measures taken aim at this. Unfortunately, most often traditional communities do not get their user rights for natural resources recognized and are simply excluded from the use of the resource with no or inadequate compensation.[20] This can be improved through dialogue and participation with the affected parties, so that mitigation and compensation packages are such as to avoid "no worse off" scenario. Enhancing local development opportunities through benefit sharing mechanisms may often be a cost-effective way of facilitating project implementation, as long as local communities perceive these mechanisms as contributing positively to their baseline conditions. Local communities can also enhance their development opportunities if they are supported by project promoters either alone or in collaboration with other stakeholders – public or private. The eventual improvement of local communities' baseline conditions can be expressed and monitored by indicators such as : per capita income, improvement of living standards, that is, housing, communications, and access to social

[20] Baland, J-M., Platteau, J-P. (1996)., Halting Degradation of Natural Resources : Is there a role for rural communities ?, Food and Agriculture Organization of the United Nations (FAO), Clarendon Press, Oxford.

infrastructure/services, measures of economic activity, that is, agricultural/livestock productivity, market access, etc. Local communities must therefore search for a balance between the risks of living in the project influence area with the opportunities it may carry and project promoters must understand that the higher the risks placed on these communities, the higher the challenge to support local development opportunities.

Also, from the project promoters' point of view, arguments justify profit sharing initiatives in socially beneficial projects. The first is that actions aimed at improving social and environmental performance may effect on profitability that differ *in the short versus the long term*. Higher levels of social responsibility may generate unrecoverable costs. It is thus easy to understand that enhancing local development initiatives – beyond what is required by a legal framework – entail costs for the project promoters from which some of its benefits are only visible in the long run as well as being difficult to measure. In addition, voluntary social investment may be hindered because the costs related to not having a responsible corporate behaviour are often hidden or unrecognized, while the savings from cutting corners seem obvious and may be considered as apparent benefits.[21] The benefit sharing measures may induce short-term decrease in profits which are followed by a more-than-compensatory increase in long-term profits. Under this vision, CSR/Benefit Sharing is about taking a long-term perspective to maximizing profits. This suggests that socially responsible investors should position themselves as long-term investors who monitor management and exert voice to correct short-termism.[22] The second argument claims that CSR can be explained by a new class of sociological and psychological ideas that have recently entered microeconomic theory in general and the individuals' agent utility function in particular ; as such, CSR can be perfectly compatible

---

[21] Testa, M. (2008)., Corporate Social Responsibility and Reputation Risk Analysis, Paper Prepared for Corporate Responsibility Research Conference 2008, Queen's University Management School/Queen's University Belfast (UK).

[22] Bénabou, R., Tirole, J. (2009)., Individual and Corporate Social Responsibility, TSE Working Paper Series 09-109, Toulouse School of Economics, Toulouse, France.

with profit maximization behaviour.[23] Standard motivational assumptions have been expanded and a literature on intrinsic (non-pecuniary, including social) aspects of motivation has emerged. This assumes that agents have preferences not only for money, but also for other social/public goods and reputation. The related departure from the neo-classical firm paradigm is closely linked to the extension of traditional individual choice theory towards a broader set of attitudes, preferences and calculations.[24] This approach is illustrated by the efforts known as "Triple Bottom Line" and represented by Sustainability Reports and/or by Social Reports where "wider values" determining social and economic values for all stakeholders, through the progressive expansion of social responsibility are taken into account.[25] For instance, ISAGEN, a Colombian utility, does report annually their contribution to social development with a "triple bottom line approach".[26]

B. THE ACUITY OF SOCIAL LICENSE

There is no commonly accepted definition of a social licence to operate. The term SLO is therefore a measure of confidence and trust society has in business to behave in a legitimate, transparent, accountable and socially acceptable way. It does not derive from a need for legal or regulatory compliance. Instead, it is deemed to be the foundation for enhancing legitimacy and acquiring future operational certainty, realising opportunities and lowering risk for the business, an unwritten contract between companies and society for companies to acquire acceptance or approval of their business operations. The terms of a SLO are often

---

[23] Reinhardt, F. L., Stavins, R.N. and Vietor, R.H.R. (2008)., "Corporate Social Responsibility Through an Economic Lens", Review of Environmental Economics and Policy, vol. 2(2), pp. 219-239, Summer.

[24] Kitzmueller, M. (2008)., Economics and Corporate Social Responsibility, EUI Working Papers
ECO 2008/37, European University Institute, Department of Economics, San Domenico di Fiesole, Italy.

[25] Testa, M. (2008)., Corporate Social Responsibility and Reputation Risk Analysis, Paper Prepared for Corporate Responsibility Research Conference 2008, Queen's University Management School/Queen's University Belfast (UK).

[26] ISAGEN (2010), Informe de Responsabilidad Empresarial 2009, Medellin.

project or location specific. Although society as a whole 'issues' the SLO, it is usually local communities who are the 'key arbiter' of the terms of the SLO due to their proximity to the company's activities and associated effects ;[27] and the relationship required for this contract to operate relies on trust and consistency between parties, quality information being provided, accountability, flexibility and transparency from all parties. Therefore, a SLO can be difficult to earn and can be easily revoked if society believes that the company is not meeting the terms of the contract. Companies need to continuously reassess the terms of the SLO to accommodate changes in social expectations.[28] Thus, SLO is also embedded in the concept of CSR which at its broadest considers the role of business in society in ethical terms. The concept now extends beyond environmental issues to those of social equity. *Boutilier and Thomson* and *Sinclair Knight Mertz* have attempted to describe what a SLO might look like, and propose that most companies and projects are located at the acceptance or approval level most of the time.[29]

1. The Voluntary Measures and Long View of Social License

Some voluntary measures are most influential for social license and are considered here below.

a) The Stakeholder Engagement, Disclosure and Governance

Ongoing dialogue and engagement with stakeholders build trust that can provide a base social capital when advancing a specific project or when faced with a crisis. To be effective stakeholder engagement must be timely, inclusive, complete, and meaningful. Timeliness entails that engagement commences before a stakeholder is affected by a corporation's actions and continues until legitimate issues are resolved or

---

[27] Prno, J., & Slocombe, D. S. 2012, Exploring the origins of 'social licence to operate' in the mining sector : Perspectives from governance and sustainability theories. Resources Policy, vol.37, no. 3, p. 346. doi : 10.1016/j.resourpol.2012.04.002.

[28] Nelsen, J. (2006)., Social licence to operate. International Journal of Mining, Reclamation and Environment, vol. 20, no.3, pp. 161-162.

[29] Achieve Magazine, 2011, Issue 4, 2013, accessed 27 March 2015, <http ://www.globalskm.com/Insights/Achieve-Magazine/Issue4-2011/article1.aspx>

the effect has ceased. While the scope and depth of engagement may vary depending on the stakeholder group, corporations must recognize that stakeholders will identify themselves. Thus, there is rarely any legitimate basis for choosing to exclude a stakeholder group from engagement. The information shared through engagement must be adequate to enable the stakeholder to fully understand how the corporation's actions may affect it and what the available options are, if any. Finally, the engagement must provide opportunities for the stakeholder to offer input, as well as demonstrate how the corporation has considered or will consider that input in its decision-making. Thus, the relationship established through the effective engagement will facilitate communication and mutual understanding when companies seek social license for a specific project, as well as when they try to retain social license during a crisis. Moreover, where stakeholder relationships are particularly strong, these bonds can sometimes be leveraged to engage other stakeholders or to overcome opposition. This can happen when relationships become sufficiently advanced that the manifest benefits cause the stakeholders to become advocates, instead of neutral parties or outright opponents. Therefore, the trust developed through the effective engagement provides a crucial cushion for an organization facing any kind of crisis. As long as the engagement efforts have been sincere, and the company has demonstrably made meaningful attempts to address stakeholder concerns, such trust will buffer the company from an immediate loss of social license, provided that the company continues to effectively engage.

As for disclosure and reporting, communication is a close cousin of stakeholder engagement. The fulsome disclosure of performance, particularly against standardized reporting criteria, can build trust with external stakeholders. This is especially true when reporting is not limited to a corporation's good performance but also includes disclosure of incidents of non-compliance with regulatory limits or self-imposed targets, accidents and near-misses, and actions taken to resolve such incidents. Thus, ongoing reporting illustrates, over time, the company's track record for engaging stakeholders, responding to concerns, mitigating impacts, and managing performance. If such reporting is credible and shows proactive management and continuous improvement, it can help raise the confidence of stakeholders that the foreseeable issues related to any specific project will be similarly well managed. This is likely to enhance social license. Similarly, a corporation's track record of crisis disclosure and reporting on outcomes may help not only to demonstrate a preparedness to respond in times of crisis but it also charts the path that the corporation's response to any future crisis will likely follow.

As for corporate governance, the transparent adoption of best principles and practices is an important factor as it contributes to general social license. Thus, best-governance principles and practices go beyond regulatory compliance, fiduciary duty to shareholders, and the management of oversight. They include, but are not limited to, articulating purpose and vision, ensuring disclosure promoting a culture of integrity and ethical behaviour, respecting stakeholder interests, and managing risk. In particular, a company's disclosure of its policies and procedures, of whistleblower protection and complaint response, for example, is an important way in which stakeholders can be assured of access to means of safely resolving issues that may arise in relation to a specific project. Similarly, disclosure of the corporation's code of ethics can boost stakeholder confidence in honest and good-faith dialogue in the context of development proposals.

b) Public Policy and Legislative Approaches in Fostering Social License

As described above, social license *per se* is not a mandatory requirement in any jurisdiction, at least to our knowledge. However, the procedures involved in securing legal license often contribute to social license. In particular, most legal licensing processes involve some form of consultation or engagement on the part of the proponent or the regulator or statutory decision-maker. The scope and depth of consultation and engagement, and the procedures by which such consultation and engagement must be undertaken, vary according to jurisdiction and regulatory authority and typically reflect both policy objectives and legal requirements. In Canada, for example, environmental assessment processes require and encourage consultation and engagement with indigenous people, the public, and other stakeholders. These processes aim to facilitate early identification and resolution of issues by providing for indigenous public, and other stakeholder input into the scope of environmental assessment, as well as into the adequacy of mitigation and management plans to avoid, eliminate, or reduce the adverse effects of development. In some cases, the issuance of approvals and permits hinges on whether the proponent has demonstrably resolved all legitimate issues raised by stakeholders affected by the project, which can rarely be achieved without obtaining some degree of basic social license. Moreover, legal license may include conditions that oblige the proponent to continue stakeholder engagement throughout the life of the project. In this regard, social license serves to assure regulators and statutory decision-makers that their decisions will be accepted by the electorate. Thus, in Canada, there are constitutional obligations on the part of the government, both provincial and federal, to consult with and perhaps accommodate First Nations that may be affected by resource development. In fact, in British Columbia, where treaties were not historically reached with First Nations at or shortly after the arrival of Europeans, outstanding First Nations claims contribute to an uncertain investment climate, because the ownership of resources may be unclear and the authority to grant a license may be shared. Some of these governance issues continue to be resolved through legal processes, thereby imposing greater uncertainty on the scope of proponent responsibilities. The government often delegates procedural aspects of indigenous consultation to proponents, who then integrate such consultation with their own engagement efforts to build relationships and trust and to resolve outstanding issues. In these circumstances, the proponent's success in obtaining social license with key stakeholders can contribute to the fulfillment of government responsibilities to those same stakeholders.

Furthermore, where indigenous people are present, it is emerging practice for companies to undertake a process of engagement characterized by sequential steps, each with progressively greater levels of trust and commitment. For example, the first bilateral milestone between a company and a First Nation may simply be a communication protocol, specifying the parties and outlining the steps to be taken for information sharing and exchange. This may be followed, in time, by a detailed impact and benefits agreement that outline each party's responsibilities for managing the potential negative effects and positive outcomes of the proposed development. Such bilateral agreements constitute and contribute to social license. Indeed, these supra regulatory agreements may be more effective in realizing community benefits than regulatory processes.[30] However, notwithstanding the effectiveness and value of such agreements, the proponent cannot and should not assume the government's role or responsibility, and, to be clear, we do not advocate the superseding of legal license by social license.[31] Internationally, the concept of free, prior, and informed consent (FPIC), particularly as it pertains to resource development in areas occupied or claimed by indigenous peoples, is gaining purchase through a range of international conventions, national legislation, and sub-national policy. Social license contributes to and may constitute FPIC in some circumstances. In addition, stakeholder engagement and the assessment and management of social risks are emerging as key principles and requisites of investment and financing mechanisms for international development projects. Examples include the Equator Principles, the World Bank and the International Finance Corporation environmental and social safeguard policies and procedures. Likewise, the growth of international, national, and sub-national government policy and regulatory frameworks and non-governmental credit risk management mechanisms employed by the

[30] Galbraith, L., Bradshaw, B., and Rutherford, M.B., (2007)., "Towards a New Supraregulatory Approach to Environmental Assessment in Northern Canada," *Impact Assessment and Project Appraisal* 25, no. 1, pp. 27–41.

[31] A very useful, but potentially outdated, overview of entrenchment of FPIC principles in international and domestic law and practices is provided in Tamang, P. (January 17–19, 2005)., "An Overview of the Principle of Free, Prior and Informed Consent and Indigenous Peoples in International and Domestic Laws and Practices" (paper presented at the Workshop on Free, Prior and Informed Consent and Indigenous Peoples, organized by the Secretariat of the UN Permanent Forum on Indigenous Issues, New York).

investment community has fostered attention to social license by emphasizing the need for demonstrably effective management of social and environmental risk. Although social license is not explicitly required or prescribed by law, elements of social license, such as stakeholder engagement, issue resolution, and risk management, is required by many jurisdictions and investors. Thus, social license is over time becoming less a voluntary initiative and more a *de facto* prerequisite to development expected by various stakeholders.

c) The Impact of Social Media on Social License as Emerging and Future Challenges

Another significant factor affecting social license is the emergence of social media as a tool for communication, dialogue, and activism.[32] Communities are now linked through the web and social media and have access to information about a company's behaviour around the world, including, in many cases, information on its efforts, and the comparable efforts of other companies, to foster social license. Thus, communities are better engaged, informed, and networked than ever before. The traditional communications landscape has long been centralized and controlled, with information shaped by a few and pushed out to many. The emergence of new technologies, however, is effectively altering the media landscape, moving content production and distribution out to the edges. This trend signals an important shift in communications and information flow from the traditional one-way "push" model common to mass media, in which a company crafts and delivers messages to its stakeholders, to a multi-directional "pull" model, in which a company and stakeholders are on a more even footing. In the latter model,

---

[32] Some content in this section is adapted from C.L. Horvath, "The Convergence of Social Media and Corporate Responsibility," Making Sense of Responsibility, web log, September 5, 2010, http ://makingsenseofresponsibility.com/2010/09/05/the-convergence-of-social-media-and-corporate-responsibility ; and C.L. Horvath, "Social Media and the Extractive Sector : The Changing Currency of a Modern License to Operate," *CIM Magazine*, September/October 2011,
http ://www.cim.org/en/Publications-and-Technical-Resources/Publications/CIM-Magazine/September-October-2011/upfront/Social_media_and_the_extrative_sector.aspx.

stakeholders themselves define their own information requirements and actively seek out the sources, connections, and networks that will meet them. The outcome is increasing democratization of information and knowledge. In fact, the development of new technologies, particularly social media platforms and mobile technologies, is occurring at a time of rapid globalization and increasing public awareness about pressing natural and social challenges. This convergence is driving a demand for greater transparency. Social media gives voice to previously isolated or remote stakeholders, who often come to the social media landscape with disproportionate credibility and trust, due in part to their perceived authenticity. Moreover, social media allows users to self-organize quickly into communities with shared interests. Trust can also be generated rapidly within online communities, and such trust creates opportunities for collaboration and action much more quickly than would be possible through traditional engagement. At the same time, there is very low tolerance among social media users for antitrust behaviour, whether it involves inappropriate data mining, breach of privacy, or attempts at message control. Consequently, unlike with traditional media, a company no longer dominates the messaging around its brand and reputation on social media. The vast majority of social media content is generated by users, and any attempt to censor or stifle content is likely to be met with distrust and suspicion, at best, and a significant backlash, at worst.

Thus, the scope and norms of the social web described above, that is, openness, trust, and authenticity, are causing a shift in the way that companies build and maintain social capital, the currency of social license. Stakeholders now increasingly expect corporations not only to communicate their corporate-responsibility initiatives but also to engage in online dialogue about environmental, social, and governance issues. These characteristics of social media may be perceived as risks. However, by virtue of its very nature, social media presents myriad opportunities to increase social capital and, by extension, social license. When used effectively, social media tools facilitate connections with a wide range of stakeholders. Moreover, they make it possible to collaborate with stakeholders throughout the value chain to identify challenges, innovate solutions, and achieve sustainability goals. Stakeholder feedback can also help a company identify and prioritize areas of performance for improvement. Whether it is to solve a technical problem or make a strategic decision, engaging stakeholders in the process of generating ideas that can help companies keep up with the pace of change and complexity of today's economy, while also building valuable social capital. Yet entering this space requires not only new technologies and networks but a new organizational mindset as well, that is, there need to be a culture of openness and collaboration that allows a company to engage effectively.

However, while social media use by corporations is becoming commonplace, its use for direct engagement with stakeholders is lagging. In 2010, SMI-Wizness[33] found that approximately 85% of almost 300 companies in North America and Europe listed on the Dow Jones Sustainability Index were using social media, but that less than half used it for any sustainability or corporate-responsibility communications, and less than a quarter of companies had a dedicated social-media channel for sustainability and corporate responsibility. The oil and gas sector lagged behind all sectors in social media use for such communications. In 2012, by contrast, SMI-Wizness found that 176 major companies around the world had allotted dedicated resources and social media channels to their sustainability dialogue.[34] Moreover, although the use of social media for sustainability and corporate-responsibility communications has increased in the last two years, the oil and gas and mining sectors continue to lag in this regard. This finding may be surprising given that in Canada, energy and natural-resource companies generally have a lot of experience in stakeholder engagement. Nonetheless, their use of social media to complement the traditional engagement methods has, by and large, been slower—perhaps for fear of losing control of the message or concern

[33] Yeomans, M. (January 2012)., "The SMI-Wizness Social Media Sustainability Index," SMI-Wizness, http ://www.socialmediainfluence.com/SMI-report/smi_sustainability_report_final.pdf.
[34] *Ibid*

about getting offside securities regulations. This gap threatens to undermine the credibility of corporate efforts to engage stakeholders, whose expectations have increasingly shifted from company-controlled communication toward balanced, two-way dialogue in which stakeholders themselves have the opportunity to define both the scope of exchange and the terms by which it is conducted. In this light, one notable exception is Suncor, whose multichannel social media presence includes in-depth sustainability and corporate-responsibility content. Through its "Oil Sands Question and Response" blog, for example, Suncor is enabling two-way dialogue with stakeholders around tough issues such as energy demand, water use, and reclamation of tailings ponds. By focusing on science-based data and expanding the conversation to tackle oil-sands issues in a broader societal context, Suncor has created safe and respectful ground for engagement[35].

Thus, companies that do not engage in dialogue through social media are increasingly conspicuous in their absence. They will likely experience declining levels of trust and respect from stakeholders, who already are complementing their own learning, networking, and activity with social media tools. In contrast, companies that are constructive and contributing members of the social web and that actively engage with stakeholders through social media are building social capital and relationships that facilitate the license to operate. Indeed, social media is effectively emerging as a critical tool in achieving and maintaining social license. This growing reliance on social media by stakeholders and proponents alike, and the risks associated with disclosure through it, may lead to an increased need for the development of guiding ethical and technical codes of conduct.[36]

2. The Tools to Assist Business Address Social License to Operate Issues

Since SLO involves the measure of confidence society has in business to behave in a legitimate, accountable and socially acceptable way, the

---

[35] *Ibid.*

[36] Raymond, N.A., Howarth, C.N. and J.J. Hutson, J.J. (2012). "Crisis Mapping Needs an Ethical Compass," *Global Brief*, no. 9, pp. 12–16.

relationship required for this contract to operate relies on trust and consistency between the parties, quality information being provided, accountability, flexibility and transparency from all the parties. These SLO elements are the same as many of those traditionally embedded in corporate social responsibility (CSR) methods and tools to engage stakeholders which many leading companies use to strengthen their SLO. Thus, we may outline here some of the tools being used by companies to build trust with the communities within which they operate and that enable them to be transparent and accountable in their performance to broader society. Material issues, fit with company, and stakeholder preference will dictate which tools are chosen. Moreover, companies are regarded as the current leaders in aspects of national or international CSR and SLO practice. They do a range of things including developing clear business strategies which identify emerging social and environmental risks. This involves constantly reviewing and refreshing what they do to stay focused on material risks for the company and its stakeholders and sustainable sources of competitive advantage ; identifying how to contribute to societal needs in a way that is material to and aligned with their core business and partnering with others to do this. They often embed sustainability into core products and services and make it part of the story they use to engage with their customers. Or being strategic about which social concerns and opportunities will, with collective action for results, create the social environment in which the business strategies can succeed ; identifying communities as key stakeholders and continually seeking to understand the environmental and economic implications of their operations. A range of stakeholder engagement tools such as locally appropriate, publicly reported social performance indicators, can be used to demonstrate their contribution to the communities/regions they operate in ; and communicating their performance regularly in an internationally accepted and credible way.

a) The Legislation and regulation

Legislation and regulation is a tool used by a number of governments internationally to encourage more sustainable and transparent business performance. In Denmark, parliament requires large companies to report on their economic, environmental and social performance, or explain why they do not report. Similarly, in South Africa companies listed on the Johannesburg Stock Exchange are required to produce a report integrating their financial and sustainability performance, or explain why they do not – a requirement of the King III Code[37]. Sweden and France also have requirements to report. This has largely come about through programmes such as the Sustainable Stock Exchange Initiative of the United Nations Principles for Responsible Investment (UNPRI). This initiative aims to explore how stock exchanges can work together with investors, regulators, and companies to enhance corporate transparency and performance on sustainability issues through encouraging responsible long-term approaches to investing. They have requested the top 30 stock exchanges worldwide to encourage better internal corporate governance by firms, and disclosure of how sustainability issues are addressed at the board level. Many, including the NASDAQ OMX, and BM&FBOVESPA, have already made a commitment to promote long-term, sustainable investment in their markets.[38]

b) The Scanning and Strategy Development

The leading companies in this area use stakeholder engagement, especially partnership, and subject matter experts to identify these emergent risks and opportunities and build them into their long-term strategies.

c) The United Nations Global Compact Frameworks

Frameworks such as the United Nations Global Compact have gained considerable support amongst the global business community. This framework aims to assist in the development, implementation, and

---

[37] Global Reporting Initiative, 2012, *Brazil, Denmark, France and South Africa governments join in commitment to sustainability reporting*, accessed 1 March 2013, <https ://www.globalreporting.org/information/news-and-press-center/Pages/Brazil,-Denmark,-France-and-South-Africagovernments-join-in-commitment-to-sustainability-reporting.aspx>

[38] United Nations n.d., *Exchanges Listing Over 4,600 Companies Commit to Promoting Sustainability,* accessed 1 March 2013, <http ://business.un.org/en/documents/10712>

disclosure of sustainability policies and practices. To operate in accordance with the framework, businesses must commit to aligning their operations and strategies with ten universally accepted principles in the areas of human rights, labour, environment and anti-corruption. The hope is that this will assist markets, commerce, technology and finance to advance in ways that benefit economies and societies globally. The Global Compact is the largest voluntary corporate responsibility initiative in the world with over 10,000 corporate participants and other stakeholders from over 130 countries. The Global Compact is described as applicable on a global and local scale to the private and public sectors and is voluntary yet accountable.[39]

d) The Standards for Social Responsibility and Stakeholder Engagement

The credible and internationally accepted standards can assist organizations to better manage their performance and demonstrate commitment to their stakeholders. Reporting to a standard, especially if data is assured by a third party, allows stakeholders to compare performance of the organization with others reporting to the standard and gives a level of confidence that the organization is aware of, and managing its performance in the area that the standard covers. A number of standards have been devised to help manage sustainability performance, social responsibility and stakeholder engagement. Two of the most widely used are ISO 26000, a guidance standard which focuses on social responsibility and AA1000SES, a standard on stakeholder engagement.

The ISO 26000 standard is intended to clarify an international consensus on what social responsibility is and to help businesses and organizations translate principles into effective actions. It is based on broad stakeholder input from developing countries, business, government, consumers, labour, non-governmental organizations and others. The standard addresses seven core subjects of responsibility :

---

[39] United Nations n.d., accessed 27 March 2015, <http ://www.unglobalcompact.org/AboutTheGC/>

accountability, transparency, ethical behaviour, respect for stakeholder interests, and respect for the rule of law, respect for international norms of behaviour, and respect for human rights. Unlike many other ISO standards, it does not contain requirements and so is not certifiable. A number of companies have already implemented the standard such as Air France, Toshiba, Panasonic, British Telecom, and Toyota.[40] We hope that corporations in Cameroon will do same.

The AA1000 Stakeholder Engagement Standard, on its part, is a generally applicable open source framework for designing, implementing, assessing, and communicating the quality of stakeholder engagement. It emphasizes that stakeholder engagement must result in outcomes valued by those involved and must be communicated in a credible way.[41] At the core of the standard are the principles of inclusivity, that is, people should have a say in the decisions that impact on them ; materiality, that is, decision makers should identify and be clear about the issues that matter ; and responsiveness which means ensuring that organizations should be transparent about their actions.[42] A number of organizations are using this standard including Miller Construction, one of the UK's largest construction companies and Takeda Pharmaceuticals and it is hoped that organization in Cameroon should follow suit.

e) The Reporting Frameworks

The reporting frameworks assist an organization to plan, monitor and report on their stakeholder engagement performance as part of their overall sustainability strategy. Often, the value from reporting is gained through the reporting process itself as it requires reporting on long term

---

[40] ISO 10 January 2013, ISO 26000 - *International forum revisits the road travelled*, accessed 27 March 2015,
<http ://www.iso.org/iso/home/news_index/news_archive/news.htm ?refid=Ref1691>

[41] AccountAbility, *AA1000 Stakeholder Engagement Standard 2011, Final Exposure Draft*, accessed 27 March 2015,
<http ://www.accountability.org/images/content/5/4/542/AA1000SES%202010%20PRINT.pdf>

[42] Centre for Corporate Citizenship n.d., accessed 27 March 2015, <http ://cccro.org/aa1000ses/ ?lang=en>

strategy and governance, key impacts, risks and opportunities and setting and reviewing targets. Reporting to an international framework allows international stakeholders to understand material issues and compare results.

Sustainability or Corporate Social Responsibility Reporting is also a form of organizational reporting, usually produced annually or bi-annually, that provides information on a company's economic, environmental, social and governance performance. Quantitative and qualitative data is presented in a variety of formats including webpages, stand-alone reports or within other reports such as an annual report. A number of New Zealand companies report their performance via sustainability reports including Ricoh, Sanfords, URS and Toyota. The Global Reporting Initiative (GRI) is regarded as the most widely used and comprehensive sustainability reporting framework. The framework aims to enable greater organizational transparency and accountability around business performance. Thousands of organizations, of all sizes, from many sectors, use GRI's Framework in order to understand and communicate their sustainability performance.[43]The GRI Guidelines are often used in conjunction with other relevant international initiatives, frameworks and guidance.

The International Integrated Reporting Council (IIRC) is a global, market-led coalition which believe communication about businesses' value creation should be the next step in the evolution of corporate reporting (beyond current sustainability reporting). It is at the helm of the development of the global framework for corporate integrated reporting which is designed to support a more resilient business environment and better decision-making. An integrated report is a concise communication (usually a periodic report) detailing how an organization's strategy, governance, performance and prospects lead to the creation of value over the short, medium and long term. These reports benefit principally the providers of financial capital but they are

---

[43] Global Reporting Initiative n.d.,*What is GRI*?, accessed 27 March 2015, <https ://www.globalreporting.org/information/aboutgri/what-is-GRI/Pages/default.aspx>

also will also be useful to the full suite of societal stakeholders. More than 80 global businesses and 50 institutional investors are involved in the IIRC's work, including Coca-Cola, Clorox, Microsoft, Hyundai, Tata, Unilever, Marks and Spencer, SAP and National Australia Bank.[44]

f) The Partnership

Partnering is a term increasingly applied to a broad range of business, community sector and government engagement. It is described as the relationship existing between private business organizations and non-for-profit community organizations formed mainly to address common-interest social issues. The relationships are intended to engage the partners on an on-going basis but are often strongly project oriented.[45] The classic definition of a partnership for sustainable development involves two or more cross-sector organizations, working jointly to accomplish a compelling goal which is unachievable by one organization on its own. Partners pool resources, talents and responsibilities for mutual benefit and to achieve the shared goal. They share the risks and successes.[46] The benefits of partnerships to all sectors include providing a way for each sector to bring the specific skills, competencies and interests of their sector to common problems or opportunities. On this basis the competencies, legitimacy and transparency of each organization are enhanced when there is collective impact mobilizing more leadership and resources by combining the human, technical, informational and financial resources with leadership in the 'space' between organizations, where there has not been leadership for the goal ; ensuring greater awareness of the priorities, needs and roles of each sector, and creating a more integrated and stable society ; creating a dynamic relationship

---

[44] The International Integrated Reporting Council n.d., accessed 27 March 2015, http ://www.theiirc.org/., The International Integrated Reporting Council, *Business Leaders : What You Need to Know,* accessed 27 March 2015, <http ://www.theiirc.org/wpcontent/uploads/2013/04/Business-Leaders-What-you-need-to-know-English.pdf>

[45] Funding Information Service n.d., *Business Community Report,* access date 25 March 2015, <http ://www.fis.org.nz/pdfs/MediaReleases/Business_community_report.pdf>

[46] Adapted from : Tennyson, R. 2003, *The Partnering Toolbook,* International Business Leaders Forum.

network offering channels of influence that can engage wider communities and impact the policy agenda ; and replacing conflict (or suspicion) with co-operation for the participants. The cost of conflict or low trust is in the medium and long term greater in both time and resources than co-operation. Partnering, on the other hand, does not come without time and resource investment.[47] Thus, the World Wildlife Fund (WWF) provides a good example of partnership in action. They have partnered with a number of businesses globally including Coca-Cola, Nokia, Sony and IKEA. Their approach to partnering with the private sector is to be constructive, transparent and solutions-oriented with agreement on measurable targets. WWF recognizes that they will not agree on all things, at all times with their partners. However, they state that agreeing to disagree in the context of a transparent framework is a key factor to sustaining credible and mutually beneficial partnerships.[48]

II. SOCIAL LICENSE - MYTH AND REALITYIES IN CAMEROON

In a broad sense, corporate social responsibility (CSR) has never really been voluntary as in most cases it is a response to market pressures and reputational risk. But increasingly, it is subject to legal pressure and legal enforcement, not necessarily in the form of conventional state regulation but rather through indirect state pressure and through the use of private law by private actors, sometimes through highly innovative uses of law.[49] Moreover, CSR is seen as a form of 'self-regulation in the shadow of the law'. Its aim is to manage the social expectations between the corporate organizations and their various stakeholders, notably in the areas of the environment, health and safety, employment, human rights and the community relations. While it may often be voluntarily adopted by the

---

[47] Robert Davies, Chief Executive of The Prince of Wales Business Leaders Forum : Partnerships- a revolution without route maps in Tennyson, R : Managing Partnerships 1998 ; IBLF.

[48] World Wildlife Foundation, *Working with businesses*, accessed 27 March 2015, <http ://wwf.panda.org/what_we_do/how_we_work/businesses/>

[49] McBarnet, D., *op cit.*

corporate organizations, it can and should be seen to serve as an extension of sound legal management, aiming to mitigate the legal and other social risks of the business organizations.[50] In this light, it is a commonly used term today even though its meaning is changing, shifting according to time and space and has often been interpreted in different ways. In general, it reflects the way in which businesses take into account the repercussions of their activities on society in order to acquire social license, which is referred to a local community's acceptance or approval of a company. It exists outside formal regulatory processes and can nevertheless be acquired through timely and effective communication, meaningful dialogue and ethical and responsible behaviour. Displaying commitment to CSR is one way to achieve social license, by enhancing a company's reputation.[51] Thus, the Cameroonian experience is not different as there is a general awareness of CSR among the producers and consumers.[52] Indeed, on a case by case basis, the Government of Cameroon (GoC) requires elements of corporate responsibility as part of the permit and project development process. Therefore, while not always mandatory, the government has increasingly required investors engaging multiple projects including hydropower investments to implement the environmental and social impacts plan.[53] In this regard, the common practice for many companies is to build bridges, health centres, and classrooms in villages near the work site. For example, in 2011, the Electricity Development Corporation (EDC) built an entire new village for the indigenous population displaced as a result of the Lom Pangar Hydropower Project (LPHP) investments in the East Region.[54]

---

[50] ILO, Regional Office for Latin America and the Caribbean. (*2007) Labour Overview, Latin America and the Caribbean*, pp. 21-23. http ://www.oit.org.pe (visited on the 12/12/2012)

[51] Social License to Operate : How to Get It, and How to Keep It

[52] Cameroon Country profile KPMG Africa Region 2012/2013, p.16. http ://www.kpmgafrica.com

[53] *Ibid*

[54] *Ibid*

A. THE ACQUISITION OF SOCIAL LICENSING IN CAMEROON – À MYTH?

As a matter of fact, through CSR, businesses in Cameroon like their counterparts in the Carribeans have committed themselves to the principles and values, both in their processes and operations and in their interaction with other social actors.[55] It is thus expected that different social actors interested in the activities of a certain enterprise will prioritize different social and environmental demands, which may, at times, contradict or compete with one another. There are many business reasons to adopt a CSR mandate aiming at compliance with social expectations beyond the minimum prescribed by the law. The maintenance of a social licence to operate can be viewed as the practical ability to operate within a particular market, necessitating that a corporation act in a manner consistent with social expectations, whether or not such expectations are contained within the legal requirements of the State. Indeed, Cameroon is a member of the Central African Economic and Monetary Community (CEMAC)[56] which has as principal objective to formulate and implement common economic and monetary policies amongst its members, among other things. However, each country in the Union is at liberty to legislate on laws governing its investments. In Cameroon, the government has undertaken and is putting into place an enabling economic environment to consolidate a partnership between the public and private sectors and good corporate governance via a proper and modern investment code like the Investment Charter[57] and the Private Investment Incentive (PII)[58]. The PII has laid down the incentive regime for private investments in

---

[55] ILO, Regional Office for Latin America and the Caribbean. (2007) Labour Overview, Latin America and the Caribbean, pp. 21-23. http ://www.oit.org.pe (visited on the 12/12/2012)

[56] The Union has as members ; Cameroon, Chad, Gabon, Equatorial Guinea, Congo, Central Africa Republic.

[57] See Law No. 2002-004 of 19 April 2002 on the Investment Charter.

[58] See Law No. 2013 /004 of 18 April 2013 to lay down Private Investment Incentives in Cameroon.

Cameroon applicable to Cameroonians and foreign entities[59], both natural or legal, residing in or out of Cameroon, in the conduct of their activities or to participate in the equity of Cameroonian companies in order to encourage productivity, investment, promote job creation and develop activities geared towards strong, sustainable economic growth and ensure the objective of emergence by the year 2035 as may be seen with resource development projects in Cameroon.

1. **Corporate Social Responsibility and social licensing in Cameroon**

While Cameroon is a relative late-comer to the discussion relating to CSR, the corporate sector, particularly in the resources field, has shown its commitment for more than a decade, and many of the major companies regularly report their activities. A common theme in the Cameroonian literature is the need for corporations to move away from the traditional *'pat-a-poor-person'* philanthropic approach to corporate governance in social licensing to a broad and holistic approach in which the philosophy of CSR becomes part of the core business.[60] Wheeler et al suggest that 'perhaps the problem is that traditionally we have tended to take too narrow the view of the stakeholder approach of CSR and sustainability because the stakeholder theory has never been just about social issues ; sustainability is not just about environmental issues and there is no necessary dichotomy between sustainability and profitability'.[61] Conversely, Van Marrewijk suggests that if CSR is too broadly defined, it will be 'too vague to be useful in academic debate or in corporate implementation'[62] Perhaps the final comment should rest with Blyth, who has suggested that 'There is no one definition of what it

[59] Section 4 of law No 2013/ 004 18 April 2013 prescribes the advantages previewed by the law for investors

[60] Duncan, A. & Richardson, K. (July, 2005)., 'Is corporate volunteering falling short ?' *Business Community Intelligence*, pp.14-22 ; Schwartz, C. (2005), 'Waking with dinosaurs on planet community', *Business Community Intelligence*, pp.11-13

[61] Wheeler, Colbert & Freeman., *op cit,* p. 20

[62] Marrewij, V. (2003)., 'Concepts and definitions of CSR and corporate sustainability : Between agency and communion', *Journal of Business Ethics,* vol. 44, no. 2/3, p. 95. (Retrieved, December 12, 2011).

takes to be a responsible corporate'. The key is to have a rigorous process for identifying those responsibilities and try to fulfill them,[63] thereby acquiring social license to operate.

2. The Corporate Governance Concern under the OHADA Uniform Act and Social Licensing

Corporate governance is intended to boost accountability and responsibility. So to foster sustainability, attention has been focused on the responsibilities of corporations not only towards their shareholders but also to the environment and the society in which they operate.[64] However, since 1993, Cameroon and other fifteen African countries have committed themselves to enhance corporate governance, by signing the OHADA[65] Treaty and thereafter eight Uniform Acts[66] amongst which is the Uniform Act on Commercial Companies and Economic Interest Groups. The OHADA Uniform Acts are part of each member-state's internal law by reason of the fact that they are directly applicable.[67] Thus, the OHADA Treaty and the uniform acts provide the mechanisms for the enhancement of corporate governance through the establishment and institutionalization of supranational institutions which include the Council of Ministers and a supranational court - the Common Court of Justice and Arbitration (CCJA), to act as the ultimate appellate court for

---

[63] Blyth, A. (2005)., 'Business behaving responsibly', *Director,* vol. 59, no. 1, p. 30

[64] Testa, M. (2008)., *op cit.*

[65] L'Organisation pour l'Harmonisation en Afrique du Droit des Affaires. In English : the Organization for the Harmonization in Africa of Business Law.

[66] As of June 25, 2006, the West African members are Benin, Burkina Faso, Côte d'Ivoire, Guinea, Guinea-Bissau, Mali, Niger, Senegal and Togo, and the Central African members are Central African Republic, Chad, Cameroon, Comores, Congo, Equatorial Guinea and Gabon. My assertions in this part II.B are based primarily on observations in Cameroon, but also on briefer visits to Senegal and Côte d'Ivoire.

[67] They cover the following disciplines (in order of adoption) : company law and economic interest groupings ; general commercial law ; law of security interests and other encumbrances ; simplified recovery procedure and methods of execution of judgments ; bankruptcy and insolvency law ; arbitration law ; accounting law ; law on transport of goods by road. *See* OHADA : Traite et Actes Uniformes Commentes et annotes, Joseph Issa-Sayegh, Paul-Gérard Pougoué / Filiga Michel Sawdogo, ed. (2d ed. 2000) (with 2003 addendum) ; *see also* www.ohada.com.

all the member-States on matters relating to the interpretation and application of the treaty and the Uniform Acts.[68] In this light, the CCJA's decisions are final and are published in hard copy and on the Internet.[69] This initiative has readily introduced some transparency from the top and thereby guarantee the uniformity of interpretation and application of the OHADA law.

Apparently, to boost corporate governance initiative, the OHADA Uniform Act on Commercial Companies and Economic Interest Groups has provided enabling provisions that constrain management. These provisions are particularly relevant when management is separated from ownership. To follow the modern trend in the USA, the OHADA Uniform Act does recognize that many businesses do not exhibit the split between management and ownership which has given rise to governance issues. For instance, under the OHADA Uniform Act on Commercial Companies and Economic Interest Groups, even the business form that can be used for a public or private company, that is, '*société anonyme*' can have just a single owner[70]. In this respect, so long as there are not more than three owners, there can even be a single manager who, whether or not an owner, can have authority to exercise board functions including those of the senior executives.[71] Where management is separated from ownership, management is not also to abuse its rights and power.[72] More generally, the management of a company formed under the OHADA Uniform Act does have the obligation to disclose to its owners important matters while also monitoring the business. Instead of relying on the

---

[68] *See* Traité relatif à l'Harmonisation en Afrique du Droit des Affaires, 4 Journal Officiel (JO) OHADA 1, available at http ://www.ohada.com/traite.php ?categorie=10 (last visited July 6, 2012)

[69] The official site of the OHADA's executive branch, the Permanent Secretariat : A private website sponsored by various donor organizations is as of the date of this writing more complete. *See* http ://www.ohada.com.

[70] See the OHADA Uniform Act on Company law. http :// www.ohada.com.

[71] The Administrateur Général ; the OHADA Uniform Act on Company law ; Article 385 (single shareholder possible) ; Article 494 (single '*administrateur général*') ; Article 495 (the single '*administrateur general*' need not be a shareholder). www.ohada.com

[72] See the OHADA Uniform Act on Company law, Articles 130 & 131. *See* http :// www.ohada.com.

fiduciary duty, the OHADA Uniform Act tends to enlist formal structures and apply express rules. For example, it provides a centralized registry and insists on the publication of essential filings. Thus, when the registry is finally computerized, it will be a source of substantial disclosure thereby enhancing corporate governance. These requirements are serious organizational forms that will otherwise shelter the owners from any liability but will be lost if they fail to register and publish constitutive documents as required by the Uniform Act. Also, businesses that do not offer limited liability need to file with the registry. Thus, these statutory provisions apply even to sole proprietors and natural persons who are actively engaged in business to also file.[73] However, the issue of CSR is still embryonic in Cameroon thereby leading to its consequential impact on the social license to operate.

B. THE REALITY OF SOCIAL LICENSE IN CAMEROON

By and large, there is general awareness of CSR among the corporation in indigenous communities in Cameroon. This has enabled the corporation to acquire social license operate. In fact, as briefly considered above, the government usually requires elements of corporate responsibility in granting the investors the project development permit. For example, there is the tendency for some corporations to invest in social infrastructure like health centers or schools, and other projects benefiting the local populations in the areas of their operations. However, while social license is not always mandatory, corporations have increasingly been required to take the environmental and social impacts into consideration. A common practice for many corporations is to provide social facilities to the villages where their work site is located and make the necessary disclosure.[74] In this light, it is one thing to say that

---

[73] OHADA Uniform Act on General Commercial law, Articles 2-7 and 19 (definition of « *commerçants* » and stipulation of obligation to file with the register) ; DCG art 202 (contracts under this AU apply only to "*commerçants*") ; OHADA Uniform Act on Commercial Companies and Economic Interest Groups, Article 270 (all owners of a "*société en nom collectif*" are « *commerçants* »). *See* http ://www.ohada.com.

[74] The US Bureau of Economic, Energy and Business Affairs ; Investment Climate Statement – Cameroon **Investment,** March 2010.

http ://www.imf.org/external/pubs/ft/reo/2008/AFR/eng/sreo1008.pdf ;

managers should disclose and monitor, but it is another to determine what kinds of behaviours need to be disclosed and monitored. As we have seen, corporate governance constraints are designed to support and enhance the underlying values. These values, as noted above, are embodied in the concept of social license. That explains why, in countries like the USA, management must exercise its disclosure and monitor duties, so as to maximize shareholders' wealth and protect other stakeholders.

1. Social License under the OHADA Uniform Act

According to Scholarship[75], OHADA Uniform Act takes a different tack ; instead of endorsing the shareholder primacy, it embraces a form of the French '*intérêt social*'. Indeed, it suggests that the likely outcome for OHADA Uniform Act is a moderate flavor of the doctrine ; neither will the OHADA Company be limited to the shareholder primacy nor will it include an obligation to all other stakeholders[76]. However, management will probably owe an obligation not only to shareholders, but also to such integral constituencies as the employees, suppliers and customers. Altogether, after this brief tour of the few concepts pertaining to governance and social responsibility under the OHADA Uniform Acts, we shall turn to the economic realities that an organized business faces under the OHADA zone.

In Cameroon, the OHADA Uniform Act on Commercial Companies and Economic Interest Groups does not regulate the relationship between an unrelated supplier and customer. Also, in the context of transactions between "traders," the contract law is entirely outside the OHADA law[77] since a Uniform Act in this regard is still pending.

---

http ://web.worldbank.org/WBSITE/EXTERNAL/COUNTRIES/AFRICAEXT/0 ; http ://www.camnet.cm/

[75] In Mamadou, K. (2003)., Le Nouveau Droit Commercial Des Pays De La Zone OHADA ; Compariasons Avec Le Droit Français 16 (noting that OHADA's concept of corporate interest is based on the French system). *See* also *loc cit.* Part II.A.2.b (discussion of French company law's adoption of corporate interest as a form of CSR).

[76] *Ibid.*

[77] See the OHADA Uniform Act on General commercial law, Article 202. *See* http ://www.ohada.com.

Reliance therefore has to be placed on the ordinary laws of the state which differ with the language zone on which we happen to find ourselves. In Anglophone Cameroon, this will be governed by the common law rules of contract while in Francophone Cameroon, it will be governed by the civil law inspired rules of contract – the French law of obligations. In any case, as a practical matter, the business form has little consequence when analyzing corporate governance ; instead, power and cultural norms dominate. Though 'political governance' is seen to be more relevant than 'corporate governance' in Cameroon, it is understandable that corporate governance also inevitably exists. This is because although commercial realities are shaped by cultural norms, economic power determines rights and obligations, even though political governance creates the effective legal system. The challenge will be to conform OHADA's technical requirements to the social realities, but also to have the sophisticated and modern aspects of the law influence some of those social realities - at least enough to permit better and cheaper access to capital.

The society has not only sanctioned the business to operate according to the profit motive, but also the business is expected to comply with the laws and regulations promulgated by the state governing the operation of businesses. As partial fulfillment of the social contract between the business and the society, firms are expected to pursue their economic missions within the framework of the law. Legal responsibilities reflect a view of codified ethics in the sense that they embody basic notions of fair operations as established by lawmakers. So, in this regard, does the law actually allow CSR of corporations? In fact, traditionally, corporations are formed to carry out business transactions in anticipation of profit for the owners. Any jurisdiction in which corporations operate has its own law on corporate governance. But remarkably the corporate design contained in hundreds of corporate laws throughout the world is nearly identical. That design creates a governing body to manage the corporation and dictates the duties of the directors. These laws create corporate purpose, which is to operate business in the interest of shareholders. In Cameroon, the OHADA Uniform Act on companies provides that : 'A commercial company shall be formed for the common interest of the partners'.[78] Similarly, the American Business Corporation Act provides *inter alia* that 'the directors and officers of a corporation shall exercise their powers and discharge their duties with a view to the interests of the corporation and of the shareholders....'[79]

This is not different under English law where directors are required to act *bona fide* in what they consider to be in the best interest of the company.[80] The summary of these provisions is that persons who manage corporations must put the interest of the corporation first. The corporation's main interest is the maximization of profit for itself and its members. The provisions therefore equate the corporation's self-interest with the interest of shareholders. Unfortunately, no mention is made of the public interest. We may therefore conclude that corporations find social issues like human rights irrelevant because they are not included in corporation's object clause and also that Directors of a company may behave as the choose vis-a-vis indigenous communities because their only obligation is to make money for the company and its members. This provisions has the unfortunate effect of shelving social responsibility.[81] Because corporate Law generally regulates corporations but not Directors, the latter usually become inattentive to social justice. They instruct their subordinates 'to make the numbers' and pay little attention to how they do so. Directors and officers know that their jobs, salaries, bonuses and stock options depend on making profits for shareholders.[82]

Therefore, most corporate donations or social activities have usually been carried out as philanthropic gestures provided that they are seen to contribute to the profit of the corporation. In fact, under English law,

---

[78] See the OHADA Uniform Act on Commercial Companies and Economic Interest Groups 1998, Article 4 para.2

[79] *Ibid*, Article 7- 6

[80] Lord Greene M R, in Re Smith and Fawcett Ltd. 1942, Ch. 304CA, p.306

[81] Hinckley, R. (January/February, 2002)., 'How corporate law inhibits Social Responsibility : A Corporate Lawyer proposes a Code of Corporate Citizenship. Business Ethics : Corporate Social Responsibility Report, p.1

[82] *Ibid*

even such philanthropic acts were not tolerated, as they were considered to be *ultra vires* to the company for as Bomen, L. stated in Hutton v. Bruner Mond & CO. ", Charity cannot sit at the boardroom table and the fact is that there are to be no cakes and ale except for the benefit of the company". The *ultra vires doctrine* is to the effect that any act done by the company which was not part of its objects could not be held to be that of the company, even if a third party suffered loss as a result of the act. The tenor of this doctrine is that for any CSR act to made, it ought to be enshrined as part of the objectives of the corporation. This put management in a very difficult position as they would be held personally liable for any acts that were out-side the objects of the company. This in no way could help the course of CSR. This doctrine does not apply only to acts done to third parties but also covered the acts done to employees of the corporation. This was the case in *Parke v. Daily News*,[83] where it was held that to use the proceeds of sale of the defunct News Chronicle and the Star News Papers to compensate employees who lost their jobs was *ultra vires*, since the company business had ended. This decision led to a huge outcry and little response by legislature.[84] This caused the courts in subsequent decisions to narrow down the doctrine of '*ultra vires*'[85] as it became evident that coupled with the constructive notice rule, they were practices geared towards the protection of the interest of the corporation and had no regard for public interest. This led to a reformation of the *ultra vires doctrine* by law.[86] The position in England today is that where a person deals with the company in good faith, any act performed by the directors should be deemed to be within the objects of the company and free from any limitations by the Memorandum and

[83] *Parke v. Daily News* (1962) ch. 927

[84] Companies Act 1980, s.74 ; now Companies Act 1985, s.719 and the Insolvency Act 1986, s.187

[85] *Charterbridge Corpn. V. Lloyds Bank* (1970) ch. 62, *Re Halt Garage Ltd* (1986) 3 All EeRr 1016 ; *Re Horsely & Weight Ltd* (1982) CH.442, CA ; *Rolled Steel Ltd v. British Steel Corporation* (1986) ch. 246, CA. They established that *ultra vires* should be limited to the question whether the company has acted within its capacity, depending on the construction of the objects cause and if it acted within the objects.

[86] Paul L. Davies ; Gowers, (1997)., Principles of Modern Company Law, 6th ed, Sweet and Maxwell, p.207-220

Articles of Association on the powers of the directors and this relieves the other party from the obligation to inquire these matters.[87] Perhaps the delegation of powers to the directors and the reformulation of the *ultra vires doctrine* are the widest latitudes that the law has given to directors of the corporations in England to commit the company to CSR. This is because the directors who embark on activities corresponding to CSR may be regarded as acting within these and will not require ratification of their actions. The position in Anglophone Cameroon is a replication of the English rules as they obtained in the English-speaking regions before the entry into force of the OHADA treaty. Similarly, in the French-speaking regions, the French concept of "*intérêt social*" was used to encourage businesses to gain the social license to operate (SLO). But with the entry into force of the OHADA Treaty and Uniform Act, the position has somewhat shifted as some of their provisions provide mechanisms for companies to acquire SLO.

This is evident when the OHADA Uniform Act on companies provides that members of the management organs of the company, directors and managing directors, within the limits provided by the Uniform Act for each form of company, shall have full powers to commit the company with respect to third parties, without having to show proof of a special instrument granting such powers. Any limitation of their legal powers by the Articles of Association shall not be binding on third parties.[88] This provision undoubtedly undermines the '*constructive notice doctrine*' in all transactions between the corporate management and the rest of the world and, this differs from the English law position where such third parties will not incur liability if they acted in good faith with the company. Perhaps, in addition to the above provision, corporate management may rely on Article 122 of the Uniform Act to carry out CSR and that will not amount to be breaking corporate rules. The Article provides that *"the company shall be bound by the acts of its managers, directors and administration which are unrelated to*

[87] Companies Act 1985 Section 35 ; Section 3A(b) and Section 15

[88] See Article 121, Uniform Act on Commercial Companies and Economic Interest Groups 1998

the company's object. So, directors who are daring and pro-CSR and having the desire to acquire social license may rely on the above provisions to exercise their powers. However, they are not expected to transform themselves to philanthropic organizations and dispose of corporate properties[89] as any such acts must not only be justified but they must also not be seen as capable of jeopardizing the corporate existence. Nevertheless, some corporations may not take it kindly with any acts amounting to CRS as these may be considered tantamount to waste of the company's resources and can be sanctioned as management fault. The question for determination is - how many or what percentage of management staff would be ready to indulge in acts that will cause them to lose their jobs?

2. Social License and Corporate Publicity in Cameroon

The power of advertisements and publicity cannot be over-emphasized when products or corporate image are being sold. The traditional advertising methods would be *"straight-faced"* payment media publicity or hiring professional private advertising firms who nonetheless make use of different media to drive home their message. However, some of the most unconventional method or tactics one of which is CSR are often used by corporations to acquire social license. Just, as religion had been one of the most powerful tools for colonialism, so too has CSR become a tool for brainwashing communities for corporate gain and survival.[90] The results of recent studies by the United Nations Institute for Social Development show that some of the CSR projects as negotiated could end up being risk projects for the host country as is the case of the Chad-Cameroon pipeline project.[91] This reinforces the observation made earlier that some corporations today use CSR as advertising tools. From the above analysis, it would be unrealistic to hold

[89] Lukong, A. (2010)., Corporate Social Responsibility : A favour or an obligation, African Law Review, vol.7, No.1, pp.141-144

[90] *Ibid,* p.145

[91] Terence, G. (September, 2008)., Article published in New Straits Times, Malaysia. Further one can validly use this to counter the argument of Mathew Grouch., *op cit.* of the Chad-Cameroon pipe-line project as a CSR report

that corporations in Cameroon today use advertising and publicity methods as CSR programs rather than being socially responsible properly speaking so as to gain the social license. This amounts to playing the ostrich because by so acting, they are neither being socially responsible nor abiding to regulations relating to advertisement and publicity. Conversely, since businesses operate in global markets with rapid communications, transparency and integrity are essential components of brand resilience. Hence, the reputation and brands that have taken years to develop can be easily lost progressively if the businesses are not socially responsible. There is thus a need for the businesses to gain social license in order to effectively and efficiently realize their economic objectives. Therefore, businesses that have built CSR at the core of their strategic orientations and culture, readily gain the needed SLO apart from the already granted legal license. Thus, there is the risk that if corporations in Cameroon are not socially responsible, they may negate their current favourable market positioning and it may be jeopardized or lost. In this regard, the corporations should not consider social responsibility as an advertising and publicity tool but they should rather consider it as a mechanism to acquire SLO, which is based on a changing set of expectations, good relationships and quality communication. Moreover, the managers of the corporations should understand and manage their performance more effectively and efficiently taking into consideration of the interests of all stakeholders, that is, having an easily communicable strategy to address the changing societal expectations that can improve relationships, brand and reputation, realize opportunities and lower risks and threats. Ultimately, these shall enable the corporations to consolidate their competitive positions and enhance their corporate culture and image, which may then lead to the realization of their economic objectives. Moreover, the tools as outlined above if appropriately implemented by the government shall boost and assist the businesses to manage better their performance and increase their societal expectations. In this regard, the tools may be considered as the baseline and synergetic panacea appropriate to enhance the concerted efforts of the government, the business community and the indigenous stakeholders to tailor public and business needs with communal needs and aspirations ; promote social awareness strategies and good governance ; and encourage communication between the corporations and the local communities and stakeholders. These initiatives could enable successful companies to humbly acknowledge their mistake, renew their commitment to timely and effective communication, meaningful dialogue, and ethical and responsible behaviour ; and thereby begin to rebuild trust and social capital which are the currency of social license.

CONCLUSION

The emergence of social license as a critical success factor in resource development in particular reflects a growing understanding of the importance of effective risk management, which is itself driven by society's expanding knowledge of the environmental, social, and economic impacts of development. This trend has been driven also by the growing recognition and acceptance of concepts such as social equity and justice. Indeed, among the lessons learned from observing attempts to develop social license, it is realized that the common aspects of success include : the early and substantial analysis of communities and stakeholders potentially affected by a project to understand local conditions, needs and customs, including communication protocols and constraints ; the early engagement and consultation with affected communities and stakeholders to identify issues and interests and establish dialogue ; the action on areas of mutual interest and enhancement of benefits targeted at specific community needs ; the sustained and transparent communication, particularly in the context of the growing role of social media in rapidly disseminating information about companies, technologies, and projects ; the effective partnering to develop commercial opportunities associated with a project. In this light, proponents committed to these actions and behaviours are more likely to realize timely social license and consequently legal license. However, like legal license, a social license is often conditional and requires follow-up action, usually in the form of ongoing communication and fulfillment of commitments. In this light, policymakers have the opportunity to create a regulatory and policy environment that can set in motion the consideration of social license in their jurisdictions. By establishing guidance and decision-making frameworks that reward corporate efforts to pursue a social license to operate, they can achieve better policy goals associated with the creation of community well-being and environmental stewardship. For their part, stakeholders and communities, acting with an enhanced expectation of a corporate interest in obtaining social license, should be prepared to engage with companies, establish a productive communication process, and work toward identifying mutual benefits from project development. Conversely, social license cannot be viewed as transactional ; it is founded on trust-based relationships that demand sustained attention. In fact, even the suspension, cancellation, or closure of a development project readily requires a transitional approach that leaves a positive balance of social capital and protects the corporation's long-term reputation. Apparently, it could be asserted that even the most experienced companies can make errors in their engagement with local communities and stakeholders. They may begin too late, fail to share complete information in a timely manner, breach communication protocols and local customs, inadvertently exclude important stakeholders, disregard important issues and concerns, or impose an unfair burden on the community.

However, in Cameroon, some degree of opposition and conflicts are faced in this process. This is because social risks arise because the expectations of external stakeholders are broader or different from those defined by legislation, regulatory approvals and/or the conditions of project financing.[92] Readily, in the hydropower or mining sectors, additional complications arise when the affected populations simultaneously claim for mitigation and compensation measures due to the external negative effects of these projects, in addition to the participation in the project benefits. Thus, enhancing the benefits to local communities and promoting good relations between project promoters and a wide set of stakeholders, is more than a viable risk

---

[92] Overseas Development Performance/ODI (2005), Meeting the Social Performance Standards of International Project Finance Institutions : Guidance for Energy Companies, London.

management strategy. Moreover, financial performance can be positive, with proactive CSR policies aiming at enhancing local development opportunities and actually contributing positively to social returns. These initiatives can then bring benefits to the local communities in the form of improved living conditions ; the investors in the form of long-term business potential, reduced reputation risks and goodwill from their neighbours ; and the country, in the form of optimized use of scarce resources, improved investment climate and through stronger multiplier effects, increased GDP growth. Thus, to enhance SLO in Cameroon, it is highly recommended that the government should put in place viable and sustainable social responsibility legislation and institutions.

LE STATUT JURIDIQUE DES PERSONNES DÉTENUES DANS LE CADRE DE LA LUTTE CONTRE BOKO HARAM

Brusil Miranda METOU

Agrégée des facultés de droit
Université de Yaoundé II, Cameroun

''À toutes les victimes des exactions de Boko Haram''

Introduction

La lutte contre Boko Haram[1], dans laquelle s'est engagé le Cameroun depuis le mois de mai 2014[2], a entraîné l'arrestation et la détention de nombreuses personnes, de diverses nationalités[3]. Ces personnes sont

---

[1] La secte Boko Haram est née dans le nord-est du Nigeria au début des années 2000 sous le nom de Jama'atu Ahlul Sunna Lidda'awati Wal Jihad (communauté des disciples pour la propagation de la guerre sainte et de l'islam). Son objectif est d'instaurer une application stricte de la loi musulmane telle qu'enseignée par le prophète pour l'étendre à l'ensemble du pays et combattre l'éducation occidentale, considérée comme un véritable péché et comme le point de départ du déclin des sociétés islamiques. C'est dans cette logique que les attaques sanglantes de Boko Haram contre les chrétiens se sont multipliées, semant un climat de terreur dans un le pays. (Voir J-P. REMRY, « Le Nigeria face au spectre d'une guerre de religion », *Le Monde*, 29 décembre 2011 http ://www.lemonde.fr/afrique/article/2011/12/29/le-nigeria-face-au-spectre-d-une-guerre-de-religion_1623966_3212.html). Également A. VICKY, « Aux origines de la secte Boko Haram », *Le Monde*, avril 2012)

[2]La déclaration faite par le président camerounais le 17 mai 2014 lors du sommet de Paris, ne faisait peser aucun doute sur l'engagement du Cameroun à lutter contre ce phénomène : « nous sommes ici pour déclarer la guerre au Boko Haram ». (Déclaration du président camerounais, Paul Biya, à l'issue du *Sommet de Paris sur la sécurité au Nigeria).*

[3] L'armée camerounaise a affirmé détenir « *plus de 1 000* » combattants suspectés d'être liés au groupe nigérian, dans la prison de Maroua, chef-lieu de la région de l'extrême nord du pays. « *Tous ont été arrêtés en territoire camerounais lors de nos opérations* » de

capturées au cours des opérations de réplique contre les assauts du groupe terroriste, ou arrêtées lors des opérations de ratissage opérées par les forces armées régulières. Aux troupes camerounaises engagées sur ce front, se sont ajoutées les forces armées tchadiennes et nigériennes, avec une proposition de création d'une force multinationale[4].

S'il est vrai que les membres des forces armées des pays impliqués dans la lutte contre Boko Haram et ceux de la force multinationale créée pour lutter contre ce phénomène sont repérables, et peuvent se voir reconnaître *ipso facto* le statut de combattant dans le cas où la lutte contre Boko Haram se transformerait en conflit armé, il est difficile de reconnaître un statut similaire aux membres de ce mouvement terroriste. La raison, toute simple sur le plan général, est pourtant juridiquement complexe. Le statut juridique des personnes arrêtées dans le cadre de cette lutte suscite chez le juriste un certain nombre d'interrogations, et pousse à des analyses.

Le mot statut découle du latin *statuere (*qui signifie fixer, établir) et désigne un texte ou un ensemble de textes fixant les garanties

---

ratissage, a précisé le colonel Joseph Nouma, commandant de l'opération Alpha de lutte contre le groupe terroriste dans la région. « *Le maximum de ce que nous savons de leur organisation (Boko Haram) vient de ces prisonniers* », a-t-il ajouté, assurant qu'ils seraient mis « *à la disposition de la justice* ». De son côté, la police nigérienne a annoncé avoir arrêté plus de 160 personnes, soupçonnées d'être membres de la secte islamiste Boko Haram, dans la région de Diffa (Annonce faite le 16 février 2015 par la police nigérienne.)

[4]Loin d'être une simple aide apportée au Cameroun, l'internationalisation de la lutte contre Boko Haram se présentait comme une nécessité pour la sauvegarde de la paix et de la sécurité dans la sous-région de l'Afrique centrale et en Afrique de l'ouest. Dès janvier 2015, la lutte contre le mouvement terroriste a pris une tournure régionale, avec la prise de conscience des membres de l'Union africaine de la nécessité d'éradiquer le phénomène. Pour ce faire, les dirigeants de la CEEAC, de l'Union africaine et les Nations unies, ont décidé de mettre en place une force multinationale chargée de la lutte contre Boko Haram. (Rapport du Secrétaire général sur les efforts déployés par le système des Nations unies pour aider les organismes nationaux, sous-régionaux et régionaux en Afrique à lutter contre le terrorisme) (Sur l'internationalisation de la lutte contre Boko Haram, voir B.M. METOU, « Lutte contre Boko Haram, le temps d'une action collective », *Bulletin SENTINELLE*, n°420 du 01er février 2015).

fondamentales accordées à une collectivité, à un corps[5]. Sur le plan juridique, le statut s'entend d'un ensemble cohérent de règles applicables à une catégorie de personnes ou d'agents, ou à une institution et qui en déterminent, pour l'essentiel, la condition et le régime juridiques[6]. La détermination du statut des personnes arrêtées et détenues dans le cadre de la lutte contre Boko Haram passe donc par la précision de l'ensemble des règles applicables à ces personnes. Si un certain nombre de textes internationaux s'appliquent aux mesures de prévention et de répression du terrorisme[7], ni les conventions internationales applicables en temps de conflit ni les conventions universelles ou régionales relatives au terrorisme[8], ne permettent de déterminer avec précision la condition

[5] Dictionnaire Larousse, mot « Statut »

[6] G. CORNU (Dir.), *Vocabulaire juridique*, Paris, PUF, 2008, p. 886. Également J. SALMON (Dir.), *Dictionnaire de droit international*, Bruxelles, Bruylant, 2001, p. 1052

[7] Le principal système juridique régional qui s'applique aux États d'Afrique subsaharienne en matière de lutte contre le terrorisme est celui constitué par l'Organisation de l'unité africaine (OUA) puis l'Union africaine (AU), qui l'a remplacée en 2002. Dans ce cadre, deux instruments majeurs ont été adoptés : la convention de l'OUA sur la prévention et la lutte contre le terrorisme (ou convention d'Alger) et son protocole additionnel. Il existe d'autres instruments juridiques sous-régionaux de lutte contre le terrorisme. Pour exemple, les États de la Communauté économique et monétaire de l'Afrique centrale (CEMAC) ont adopté à Libreville (Gabon) le 27 mai 2004 le règlement n°08/05-UEAC-057-CM-13 portant adoption de la convention relative à la lutte contre le terrorisme en Afrique centrale (Les pays signataires sont le Cameroun, la République centrafricaine, la République du Congo, la République démocratique du Congo, la République gabonaise, la République de Guinée équatoriale, la République démocratique de Sao Tome et Principe, la République du Tchad. (Document de l'OUA AHG/Decl.132(XXXV).

[8] Le chapitre VII de la Charte des Nations unies accorde le pouvoir au Conseil de sécurité pour prendre des décisions qui engagent tous les États membres des Nations unies, afin de maintenir ou restaurer la paix et la sécurité internationales. À cet égard, le Conseil de sécurité peut imposer diverses formes de sanction et, si d'autres mesures s'avèrent inadéquates, autoriser l'action militaire. Depuis le début des années 90, le Conseil de sécurité a adopté de nombreuses résolutions imposant des sanctions aux régimes accusés de soutenir le terrorisme, y compris des sanctions militaires. Le 12 septembre 2001, dans sa résolution 1368, le Conseil de sécurité a adopté une mesure sans précédent en affirmant que le "terrorisme" constitue une menace à la paix et la sécurité internationales (la résolution dispose ainsi : "*Résolu* à combattre par tous les moyens les menaces à la paix et à la sécurité internationales causées par les actes

juridique des personnes arrêtées et détenues dans le cadre de la lutte contre le terrorisme. Il en est ainsi parce que la lutte contre le terrorisme est difficilement qualifiable de guerre ou de conflit armé. Sur le plan international, il s'agit d'un type particulier de combat, complètement déstructuré et anachronique, qui bouleverse l'ensemble du dispositif juridique applicable jusqu'alors, et même la doctrine militaro-stratégique de la communauté internationale. Sur le plan interne, l'encadrement juridique du combat mené par les États pour maintenir la paix et la sécurité sur leur territoire, et parer aux incursions des mouvements terroristes demeure embryonnaire, alors même que depuis quelques années, un terrorisme davantage organisé et tendant à se rapprocher d'un modèle militaire étatique se développe un peu partout dans le monde[9]. Comme l'explique Emmanuel Gross, « pour les terroristes, le champ de bataille est l'*hinterland* civil, non le front militaire »[10]. Le mode opératoire des groupes armes consiste à agir sous l'apparence de civils ou à utiliser la population comme bouclier humain, sans se transformer en armée identifiable.

Le sort des personnes arrêtées et détenues dans le cadre de la lutte contre Boko Haram en particulier et dans la lutte contre le terrorisme en général, et la détermination du droit qui leur est applicable conduisent à un clivage entre ceux qui jugent qu'ils relèvent du statut de terroristes et doivent seulement bénéficier des protections minimales relatives aux droits de l'Homme, et ceux qui estiment qu'ils ont droit au statut de

---

terroristes", résolution 1368 (2001) du Conseil de sécurité, 12 septembre 2001). La résolution 1373 (2001) du 28 septembre 2001, crée une obligation internationale d'adopter un certain nombre de mesures spécifiques visant à combattre le terrorisme, sera tout aussi importante et sans précédent. La résolution 1373 "demande" également aux États de prendre d'autres mesures pour empêcher et réprimer les actes terroristes, dont le dépistage des demandeurs d'asile avant de leur accorder le statut de réfugié, et la criminalisation en droit national du financement des organisations terroristes (Doc. N.U. S/RES/1373 (2001).

[9] La menace islamiste radicale, illustrée notamment par la nébuleuse Al-Qaïda, figure de proue du djihadisme est aujourd'hui concurrencée par des groupes africains de création récente à l'instar d'AQMI, de Boko Haram ou même de l'EI (ex-EIIL ou Daesch).

[10] E. GROSS, cité par QIAO LIANG, WANG XIANGSUI, *La guerre hors limites,* Paris, Rivages, 2003.

combattant entraînant la pleine application du *jus in bello*. Il faut rappeler que depuis les attentats du 11 septembre 2001 aux États-Unis[11], la lutte contre le terrorisme a pris une nouvelle tournure et que, bien qu'elle ait gagné en intensité, les problèmes qu'il pose sont restés identiques et sans solutions. L'ensemble des mécanismes de répression du terrorisme ont un caractère essentiellement interétatique alors que les terroristes, qui s'organisent par-delà les frontières d'un État, échappent à tout encadrement[12]. Ils sont frappés tout au plus des sanctions du Conseil de sécurité qui, par moments, sont difficiles à produire des effets escomptés.

Le critère de détermination du droit applicable aux personnes arrêtées et détenues dans le cadre de la lutte contre Boko Haram réside dans le lien de causalité entre les opérations militaires entreprises par les États impliqués dans cette lutte (Cameroun, Niger et Tchad) et les opérations de police menées. Le terrorisme[13] décrit un phénomène étudié par de

[11] Comme l'a relevé KALLIOPI K. KOUFA, « Depuis les événements du 11 septembre, les actes de terrorisme se sont multipliés d'un bout à l'autre du monde, liés avant tout à un certain nombre de situations de crise en divers points chauds. Les réponses au terrorisme, expressions parfois d'un sentiment de panique ou d'urgence, se sont elles-mêmes avérées spectaculaires. D'ailleurs, pour une bonne part, l'activité politique et juridique liée au terrorisme continue à révéler des réactions proches de la panique... Or, ces réactions qui confinent à la panique peuvent avoir de graves incidences sur le droit international et sur le droit relatif aux droits de l'Homme, ainsi que sur le droit humanitaire » (Documents des Nations unies E/CN.4/Sub.2/2002/35, du 17 juillet 2002, paragraphe 59).

[12] Cela ne signifie nullement que les actes terroristes ne sont pas réprimés en droit international.

[13] Le mot « Terrorisme » dérive de terreur. Le terme et le sens de terreur sont empruntés (vers 1356) au latin « *terror* » qui signifiait «effroi épouvantable, inspirant de l'effroi », lui-même dérivant de « *terrère* » qui signifiait « effrayer, épouvanter ». François Noël Babeuf va créer, en 1794 le mot « terroriste » pour qualifier les partisans et agents du système de la terreur. Le terme "terreur" a été employé pour la première fois afin de décrire la volonté de Robespierre de terroriser les royalistes pendant la Révolution française. Depuis lors, le terme a é té utilisé pour décrire toute une série d'actes ou de situations qui varient selon le contexte et l'auteur de la qualification. À partir de la fin du 19e siècle le mot va connaître une certaine émancipation et c'est à ce moment précis que vont apparaître plusieurs définitions qui vont contribuer à jeter le flou sur la

nombreuses disciplines, dont le droit, la sociologie et les sciences politiques. Cependant, il n'y a aucune conception commune de la signification de ce terme qui désigne des choses différentes selon le contexte de son emploi et selon l'auteur[14]. Si la communauté internationale n'a toujours pas adopté de définition substantielle du terrorisme, divers déclarations, résolutions et traités universels « sectoriels » concernant des aspects particuliers du phénomène en énumèrent des éléments fondamentaux[15]. Ainsi, de nombreuses

---

notion. Le terme terrorisme se verra attribuer deux sens : il y aura d'un côté le sens traditionnel, c'est-à-dire celui lié aux origines historiques de ce mot et d'un autre côté le sens politique du mot. De l'union de ses deux va naître une multitude de définitions. Le terrorisme va devenir semblable à l'hydre de Lerne, ce monstre mythologique à sept têtes qui terrorisait la Grèce antique, et dont le nombre de têtes augmentait à chaque fois que l'on essayait d'en couper une. Il en va de même pour le terrorisme qui lorsqu'on tente de le définir opère des mutations qui rendent difficile cet exercice. Comme le note le rapporteur spécial des Nations unies sur le terrorisme, Kalliopi K. Koufa : "(...) certains auteurs ont souligné, à juste titre, la tendance qui existe chez les spécialistes à confondre définition et jugement de valeur, de sorte qu'ils qualifient de terrorisme les actes ou les comportements violents qu'ils rejettent et, à l'inverse, refusent d'employer ce terme lorsqu'il s'agit d'activités ou de situations qu'ils approuvent. D'où la formule bien connue : 'Terroriste pour l'un, combattant de la liberté pour l'autre'." (*Terrorisme et droits de l'homme (Rapport intérimaire)*, Rapport de la Rapporteuse spéciale, Mme Kalliopi K. Koufa, Doc. N.U. E/CN.4/Sub.2/2001/31, 27 Juin 2001, para. 25, p. 8.

[14] En effet, bien que le terme "terrorisme" ait été inclus dans des conventions internationales et des résolutions du Conseil de sécurité des Nations unies, il n'existe aucune définition générale du terrorisme en droit international. Jusqu'à présent, le projet de convention générale sur le terrorisme n'a pu être adopté aux Nations unies ; une définition exacte de ce phénomène étant inexistante. Seuls les actes considérés comme relevant du terrorisme sont énumérés dans divers textes juridiques, ce qui rend difficile l'appréhension du statut des personnes arrêtées dans le cadre d'une guerre contre le terrorisme. Le terrorisme oppose deux ou plusieurs entités dans une guerre au cours de laquelle certaines entités, notamment les États, sont tenues de respecter un certain nombre de règles et principes tandis que les groupes terroristes ne sont tenus par aucune obligation, si ce n'est celle d'ordre général, de respecter les droits de l'Homme.

[15] Il y a eu plusieurs tentatives infructueuses pour définir le terrorisme au sein des Nations unies. Aucune définition ne peut être tirée du droit international coutumier non plus, même si beaucoup de crimes internationaux qualifiés par les États de "terroristes" relèvent du droit coutumier. L'Assemblée générale réfléchit actuellement à

conventions internationales définissent des infractions terroristes pour les prohiber, sans fournir une définition générale du "terrorisme"[16]. Or, c'est à travers une définition générale du terrorisme que l'on pourrait préciser le statut juridique des personnes impliquées de par et d'autre dans ce genre de combat. En effet, dans la lutte contre le terrorisme, la détermination des statuts devient incontournable pour établir les mesures

---

l'adoption d'une convention générale contre le terrorisme, qui viendrait compléter les conventions antiterroristes sectorielles existantes. Le projet d'article 2 contient une définition du terrorisme qui inclut le fait de causer, tenter ou menacer de causer, «illicitement ou intentionnellement » : «*a*) la mort d'autrui ou des dommages corporels graves à autrui ; ou *b*) de sérieux dommages à un bien public ou privé, notamment un lieu public, une installation gouvernementale ou publique, un système de transport public, une infrastructure, ou à l'environnement ; ou *c*) des dommages aux biens, lieux, installations ou systèmes... qui entraînent ou risquent d'entraîner des pertes économiques considérables, lorsque le comportement incriminé, par sa nature ou son contexte, a pour but d'intimider une population ou de contraindre un gouvernement ou une organisation internationale à faire ou à ne pas faire quelque chose ». Le projet d'article 2 définit ensuite comme une infraction le fait de se rendre complice d'une infraction visée, d'organiser la commission d'une infraction ou d'ordonner à d'autres de commettre celle-ci, ou de contribuer à la commission de telles infractions par un groupe de personnes agissant de concert. Si les États membres se sont mis d'accord sur bon nombre des dispositions du projet de convention générale, des divergences de vues sur la question de savoir s'il faut ou non exclure les mouvements de libération nationale du champ d'application de la convention les ont empêchés de parvenir à un consensus sur l'adoption du texte intégral. Les négociations se poursuivent. De nombreux États définissent le terrorisme en droit national en reprenant, à des degrés divers, ces éléments.

Les problèmes particuliers posés par la définition du terrorisme et le principe de la légalité sont considérés de façon plus détaillée au chapitre III, section G.

[16] Le terrorisme est un phénomène dont l'appréhension juridique suscite des interrogations si l'on demeure dans le cadre classique des relations interétatiques, encadrées par des conventions internationales applicables en temps de paix et en temps de guerre[16]. Comme le conclut le Comité international de la croix-rouge (CICR), « Le terrorisme est un phénomène. Or, tant dans la pratique que du point de vue juridique, on ne peut pas livrer une guerre contre un phénomène. On peut seulement combattre une partie identifiable à un conflit. Pour toutes ces raisons, il serait plus judicieux de parler de "lutte contre le terrorisme" plutôt que de "guerre contre le terrorisme" la première revêtant de multiples facettes » (Comité international de la croix-rouge, *Droit International Humanitaire : questions et réponses*, 15 mai 2004, p. 3, disponible à l'adresse : http ://www.icrc.org/fre/resources/documents/faq/terrorism-faq-050504.htm)

de traitement réservé aux personnes capturées au cours de ces opérations. La tension entre le respect des droits de l'Homme et la lutte contre le terrorisme réside dans l'absence de définition du statut juridique des personnes arrêtées et détenues au cours de ces opérations. Dans ce genre de situation, les États «... ont le choix entre deux mauvaises solutions : soit combattre les groupes armés en respectant strictement les normes édictées par les conventions internationales, ce qui signifie s'interdire d'entrer dans les zones habitées, de fouiller les maisons pour y chercher des caches d'armes et des activistes (...), soit combattre dans le milieu urbain ou para urbain. Et c'est prendre le risque non seulement de commettre des « dérapages », mais aussi de susciter des effets pervers en chaîne : soutien accru de la population locale aux combattants, protestations internationales, contestation au sein même de leur propre opinion publique »[17]. Le terrorisme semble être à plusieurs égards un piège à la démocratie et de l'État de droit, même pour plusieurs États occidentaux. Or, les pays africains qui sont actuellement engagés dans ce type de combat ne sont pas dotés de mécanismes juridiques de répression appropriés, et leur système judiciaire comporte des failles qui ne garantissent pas toujours le droit à un procès équitable.

La question devient plus complexe au regard du traitement réservé aux personnes détenues, en fonction de leur nationalité. Lorsqu'il s'agit du national de l'État qui combat le terrorisme, il tombe sous le coup du dispositif juridique applicable à la répression des atteintes à la sûreté de l'État[18]. Cette personne peut alors être traitée conformément au droit interne de l'État en question. Mais, lorsque la personne arrêtée n'est pas le national de ce pays, deux situations d'irrégularité se présentent : si elle a été arrêtée alors qu'elle se trouvait de façon irrégulière sur ce territoire et qu'elle ne participait pas aux hostilités, elle est soupçonnée d'appartenir au réseau terroriste. La situation devient encore plus

---

[17] C. SAMY, « Pourquoi les démocraties en guerre contre le terrorisme violent-elles les droits de l'homme ? », *Critique internationale*, 2008/4 n° 41, p. 9-9.

[18] À cet égard, le Cameroun a adopté en décembre 2014, la loi n° 2014/028 du 23 décembre 2014 portant répression des actes de terrorisme. Cette loi a fait l'objet de critiques de la part des politiciens et de la société civile.

complexe lorsque cette personne étrangère a été capturée sur le terrain des hostilités. À l'irrégularité de la situation sur le territoire s'ajoute l'irrégularité de la position dans la zone du conflit et dans la participation au conflit. Or, il n'existe pas, jusqu'à présent, un corpus normatif applicable aux combats menés par les États contre les réseaux terroristes dans le monde. De l'identification du bloc normatif en question devrait découler le statut juridique des personnes appartenant aux mouvements terroristes. Les groupes terroristes ne respectent aucune règle juridique internationale et agissent de manière absolument contraire aux valeurs d'humanité, de proportionnalité et de discrimination telle qu'il résulte du droit international humanitaire, alors que les États sont tenus de respecter à leur égard un certain nombre de règles. C'est finalement, en filigrane, toute la problématique du statut des membres des mouvements terroristes qui se pose, ces derniers n'entrant dans aucune catégorie spécifiée par les textes actuellement en vigueur. Le droit international humanitaire et des conflits armés a un champ d'application bien défini, et les terroristes ne tombent pour l'heure aucunement sous le coup des règles qu'il édicte, soit parce que les spécificités de ces mouvements ne correspondent pas aux critères définis par ces règles, soit encore en raison d'une exclusion expresse de ces groupes du domaine du droit international, comme c'est notamment le cas pour les conventions de Genève ou le Statut de Rome[19]. Le flou juridique qui entoure les

---

[19] Des voies s'élèvent depuis plusieurs années pour soutenir que le droit international humanitaire est dépassé (« outdated »), et qu'il méritait d'être révisé (Voir C. ROSETT, « POWs. CUBA : The Red Cross needs to get real. », *Wall Street Journal* (23 janvier 2002) A33 ; H. KAMER, «Gulliver auf Guantánamo ? », *Neue Zürcher Zeitung* (26/27 janvier 2002) 3 ; et certaines remarques du secrétaire américain à la défense D. Rumsfeld lors d'une conférence de presse du 8 février 2002, en ligne : U.S. Department of Defence). Depuis l'apparition des conflits internes, du terrorisme et des actes de piraterie, de nombreuses personnes estiment qu'il faudrait construire un nouveau droit humanitaire, plus adapté au contexte des conflits actuels et cause de rupture de la paix et de la sécurité internationales (Voir R. WEDGEWOOD, "Personal View : Prisoners of a different war : The Geneva convention applies to conventional soldiers, not to the terrorists being held at Camp X-Ray", *Financial Times*, (30 janvier 2002), en ligne : (http ://globalarchive.ft.com/globalarchive/article.html ?id=020130001411&query=ca mp+x-).

mouvements terroristes gangrène assurément la mise en œuvre des mesures coercitives prévues par les textes pour réprimer la commission de crimes internationaux. Les groupes terroristes n'entrant pas dans le champ d'application des droits de Genève et de La Haye, il n'est pas possible de sanctionner leurs actes sur le fondement de ces règles.

La présente réflexion a un intérêt à la fois scientifique et pratique. Sur le plan scientifique, elle vise une évaluation des textes applicables au terrorisme pour faire ressortir les catégories juridiques qui s'y trouvent. Au moment où la lutte contre le terrorisme gagne en ampleur et touche les États africains, il est nécessaire de mener une réflexion sur la détermination des règles applicables au traitement des personnes arrêtées et détenues dans le cadre de ce combat. Sur le plan pratique, il est évident que la lutte contre Boko Haram aura comme conséquence directe et indéniable, le déferrement des membres de Boko Haram devant les tribunaux. Dans ce cas, ils se verront appliquer un dispositif juridique particulier et les juges des divers pays impliqués dans la lutte contre Boko Haram auront à la fois l'obligation de garantir à ces personnes un procès équitable, mais aussi d'invoquer à leur encontre des textes applicables et adéquats pour ne pas se voir reprocher la violation du principe fondamental d'impartialité. Or, il est évident que le contentieux en lien avec la lutte antiterroriste est appelé à se développer considérablement, au regard de la situation actuelle. Il s'agit même du principal défi qui attend les États africains engagés dans la lutte antiterroriste, car il semble à première vue difficile de concilier lutte efficace contre le terrorisme et respect des garanties procédurales. Face à une menace terroriste grandissante, la plupart des États africains ont renforcé leur arsenal législatif en la matière. L'ensemble de ces moyens juridiques dont se dotent les États pour faire face à la menace terroriste sont susceptibles de porter atteinte à différents droits et libertés garantis sur le plan international et sur le plan interne. Au-delà de la répression des auteurs des actes terroristes, l'État a encore intérêt à sauvegarder son image d'un État de droit, c'est-à-dire un État dans lequel la garantie des droits de tous et de chacun est assurée. Dans ce débat, ce sont essentiellement les garanties procédurales qui seront mises en cause à travers la multiplication des lois d'exception[20].

La précision de l'ensemble des règles applicables aux personnes étrangères arrêtées et détenues dans le cadre de la lutte contre Boko Haram passe par une analyse judicieuse des textes juridiques applicables au terrorisme, ce qui fait appel à la méthode juridique. Mais cette analyse des textes ne saurait se passer d'une exploitation des informations sur le terrain, ainsi que la pratique des États-Unis d'Amérique en la matière. Cette approche permet de constater qu'il y a une indétermination déconcertante du statut juridique des personnes arrêtées dans le cadre de la lutte contre Boko Haram (I), ce qui rend polémique tout traitement qui leur est administré (II).

I. Une indétermination déconcertante

Il existe un éventail de textes internationaux relatif au terrorisme, et il peut paraître troublant de constater que ces textes ne donnent aucune précision sur la condition juridique des personnes capturées dans le cadre de la lutte contre le terrorisme. Les textes relatifs au terrorisme s'avèrent inadaptés (A), ce qui rend les qualifications avancées inappropriées (B).

A. Des textes inadaptés

Au silence des conventions sectorielles sur le terrorisme s'ajoute l'inadaptation de l'ensemble du droit international humanitaire.

1. Le silence des conventions sectorielles sur le terrorisme

L'on recense actuellement environ 16 instruments universels relatifs à la prévention et la répression du terrorisme[21]. Ces instruments portent

---

[20] Dans de nombreux pays, les lois d'exception ont fait l'objet de vives critiques, et certaines mêmes ont été annulées par la cour constitutionnelle (cas du Kenya).

[21] La convention de 1963 relative aux infractions et à certains autres actes survenant à bord des aéronefs ; La convention de 1970 pour la répression de la capture illicite d'aéronefs ; La convention de 1971 pour la répression d'actes illicites dirigés contre la sécurité de l'aviation civile ; la convention de 1973 sur la prévention et la répression des infractions contre les personnes jouissant d'une protection internationale (concernant les attaques contre les hauts responsables gouvernementaux et les diplomates) ; la convention internationale de 1979 contre la prise d'otages ;la convention de 1980 sur la

sur des questions spécifiques, allant de la capture illicite d'aéronefs et de la prise d'otages à la répression des attentats terroristes à l'explosif. À ces instruments universels s'ajoutent des textes régionaux relatifs à certains aspects du terrorisme[22]. Ces accords mettent en place une approche "sectorielle" ou progressive du terrorisme, dans la mesure où chacun traite de comportements criminels différents. Ils contribuent au régime juridique général contre le terrorisme et constituent un cadre pour la coopération internationale en matière de prévention et de répression de ces actes. Les conventions internationales ne contiennent généralement

---

protection physique des matières nucléaires (concernant l'acquisition et l'utilisation illicites de matières nucléaires) ; le protocole de 1988 pour la répression des actes illicites de violence dans les aéroports servant à l'aviation civile internationale (texte complémentaire à la convention de 1971 pour la répression d'actes illicites dirigés contre la sécurité de l'aviation civile ; la convention de 1988 pour la répression d'actes illicites contre la sécurité de la navigation maritime (texte sur les activités illicites à bord de navires, conclu à Rome) ; le protocole de 1988 à la convention pour la répression d'actes illicites contre la sécurité des plates-formes fixes situées sur le plateau continental (texte sur les activités illicites visant les plates-formes fixes au large, conclu à Rome) ; la convention de 1991 sur le marquage des explosifs plastiques et en feuilles aux fins de détection (concerne les activités de marquage chimique pour faciliter la détection des explosifs plastiques, par exemple pour lutter contre les sabotages à bord d'un aéronef) ; la convention internationale de 1997 pour la répression des attentats terroristes à l'explosif ; la convention internationale de 1999 pour la répression du financement du terrorisme ; la convention internationale de 2005 pour la répression des actes de terrorisme nucléaire ; la convention de 2010 sur la répression des actes illicites dirigés contre l'aviation civile internationale.

[22] En Afrique, deux instruments majeurs ont été adoptés : la convention de l'OUA sur la prévention et la lutte contre le terrorisme (ou convention d'Alger) et son protocole à la convention de l'OUA sur la prévention et la lutte contre le terrorisme. Certains autres pays africains (Comores, Djibouti, Mauritanie, Soudan et Somalie), sont membres de la Ligue des États arabes et de l'Organisation de la conférence des États islamiques qui ont respectivement adopté la *Convention Arabe sur la suppression du terrorisme* et la *Convention de l'Organisation de la conférence islamique sur la lutte contre le terrorisme international.* Il existe des textes sous-régionaux de lutte contre le terrorisme. Les États de la Communauté économique et monétaire de l'Afrique centrale (CEMAC) ont adopté à Libreville (Gabon) le 27 mai 2004, un règlement portant adoption de la *Convention relative à la lutte contre le terrorisme en Afrique centrale.* L'Union économique et monétaire ouest-africaine (UEMOA) a également adopté des textes sur le financement du terrorisme.

que des obligations pour les États[23], sans pour autant contribuer à la détermination de la condition du terroriste capturé. Or, le terrorisme d'État est difficile et rare, ce qui entraîne immédiatement l'inapplicabilité de ces instruments juridiques dans le cadre de la lutte contre Boko Haram. En effet, aucune des conventions mentionnées ne fait allusion aux groupes terroristes et à leurs membres. Par conséquent, lesdits instruments ne contiennent pas de réglementation spécifique permettant d'imposer un traitement spécifique aux membres des mouvements terroristes détenus.

De même, les résolutions du Conseil de sécurité adoptées dans le cadre de la lutte contre le terrorisme, et dans lesquelles il qualifie le terrorisme de menace à la paix et à la sécurité internationales, ne visent généralement que les États, même si l'on y retrouve parfois des sanctions prononcées à l'encontre des membres de mouvements terroristes[24].

Par ailleurs, la jurisprudence tente de cerner le crime de terrorisation sans pour autant préciser le régime juridique applicable à l'auteur de ce crime. Ainsi, en 2003, le Tribunal pénal international pour l'ex-

[23] Ils font obligation aux États de prendre des mesures particulières pour prévenir les actes terroristes et interdisent les infractions liées au terrorisme, notamment en obligeant les États parties à ériger certaines conduites en infractions pénales, établir certains critères juridictionnels (y compris le fameux principe *aut dedere aut judicare*, «extrader ou juger ») et assurer une base juridique pour la coopération en matière d'extradition et d'entraide judiciaire.

[24] Parmi les résolutions du Conseil de sécurité relatives au terrorisme qui ont été adoptées en vertu du chapitre VII (articles 39 à 51) de la Charte des Nations unies figurent les résolutions 1267 (1999), 1373 (2001) et 1540 (2004). Sur la base du Chapitre VII de la Charte des Nations unies, le Conseil a adopté sa résolution 1373 (2001), dans laquelle il déclare explicitement que tout acte de terrorisme international constitue «une menace à la paix et à la sécurité internationales » et que les « actes, méthodes et pratiques du terrorisme sont contraires aux buts et aux principes de l'Organisation des Nations Unies ». Le Conseil a également demandé à tous les États d'ériger en infractions pénales les actes de terrorisme, les actes de soutien et de préparation d'infractions terroristes ainsi que le financement du terrorisme ; de dépolitiser les infractions de terrorisme ; de geler les fonds des personnes qui commettent ou tentent de commettre des actes de terrorisme ; et de renforcer la coopération internationale en matière pénale.

Yougoslavie a condamné pour la première fois un individu pour sa responsabilité dans le crime de guerre de terrorisation de la population civile à Sarajevo, en vertu de l'article 3 de son statut. Le Tribunal a conclu que le crime de terrorisation de la population civile était constitué du fait de la réunion des éléments communs aux autres crimes de guerre ainsi que d'autres éléments tirés de la convention pour la répression du financement du terrorisme[25]. À cette imprécision sectorielle s'ajoute l'inadaptation des règles de droit international humanitaire.

2. L'inadaptation des règles de droit international humanitaire et des conflits armés

L'application du droit international humanitaire à la lutte contre Boko Haram suppose un rapprochement entre la guerre et le terrorisme, ce qui n'est pas nécessairement le cas.

a. La nature juridique imprécise de la lutte contre Boko Haram

Le terrorisme international, défini comme « un fait illicite (...) commis par un individu ou un groupe d'individus (...) contre des personnes ou des biens, dans la poursuite d'un objectif idéologique », s'inscrit dans le cadre du droit de la paix, quand bien même il se caractériserait par une « violence grave » et serait susceptible de « mettre en danger la paix et la sécurité internationales »[26]. Il découle d'une telle définition que les membres présumés de Boko Haram entrent difficilement dans la catégorie de combattants d'une armée régulière, d'une milice ou d'un groupe armé menant une guérilla au sens des

---

[25] Tribunal pénal international pour l'ex-Yougoslavie, *Procureur* c. *Gali´c,* Affaire IT-98-29, arrêt du 5 décembre 2003. Le Tribunal a ajouté les éléments spécifiques suivants (par. 133) : «1. Actes de violence dirigés contre la population civile ou des personnes civiles ne participant pas directement aux hostilités, qui entraînent parmi elles la mort ou des atteintes graves à l'intégrité physique ou à la santé.

2. L'auteur a intentionnellement soumis à ces actes de violence la population civile ou des personnes civiles ne participant pas aux hostilités.

3. L'infraction susmentionnée a été commise dans le but principal de répandre la terreur parmi la population civile ».

[26] H. TIGROUDJA, « Quel(s) droit(s) applicable(s) à la « guerre au terrorisme ». *Annuaire français de droit international,* volume 48, 2002. pp. 81-102, p. 83

conventions de Genève et de leurs protocoles additionnels[27]. Il en est ainsi parce que le droit international humanitaire n'est applicable qu'en cas de conflit armé, alors que le terrorisme est perpétré en temps de paix et parfois en temps de guerre.

Les règles de droit international humanitaire s'appliquent de manière égale à toutes les parties à un conflit armé qui y consentent de diverses façons[28]. Il serait difficile de voir les mouvements terroristes consentir au respect des règles humanitaires. Même si la guerre et le terrorisme international ont en commun l'utilisation de la violence et peuvent avoir des effets similaires sur la sécurité internationale, deux éléments au moins les distinguent : leurs buts et leurs auteurs[29]. Le droit applicable au terrorisme international est prédéterminé par le cadre dans lequel il intervient (droit de la paix ou droit de la guerre), mais jusqu'à présent, même lorsque le terrorisme a pris ses formes les plus graves et lorsqu'il a entraîné l'usage de la force, il n'a jamais eu, à lui seul, pour effet de substituer l'application d'un régime (droit de la guerre) à l'autre (droit de la paix)[30]. Faire de la lutte contre le terrorisme une « guerre » suppose que l'on puisse négocier avec les terroristes qui, par essence, rejettent le droit. C'est implicitement reconnaître aux mouvements terroristes, un pouvoir similaire à celui d'un État et une capacité internationale découlant de sa personnalité juridique. Ce serait créer le monstre chargé de mettre fin à l'existence d'une société internationale des peuples civilisés. L'assimilation de la lutte contre Boko Haram à une guerre, tout simplement pour entraîner l'application du droit international

[27] Un élément fondamental de la notion de conflit armé est l'existence de « parties » belligérantes. Dans un conflit armé international, les parties au conflit sont deux ou plusieurs États (ou des États et des mouvements de libération nationale), tandis que, dans un conflit armé non international, les parties peuvent être, soit un État et des groupes armés (par exemple, des forces rebelles), soit uniquement des groupes armés. Dans un cas comme dans l'autre, les parties au conflit armé ont une formation de type militaire ainsi qu'une organisation et un commandement plus ou moins structurés. Elles sont donc en mesure de respecter et de faire respecter le droit humanitaire.

[28] Conclusions des accords de paix, etc. Mais il est difficile d'imaginer des négociations avec des groupes terroristes.

[29] H. TIGROUDJA, « Quel(s) droit(s) applicable(s) à la « guerre au terrorisme », *op cit.*

[30] *Ibid.*, p. 84.

humanitaire, ferait donc naître ce qu'un auteur a appelé un « faux droit de la guerre »[31]. Dans le cadre de la lutte contre Boko Haram, les États (Cameroun, Niger, Tchad) ne s'attaquent pas à des combattants identifiables. Il flotte même dans la lutte contre Boko Haram un air de métaphysique relativement au mode opératoire des membres de ce mouvement. La prétention de l'applicabilité des règles de droit international humanitaire serait un moyen de reconnaître et même d'approuver la possibilité de faire rentrer les mouvements terroristes dans un ordre juridique, par le biais d'une situation qui pourrait provoquer l'obligation, même pour ces mouvements, de respecter le droit international humanitaire. Ainsi, se placer sur le terrain du droit de la guerre revient à placer les terroristes dans une logique de combat, avec pour seul principe que « les belligérants n'ont pas un choix illimité des moyens de nuire à l'ennemi » comme le rappelle l'article 22 de la convention III de La Haye de 1899[32].

b.a. Difficile assimilation à une guerre

Des problèmes de qualification de la situation actuelle dans le nord du Cameroun surgissent, avant même qu'il ne se pose le problème du statut juridique des personnes arrêtées dans le cadre de cette lutte : s'agit-il d'une guerre contre le terrorisme, comme celle qu'ont menée les États-Unis d'Amérique en Afghanistan après les évènements du 11 septembre 2001[33], d'un conflit armé ou alors d'une lutte armée ? La guerre est un phénomène régi par le droit international dont le déclenchement

---

[31] Ph. WECKEL, « Le statut des détenus de Guantanamo », *RGDIP,* 2002, p. 366.

[32] H. TIGROUDJA, « Quel(s) droit(s) applicable(s) à la « guerre au terrorisme », *op. cit.*, p. 92

[33] Dans son discours sur l'état de l'Union du 29 janvier 2002, le président américain a utilisé le mot « guerre » à douze reprises, et a laissé entrevoir qu'après la victoire en Afghanistan, la «guerre » allait continuer contre des États comme l'Iran, l'Iraq et la Corée du Nord. Si on a beaucoup parlé de « guerre », on n'a, en revanche, pas beaucoup entendu parler de droit, et encore moins de droit international suite à ces évènements, et ceci, bien que la réaction des États-Unis ait porté, le temps d'une journée, le nom de «justice immuable » (M. SASSÒLI, « La «guerre contre le terrorisme », le droit international humanitaire et le statut de prisonnier de guerre », *The Canadian Yearbook of international law",* vol. 39, 2001, p.1)

entraîne l'application d'un corpus juridique spécifique, destiné à régir les rapports entre les belligérants, mais aussi à assurer aux personnes impliquées ou présentes sur le terrain des hostilités une protection singulière. La lutte contre Boko Haram entraîne donc, de façon quasi identique, la transposition des questions suscitées par la guerre menée contre les talibans par les États-Unis d'Amérique et les débats autour du statut des détenus de Guantanamo. La lutte contre le terrorisme est d'une nature juridique ambiguë. Sur le plan juridique, il est difficile de l'assimiler à une guerre[34] ou à un conflit armé, deux situations qui déclenchent l'application du corpus normatif du droit humanitaire[35]. L'usage récurrent de la métaphore « guerre contre Boko Haram », est une notion ambiguë. Cette lutte ne peut être régie par le droit international humanitaire que si les activités menées au nom de Boko Haram atteignent le seuil d'un conflit armé au sens juridique du terme. Les guerriers asymétriques utilisent des moyens qui leur permettent de

[34] La guerre est un état ou une situation déclenché par une confrontation armée entre deux ou plusieurs États ou par une simple déclaration à cet effet, et auxquels s'applique un corps de règles de droit international distinct de celui applicable en temps de paix (droit de la guerre, droit de la neutralité) (J. SALMON (Dir.), *Dictionnaire de droit international public, op. cit.*, p. 537).

[35] Le cadre juridique instauré par le droit international humanitaire distingue deux types de conflits armés (Article 2 commun aux conventions de Genève ; TPIY, *Le Procureur c/ Dusko Tadic*, Jugement, IT-94-1-T, 7 may 1997, par. 561-568 ; voir également TPIY, *Procureur c/ Fatmir Limaj*, Jugement, IT-03-66-T, 30 november 2005, para. 84) Les conflits armés internationaux opposent au moins deux États, tandis que les conflits armés non internationaux opposent les forces gouvernementales à des groupes armés non étatiques, ou des groupes armés entre eux. D'ordinaire, les conflits armés internationaux sont aisés à identifier : les parties sont prédéterminées puisqu'elles opposent des entités étatiques. Lorsqu'une difficulté de qualification se pose, elle relève habituellement de la question de savoir si les actes d'hostilités peuvent être imputés à un État. Cette approche n'est pas opératoire dans le cas d'un conflit armé non international. Il convient alors d'examiner le niveau d'organisation des parties et le degré d'intensité des affrontements entre ces groupes eux-mêmes ou entre ces groupes et l'État, pour voir s'il atteint le niveau requis, afin de qualifier la situation de conflit armé non international (CICR, *Commentaire à l'art. 1 du Protocole additionnel (II) aux Conventions de Genève du 12 août 1949 relatif à la protection des victimes des conflits armés non internationaux* (Protocole II), 8 juin 1977 p.372).

contourner la puissance militaire classique. Ils surgissent par petits groupes lors d'attaques ponctuelles dans le but de déstabiliser le fort[36].

Il est évident que cette situation est exceptionnelle et nécessite le déploiement d'un dispositif juridique spécifique. Pour autant, il serait tout aussi difficile de l'assimiler aux circonstances exceptionnelles prévues par le dispositif constitutionnel[37] de chaque État et dans lesquelles s'applique un droit spécifique qui déroge aux droits de l'Homme[38]. Selon que le conflit armé est international ou non, les règles applicables diffèrent et le statut des personnes impliquées dans le conflit varie. La plupart des mesures prises par des États pour prévenir ou réprimer des actes terroristes ne sont pas assimilables à des actes de guerre[39]. Le terrorisme étant considéré comme un phénomène, il est impossible de livrer une guerre contre un phénomène. On ne peut combattre qu'une partie identifiable à un conflit. La lutte est par contre considérée comme une action pour ou contre quelque chose, soutenue par la mise en œuvre de moyens appropriés. Il serait par conséquent plus judicieux de parler de

---

36 C. SAMY, « Pourquoi les démocraties en guerre contre le terrorisme violent-elles les droits de l'homme ? » *op. cit.*, p. 12.

37 L'article 9 de la Constitution du Cameroun, telle que révisée en 2008, dispose que : « (1) Le Président de la République peut, lorsque les circonstances l'exigent, proclamer par décret, l'état d'urgence qui lui confère des pouvoirs spéciaux dans les conditions fixées par la loi.
(2) Le président de la République peut, en cas de péril grave menaçant l'intégrité du territoire, la vie, l'indépendance ou les institutions de la République, proclamer, par décret, l'état d'exception et prendre toutes mesures qu'il juge nécessaires. Il en informe la Nation par voie de message ».

38 L'article 4 du pacte international relatif aux droits civils et politiques permet aux États de déroger aux droits de l'Homme dans des circonstances exceptionnelles : "1. Dans le cas où un danger public exceptionnel *menace l'existence de la nation* et est proclamé par un acte officiel, les États parties au présent pacte peuvent prendre, dans la stricte mesure où la situation l'exige, des mesures dérogeant aux obligations prévues dans le présent Pacte".

39 Des mesures telles que la collecte de renseignements, la coopération policière et judiciaire, l'extradition, les sanctions pénales, les enquêtes financières, le gel des avoirs ou les pressions diplomatiques et économiques exercées sur les États accusés de soutenir des terroristes présumés ne sont généralement pas considérées comme des actes de guerre.

« lutte contre le terrorisme » plutôt que de « guerre contre le terrorisme », la première revêtant de multiples facettes. Dans ce cas, plusieurs mesures de maintien de l'ordre dans un État peuvent être prises pour lutter contre une attaque extérieure, comme c'est le cas avec les incursions régulières de Boko Haram au Cameroun, au Niger et au Tchad.

c. Le caractère mouvant des positions terroristes

Un autre facteur de complication est la situation où un État se défend contre des attaques armées perpétrées par des mouvements armés situés hors de son territoire, mais que son gouvernement ne peut contrôler véritablement. C'est là l'une des premières caractéristiques de la lutte contre Boko Haram, puisqu'il est avéré que le Nigeria n'a pu contenir les assauts de ce mouvement sur son territoire et qu'il a même perdu le contrôle de certaines parties de son territoire national au profit de cette nébuleuse. Dans un tel contexte, les acteurs évoluent au fil du temps et, de ce fait, Boko Haram recrute des membres dans presque tous les pays. Par conséquent, ses membres n'ont plus seulement la seule nationalité nigériane. La situation, déjà complexe d'un point de vue légal, le devient d'un point de vue factuel. La distinction des phases de phénomène devient importante pour le cerner : incursions régulières des membres de Boko Haram en République du Cameroun, prises d'otages, enlèvements de jeunes et de femmes, assassinats, laxisme de l'armée nigériane, décision du Cameroun de lutter contre le mouvement depuis le Cameroun pour protéger son territoire, refus d'octroi d'un droit de poursuite au Cameroun par le Nigeria, intensification des frappes de Boko Haram dans le lac Tchad, décision du Tchad de s'engager dans la lutte, déploiement des armées du Cameroun et du Tchad dans la lutte, attaques de Boko Haram au Niger, entrée du Niger dans la lutte, sommet de la CEEAC sur Boko Haram, décision de création et de déploiement d'une force multinationale mixte pour lutter contre le mouvement terroriste, etc. Toutes ces phases sont celles au cours desquelles les situations juridiques des personnes directement impliquées dans les actions de Boko Haram ont évolué considérablement. En effet, au cours de chacune de ces phases, la condition juridique des personnes arrêtées peut évoluer, selon sa nationalité, le lieu de sa captivité et la nature de la lutte menée à ce moment.

Si les circonstances de l'arrestation des personnes détenues sont nécessairement celles de la répression du terrorisme, il faudrait qu'il existe un lien de causalité entre lesdites arrestations et la lutte en cours. Certes, dans le cadre des enquêtes, certaines personnes soupçonnées d'être des membres de Boko Haram font l'objet d'arrestations, même si elles ne participent pas directement aux activités de ce mouvement. Elles peuvent donc avoir mené des activités terroristes en dehors de la période de combat et par conséquent, c'est le droit interne de chacun des États concernés qui est applicable, avec tous les aménagements procéduraux et les limitations aux droits que la lutte contre cette infraction particulière autorise. Ces droits déterminent strictement les conditions dans lesquelles une personne peut être privée de sa liberté et comprennent le droit à un tribunal et le droit à réparation pour une détention illégale. La lutte contre Boko Haram n'est donc ni une guerre ni un conflit armé. C'est un combat atypique qui en principe devrait générer l'application des règles *sui generis* à la situation dans les zones de combat. La détermination du droit applicable aux personnes détenues ne peut se faire qu'au cas par cas, dans la mesure où toutes ces personnes n'ont pas été arrêtées au même moment ni pour les mêmes raisons. Elles n'ont pas non plus la même qualité[40]. Ces différentes situations entraînent des qualifications inappropriées.

B. Des qualifications inappropriées

Face à l'imprécision juridique, plusieurs qualifications sont envisageables. Ces qualifications reposent sur des critères épars : la nationalité des personnes arrêtées et détenues, le lieu de leur arrestation, les circonstances de leur arrestation, le matériel en leur possession au moment de leur arrestation. Leur assimilation à des combattants terroristes semble difficile à une exploitation juridique.

1. L'inadéquation des statuts en présence dans la lutte envisagée

---

[40] H. TIGROUDJA, « Quel(s) droit(s) applicable(s) à la « guerre au terrorisme », *op. cit.* , p. 93.

a. Le difficile rapprochement avec prisonniers de guerre

Le droit international humanitaire, qui repose sur le principe fondamental de la distinction, distingue entre deux catégories de statuts dans un conflit : les civils et les combattants. Le statut de prisonnier de guerre repose sur l'appartenance à une « Haute Partie contractante », à savoir l'appartenance aux forces armées régulières d'un État. Selon l'article 4 § A (1) de la 3e Convention : « Sont prisonniers de guerre, au sens de la présente Convention, les personnes qui, appartenant à l'une des catégories suivantes, sont tombées au pouvoir de l'ennemi : les membres des forces armées d'une Partie au conflit, de même que les membres des milices et des corps de volontaires faisant partie de ces forces armées. »[41] Le commentaire des conventions de Genève élaboré par le Comité international de la croix- rouge estime que : « *Se trouvant aux mains de l'ennemi, un individu doit avoir un statut selon le droit international : il est soit un prisonnier de guerre couvert par la IIIe Convention, soit une personne civile couverte par la IVe Convention, soit encore un membre du personnel sanitaire des forces armées couvert par la Ire Convention. Il n'y a pas de statut intermédiaire ; aucune personne se trouvant aux mains de l'ennemi ne peut être en dehors du droit et c'est là, nous semble-t-il, une solution satisfaisante, non seulement pour l'esprit, mais aussi et surtout du point de vue humanitaire* »[42]. Il est vrai que l'assimilation au prisonnier de guerre se présente, selon un auteur, comme « l'ultime rempart de protection dans une situation profondément inhumaine telle que la guerre dans laquelle les autres

---

[41] Allant dans le même sens, l'article 44 (3) du protocole additionnel fournit des éléments caractérisant le combattant ayant droit au traitement d'un prisonnier de guerre en disposant qu'« un combattant conserve son statut de combattant à condition que, dans de telles situations, il porte ses armes ouvertement pendant chaque engagement militaire ; et pendant le temps où il est exposé à la vue de l'adversaire alors qu'il prend part à un déploiement militaire qui précède le lancement d'une attaque à laquelle il doit participer ».

[42] J. S. PICTET (dir.), *Les Conventions de Genève du 12 août 1949, Commentaire, Convention de Genève relative à la protection des personnes civiles en temps de guerre*, vol. 4, Genève, CICR, 1956, p. 58.

garde-fous juridiques ont tendance à disparaître »[43]. Les quatre conventions de Genève laissent supposer que toute personne capturée sur le champ de bataille doit être présumée prisonnier de guerre jusqu'à ce qu'une cour compétente statue autrement[44]. Mais, le statut de prisonnier de guerre est conditionné par l'appartenance à l'une des parties en conflit. Or, il est difficile d'assimiler Boko Haram à une rébellion, encore moins à un mouvement armé en territoire camerounais. Il s'agit d'un mouvement terroriste et reconnaître le statut de prisonnier de guerre aux membres de Boko Haram arrêtés serait légaliser le terrorisme en droit international. D'ailleurs, les États-Unis considèrent que l'attribution du statut de prisonnier de guerre aux combattants terroristes serait une sorte de légalisation du terrorisme[45]. Les membres de Boko Haram capturés dans le cadre de la lutte contre ce phénomène pourraient, dans une certaine mesure, bénéficier d'un traitement similaire à celui des prisonniers de guerre, sans pour autant être considérés comme étant des

---

[43] M. SASSOLI, « Combattants et Combattants Illégaux », In V. CHÉTAIL, *Permanence et Mutation du Droit des Conflits Armés*, Bruxelles, Bruylant, 2013. p. 151-184, p. 154

[44] Voir D. BIGO et C. OLSSON, « Guantanamo. Sortir du silence, refuser l'impunité », *Cultures & Conflits* [En ligne], 56 | hiver 2004, mis en ligne le 07 janvier 2010, consulté le 23 février 2015 sur : http ://conflits.revues.org/1626. Ces auteurs considèrent d'ailleurs que " même les prisonniers à Guantanamo qui n'ont pas été arrêtés sur le champ de bataille (*certains ont été arrêtés en Gambie, d'autres en Bosnie-Herzégovine - NDLR*) doivent au titre de la quatrième convention de Genève, également bénéficier d'une protection juridique, même si celle-ci est moindre que pour les prisonniers de guerre".

[45] voir *A Message from the President of the United States Regarding Protocol II Additional to the 1949 Geneva*
Conventions, and Relating to the Protection of Victims of Non-International Armed Conflicts, 100e Cong., Washington D.C., United States Government Printing Office, 1987, pp. 100-102 et D. J. FEITH, « Law in the
service of terror : the strange case of the additional protocol », *The National Interest*, 1985, n°1, pp. 36-47, en particulier, p. 47). L'ancien secrétaire d'État américain à la Défense déclarait à propos des détenus de Guantanamo que : « Ce ne sont pas des prisonniers de guerre. Ce sont des tueurs, parmi les plus dangereux, les mieux entraînés et les plus cruels de la planète ».

prisonniers de guerre. Ce traitement permettrait de ménager celui qui n'est ni un simple civil ni un combattant régulier.

b. La situation compliquée de combattant ennemi

Les mouvements terroristes recrutent dans tous les pays et désormais, même les nationaux des pays en lutte contre Boko Haram sont arrêtés sur le terrain des affrontements. Ils sont dans ce cas dans une situation délicate. En tant que nationaux camerounais, nigériens ou tchadiens arrêtés dans le cadre de la lutte contre Boko Haram, ils ne sauraient être assimilés aux étrangers capturés en même temps. Un problème similaire s'est posé dans le cadre de la guerre américaine contre le terrorisme en Afghanistan. L'exécutif américain a créé par décret un statut spécial pour les citoyens américains ayant combattu auprès d'Al Qaida, celui de « combattant ennemi »[46]. Le terme « combattant ennemi » ou encore « combattant ennemi illégal » (*« unlawful combattant »*), défini dans les USA Patriot Act[47], a été utilisé par le gouvernement des États-Unis pour qualifier les prisonniers capturés dans le cadre de la « Guerre contre le terrorisme » se trouvant dans le centre de détention de Guantanamo ou dans d'autres centres de détention clandestins de la CIA ou du Pentagone, notamment en Afghanistan et en Irak. Définir ces prisonniers comme « combattants illégaux » ou « ennemy combattant » permettait aux États-Unis de ne pas leur appliquer la convention de Genève relative aux prisonniers de guerre. On a même parlé de « détenus fantômes » pour désigner ceux des détenus dont les noms et nationalités étaient inconnus[48]. La capture des détenus fantômes contredit le droit

[46] Le Monde, « Combattants ennemis et combattants irréguliers », 30 juin 2004.

[47] Le USA PATRIOT ACT est une loi antiterroriste qui a été votée par le Congrès des États-Unis et signée par George W. Bush le 26 octobre 2001. Cette loi a créé le statut de combattant ennemi ou combattant illégal qui permet au gouvernement des États-Unis de détenir sans limites et sans inculpation toute personne soupçonnée de projet terroriste. Dans la pratique, cette loi autorise les services de sécurité à accéder aux données informatiques détenues par les particuliers et les entreprises, sans autorisation préalable et sans en informer les utilisateurs.

[48] Le 8 avril 2002, selon le gouvernement américain, 242 personnes étaient détenues par les États-Unis en Afghanistan, et 299 autres sur la base de Guantánamo Bay. Ces prisonniers seraient des ressortissants de divers pays : Afghanistan, Algérie, Arabie

international, en particulier l'article 5 de la troisième convention de Genève, qui indique qu'en cas de doute, c'est à un tribunal qu'il revient de déterminer si un individu présente ou non les caractéristiques constitutives d'un « prisonnier de guerre », et que ledit individu doit être protégé en tant que tel jusqu'au prononcé du jugement[49]. Dans le cadre de la guerre en Afghanistan, le gouvernement américain prétendait que ces personnes sont détenues en tant que "combattants ennemis en relation avec un conflit armé", et n'acceptait pas qu'ils aient droit à une protection en vertu du droit international des droits de l'Homme[50]. En 2009, le gouvernement américain a aboli le statut de combattant ennemi[51].

Saoudite, Azerbaïdjan, Bahreïn, Belgique, Chine, Danemark, Espagne, Égypte, France, Iran, Koweït, Ouzbékistan, Pakistan, Qatar, Royaume-Uni, Russie, Suède, Turquie et Yémen. Huit de ces États sont membres du Conseil de l'Europe. Les ressortissants d'autres pays pourraient être détenus en Afghanistan et à Guantanamo Bay (d'après Amnesty International, il pourrait y avoir plus de 600 prisonniers de 40 nationalités détenus sur la base américaine). Apparemment des ressortissants géorgiens ont aussi été livrés aux États-Unis pour interrogatoire à Guantanamo Bay à l'automne 2002. Une personne en Bosnie-Herzégovine a été exposée au risque d'être transférée à Guantanamo Bay, mais elle a pu être libérée d'un centre de détention préventive de la SFOR, suite à une mesure provisoire de la Chambre des droits de l'homme de Bosnie-Herzégovine. L'armée américaine a reconnu que parmi les détenus interrogés à Guantanamo Bay se trouvaient des enfants âgés de seize ans et moins.

[49] Pour plus de détails, voir Daniel Sabbagh, « Sécurité et libertés aux États-Unis dans l'après-11 septembre : un état des lieux », *Critique internationale* n°19 - avril 2003, disponible sur http ://www.ceri-sciencespo.com/publica/critique/article/ci19p17-23.pdf consulté ce 14/11/2011.

[50] Longtemps soutenue par le gouvernement Bush qui veut que les détenus n'aient droit à aucune application de la Convention, pas même afin de déterminer leur statut éventuel de prisonniers de guerre. Son argument se fonde sur le fait qu'Al-Qaïda n'est pas une force militaire en dépit du fait que les forces armées américaines visent à la détruire ; il s'agit plutôt, à ses yeux, d'une organisation criminelle pure et simple, et ses combattants ne sont pas des combattants légaux, pour la simple et bonne raison que la Convention n'est pas destinée à s'appliquer à des terroristes criminels.

[51] Le ministère de la Justice a précisé dans un communiqué en 2009 avoir soumis devant un tribunal fédéral une nouvelle règle justifiant la détention par l'État de prisonniers à Guantanamo. La définition "n'emploie pas l'expression d' « ennemi combattant » et la détention d'un suspect de terrorisme "se basera sur les lois internationales", souligne le communiqué. Cela implique que seuls seront détenus "ceux

c. La situation complexe de combattants illégaux

La notion de « combattant illégal » [52] n'existe pas en droit international et plus précisément en droit international humanitaire. Elle est cependant utilisée aux États-Unis depuis le 19e siècle, plus particulièrement au moment de la Guerre d'Indépendance, pour qualifier les milices, puis au moment de la guerre de Sécession. En 1863, le Code Lieber (ou « Instructions pour les armées en campagne des États-Unis d'Amérique ») semblait, en outre, établir implicitement une distinction entre belligérants « légaux » et illégaux ». Ainsi, la section IV traitant des « *Ennemis armés n'appartenant pas à l'armée ennemie* » ; « *Éclaireurs* » ; « *Rebelles de guerre* » ; « *saboteurs* » créait des catégories de personnes échappant au statut de prisonnier de guerre. Mais c'est la Cour suprême des États-Unis qui a établi une distinction entre « lawful » et « unlawful combatants », dans l'affaire *Ex Parte Quirin.* Il s'agissait du cas de huit individus nazis qui, après avoir débarqué aux États-Unis (à New York et en Floride) furent arrêtés en possession d'explosifs, et vêtus de vêtements civils au lieu de leur uniforme traditionnel. La Cour suprême a alors

---

qui ont apporté un soutien important à Al-Qaïda ou aux talibans", précise le département de la Justice. "Les nouvelles normes reposent sur le droit international de la guerre (...) et stipulent clairement que le gouvernement n'a pas l'autorité de détenir ces personnes au titre d'un soutien mineur ou non avéré à Al-Qaïda et aux talibans", explique le communiqué. "Alors que nous travaillons à la mise en place d'une nouvelle politique concernant ces détenus, il est essentiel que nous agissions d'une manière qui renforce notre sécurité nationale, mais qui soit aussi en accord avec nos valeurs et avec la loi", déclarait alors le ministre de la Justice, Eric Holder. "En retirant le terme d'ennemi combattant l'administration Obama a fait un pas de plus vers la clarification de sa position sur les détenus de Guantanamo", selon Amnesty International.

[52] M. SASSOLI, « Combattants et Combattants Illégaux », In V. CHÉTAIL, *Permanence et Mutation du Droit des Conflits Armés*. Bruxelles : Bruylant, 2013. p. 151-184. Cet auteur précise que Trois éléments caractérisent le régime juridique des combattants : premièrement, eux seuls ont le droit de prendre part directement aux hostilités, deuxièmement ils peuvent être attaqués – jusqu'à ce qu'ils se rendent ou jusqu'à ce qu'ils soient mis hors de combat – et troisièmement lorsqu'ils tombent au pouvoir de l'ennemi ils deviennent des prisonniers de guerre. L'obligation qui leur est faite de se distinguer de la population civile fait également partie de la définition, en tant que condition que doit remplir un individu pour se voir reconnaître le statut de combattant.

considéré ces personnes comme des combattants « illégaux »[53]. Les « combattants illégaux » échappent donc au statut de prisonnier de guerre et, *de facto,* à la protection des conventions de Genève[54]. C'est pour remédier à cette situation que fut signé le protocole I des conventions de Genève, en 1977. En 2001, l'administration du président G. Bush s'est appuyée sur la jurisprudence *Quirin* pour définir la notion de « combattant illégal », au regard des attentats du 11 septembre, en déclarant dans le *Military Order* du 13 novembre 2001, mais aussi et surtout dans le *Military Commissions Act* de 2006 qu'un combattant illégal est : « (i) *a person who has engaged in hostilities or who has*

53" *Neither the Taliban nor the al Qaeda are prisoners of war",* A Fleisher, Conférence de presse du 7 février 2002. « By universal agreement and practice the law of war draws a distinction between the armed forces and the peaceful populations of belligerent nations and also between those who are lawful and unlawful combatants. Lawful combatants are subject to capture and detention as prisoners of war by opposing military forces. Unlawful combatants are likewise subject to capture and detention, but in addition they are subject to trial and punishment by military tribunals for acts which render their belligerency unlawful. The spy who secretly and without uniform passes the military lines of a belligerent in time of war, seeking to gather military information and communicate it to the enemy, or an enemy combatant who without uniform comes secretly through the lines for the purpose of waging war by destruction of life or property, are familiar examples of belligerents who are generally deemed not to be entitled to the status of prisoners of war, but to be offenders against the law of war subject to trial and punishment by military tribunals ». Cette notion a ensuite été reprise, sans pour autant que soit explicitement déniée l'application de la convention IV, par une juridiction britannique dans l'affaire *Osman Bin Haji Mohamed Ali et al* puis par une cour militaire israélienne dans l'affaire *Omar Mahmud Kassem* (Cour militaire israélienne siégeant à Ramallah, *Military Prosecutor v. Omar Mahmud Kassem et al,* 13 April 1969, référencée dans *Israël Law Review*, n° 42, 1971, pp. 470-483.).

54 Une telle situation a été prise en compte au sein du CICR suite à la Seconde Guerre mondiale, comme l'illustre le commentaire de l'article 45 du premier protocole additionnel : « De véritables bouleversements politiques avaient accompagné les opérations militaires de la Seconde Guerre mondiale [...]. Il en était résulté des situations anormales, confuses, caractérisées par l'inextricable enchevêtrement des rapports de droit international. Des groupements nationaux continuaient à prendre une part active aux hostilités alors que l'adversaire leur déniait ce droit, ne les considérait pas comme des combattants réguliers, mais comme des francs-tireurs, c'est-à-dire comme des individus participant volontairement aux opérations militaires sans faire partie des forces armées ».

purposefully and materially supported hostilities against the United States or its co-belligerents who is not a lawful enemy combatant (including a person who is part of the Taliban, al Qaeda, or associated forces) »[55]. Cependant, comme l'a relevé un rapport de l'Assemblée parlementaire de l'Union européenne, la notion de "combattants illégaux" est inconnue du droit international et ne correspond à aucun statut légal. Aucun soldat n'a jamais été traduit en justice en tant que combattant ; même devant les tribunaux pour crimes de guerre, ce sont généralement des officiers ou ceux qui donnaient des ordres qui ont été traduits en justice, mais un simple soldat n'a pas été jugé[56].

d- L'émergence du statut de « combattant terroriste étranger »

Le phénomène du terrorisme a mis en évidence celui des combattants étrangers dans divers groupes terroristes[57]. Le combattant étranger est considéré comme l'individu qui rejoint une insurrection au cours d'une guerre civile, mais qui n'est pas citoyen des États en conflit. Thomas Hegghammer fournit une définition plus étoffée en établissant quatre critères. Le combattant étranger est un individu qui a rejoint une insurrection et qui opère en son sein ; qui n'a pas la citoyenneté ou de parenté avec les Parties en conflit ; qui n'est pas affilié à une organisation militaire officielle ; et qui n'est pas payé. On parle souvent à leur propos de « combattants étrangers terroristes »[58]. Cette notion a été consacrée

---

[55] De là, le gouvernement américain estime que les prisonniers de Guantanamo relèvent de ce statut de « prisonniers illégaux » et, par là même, échappent à la protection des conventions de Genève.

[56] Union européenne, Assemblée parlementaire, Droits des personnes détenues par les États-Unis en Afghanistan et sur la base de Guantánamo Bay, Rapport Commission des questions juridiques et des droits de l'Homme, 26 mai 2003

[57] Leur nombre est estimé entre 3 000 et 15 000. On peut l'augmenter à 20 000 en incluant l'Irak et la Libye. À titre de comparaison, le théâtre irakien depuis 2003 comptabilisait 4 000 à 5 000 combattants étrangers, l'Afghanistan 1 000 à 1 500. La Syrie est probablement le pays où le plus grand nombre de combattants étrangers est en activité simultanément. De plus, l'étendue géographique de l'origine de ces combattants est sans précédent avec au moins 81 pays.

[58] Cité sur Les « combattants terroristes étrangers » et le droit international humanitaire, accessible à l'adresse https ://dommagescivils.wordpress.com/ , consulté le 03 avril 2015.

par la résolution 2178 (2014) du Conseil de sécurité des Nations unies le 24 septembre 2014[59]. Cette résolution les définit comme les « individus qui se rendent dans un État autre que leur État de résidence ou de nationalité, dans le dessein de commettre, d'organiser ou de préparer des actes de terrorisme, ou afin d'y participer ou de dispenser ou recevoir un entraînement au terrorisme, notamment à l'occasion d'un conflit armé ». Cette catégorie de combattant[60] se singularise par la menace globale qu'ils posent. Qui dit combattant, dit conflit armé. Si le combattant étranger est celui qui a rejoint une insurrection, il prend part juridiquement, et *a priori,* à un conflit armé non international. D'une part, comme le précise la résolution 2178 (2014), ils « contribuent à intensifier les conflits, à les prolonger et à en compliquer singulièrement le règlement ». D'autre part, « ils peuvent (…) être une menace considérable pour les États dont ils viennent, ceux par lesquels ils transitent et ceux où ils se rendent, ainsi que les États qui jouxtent les zones de conflit armé où ils combattent et qui doivent faire face à de sérieux problèmes de sécurité ». Dès lors, « la menace que représentent les combattants terroristes étrangers peut atteindre toutes les régions et tous les États membres, même ceux qui sont éloignés des zones de conflit ». Il y a d'ailleurs, dans la prise en compte de cette notion, les risques de substitution ou de superposition de statuts. En effet, le statut de réfugié risque d'être utilisé par des combattants étrangers qui se seraient fait passer pour des populations civiles pour traverser les frontières internationales. C'est la raison pour

---

[59] Dans cette résolution, le Conseil de sécurité ''*Constatant avec inquiétude* que les combattants terroristes étrangers contribuent à intensifier les conflits, à les prolonger et à en compliquer singulièrement le règlement, et qu'ils peuvent aussi être une menace considérable pour les États dont ils viennent, ceux par lesquels ils transitent et ceux où ils se rendent, ainsi que les États qui jouxtent les zones de conflit armé où ils combattent et qui doivent faire face à de sérieux problèmes de sécurité, *notant* que la menace que représentent les combattants terroristes étrangers peut atteindre toutes les régions et tous les États Membres, même ceux qui sont éloignés des zones de conflit, et *se disant profondément préoccupé* de voir que les combattants terroristes étrangers mettent leur idéologie extrémiste au service de l'apologie du terrorisme.

[60] Le combattant est un membre des forces armées d'une partie à un conflit qui participent directement aux hostilités. (J. SALMON (Dir.) *Dictionnaire de droit international public, op. cit.*, p. 194).

laquelle, les États « de veiller, conformément au droit international et notamment au droit international des droits de l'homme et au droit international des réfugiés, à ce que le statut de réfugié ne soit pas détourné à leur profit par les auteurs, organisateurs ou complices d'actes terroristes, y compris les combattants terroristes étrangers ».

La notion de « combattant terroriste étranger » est bicéphale : c'est un « combattant étranger », c'est-à-dire un individu qui a quitté son pays d'origine et qui a rejoint un groupe terroriste l'étranger par idéologie, croyance ou affinité. C'est également un terroriste, ce qui signifie deux choses. Soit c'est un individu qui part vers des pays sur les territoires desquels les organisations terroristes disposent de camps d'entraînement lui dispensant une « formation » qui lui permettra d'opérer des attentats à son retour dans son pays d'origine. Soit c'est un combattant qui commet des actes terroristes sur le territoire où se déroule le conflit armé. Dans le premier cas, le terroriste est le criminel qui commet un attentat en temps de paix, tel qu'il découle de l'énumération faite à l'article 2 du projet de convention générale sur le terrorisme[61]. Il faut distinguer le combattant

[61] Selon l'article 2 du projet de convention générale sur le terrorisme international, commet cette infraction « quiconque cause par quelque moyen que ce soit, illicitement et intentionnellement :

a) La mort d'autrui ou des dommages corporels graves à autrui ;

b) De sérieux dommages à un bien public ou privé, notamment un lieu public, une installation gouvernementale ou publique, un système de transport public, une infrastructure, ou à l'environnement ; ou c) Des dommages aux biens, lieux, installations ou systèmes mentionnés à l'alinéa b) du paragraphe 1 du présent article, qui entraînent ou risquent d'entraîner des pertes économiques considérables ; lorsque le comportement incriminé, par sa nature ou son contexte, a pour but d'intimider une population ou de contraindre un gouvernement ou une organisation internationale à faire ou à ne pas faire quelque chose.

2. Commet également une infraction quiconque menace sérieusement et de manière crédible de commettre une infraction visée au paragraphe 1 du présent article.

3. Commet également une infraction quiconque tente de commettre une infraction visée au paragraphe 1 du présent article.

4. Commet également une infraction, quiconque :

a) Se rend complice d'une infraction visée aux paragraphes 1, 2 ou 3 du présent article ; ou

b) Organise la commission d'une infraction visée aux paragraphes 1, 2 ou 3 du présent

étranger du terroriste international (les deux étant souvent confondus sous le terme de « jihadiste ») qui s'est spécialisé dans la commission d'actes de violence en dehors d'une zone d'hostilité.

2. L'assimilation jurisprudentielle aux criminels

Les personnes arrêtées et détenues dans le cadre de la lutte contre Boko Haram pourraient être traitées comme des criminels, puisqu'elles ne sont pas, en tout état de cause, des populations civiles. Elles sont le plus souvent arrêtées sur le terrain des conflits, avec ou non des preuves à l'appui[62]. Le règlement n° 08/05-UEAC-057-CM-13 portant adoption de la Convention relative à la lutte contre le terrorisme en Afrique centrale emploie le terme de ''malfaiteur'' en son article 5 en matière d'extradition, pour désigner ''tout individu recherché pour une infraction à caractère terroriste et dont l'extradition est demandée par tout autre État partie''. Ce terme est très englobant et sert à désigner celui qui commet des délits et des crimes. En ce sens, le ministre camerounais de la Communication à affirmer dans une conférence de presse que : « Ne nous y trompons pas, les criminels, ce sont les adeptes de Boko Haram qui tuent, pillent, enlèvent et égorgent. Et non les forces de défense et de sécurité qui sont là pour défendre les populations, protéger la paix et la stabilité de notre cher et beau pays, au péril de leurs vies »[63].

---

article ou donne l'ordre à d'autres personnes de la commettre ; ou c) Contribue à la commission d'une ou plusieurs des infractions visées aux paragraphes 1, 2 ou 3 du présent article par un groupe de personnes agissant de concert. La contribution doit être délibérée et faite :

i) Soit pour faciliter l'activité criminelle ou le dessein criminel du groupe, lorsque l'activité ou le dessein implique la commission d'une infraction visée au paragraphe 1 du présent article ;

ii) Soit en pleine connaissance de l'intention du groupe de commettre une infraction visée au paragraphe 1 du présent article ».

[62] H. TIGROUDJA, « Quel(s) droit(s) applicable(s) à la « guerre au terrorisme », *AFDI*, volume 48, 2002, pp. 81-102.

[63] « Allégations de torture et d'exécutions sommaires proférées par L'ONG REDHAC à l'encontre des forces de défense et de sécurité camerounaises dans le cadre de la lutte contre Boko Haram », *Conférence de presse, propos liminaire de Mr. Issa Tchiroma Bakary*, ministre de la Communication, Yaoundé, 13 mars 2015.

La construction juridique de l'incrimination du terrorisme aurait ici une finalité : garantir l'indispensable jugement, trouver le moyen juridique d'engager des poursuites pénales contre les auteurs des actes de terrorisme, leurs complices, leurs organisateurs. La résolution 1456 (2003) du Conseil de sécurité précise à cet égard que : « Tous les actes de terrorisme, quels qu'ils soient, sont criminels et injustifiables quels qu'en soient les motifs, où qu'ils soient commis et quels qu'en soient les auteurs ; ils doivent être condamnés sans équivoque, surtout lorsqu'ils frappent ou blessent des civils sans discrimination »[64]. Selon les officiels camerounais, « les malfaiteurs du groupe terroriste Boko Haram avaient pris la funeste habitude de s'infiltrer au sein des populations, pour attaquer les convois civils et militaires. À répétition, ils massacraient de paisibles citoyens, brûlaient des villages entiers et emportaient à chaque fois des centaines de têtes de bétail appartenant aux éleveurs de la Région »[65].

Par ailleurs, la prohibition des actes de terrorisme en guerre est énoncée dans deux instruments de *soft law* : le projet de règles limitant les risques courus par la population civile en temps de guerre du CICR publié en 1956 et la déclaration de Turku sur les règles minimales d'humanité de 1990[66]. Le crime de terrorisation de la population civile a été précisé dans le jugement de l'affaire *Galic* rendu par la chambre de première instance du TPIY[67]. Un tel crime est constitué lorsque sont réunis les trois éléments suivants :

- actes de violence dirigés contre la population civile ou des personnes civiles ne participant pas directement aux hostilités, qui entraînent parmi elles la mort ou des atteintes graves à l'intégrité physique ou à la santé ;

[64] Voir Document S/RES/1456 (2003) du 20 janvier 2003.

[65] *Conférence de presse, propos liminaire de M. Issa Tchiroma Bakary*, ministre de la Communication, Yaoundé, 13 mars 2015.

[66] Article 6.

[67] TPIY, Jugement du 05 décembre 2003, Le Procureur c. Galic, § 102.

- l'auteur a intentionnellement soumis à ces actes de violence la population civile ou des personnes civiles ne participant pas aux hostilités ;

- l'infraction susmentionnée a été commise dans le but principal de répandre la terreur parmi la population civile.

Cette terreur est décrite par le TPIY comme une « peur extrême »[68], distincte et allant au-delà de celle que l'on peut éprouver en période de guerre. C'est [...] une privation intentionnelle du sentiment de sécurité. C'est la peur primitive que les gens ressentent lorsqu'ils voient quelqu'un se faire tuer sous leurs yeux, c'est ce moment de panique quand ils essaient de porter secours à la victime tout en guettant les prochains coups de feu (...). Ce n'est pas seulement [...] la peur inspirée par la proximité des combats. Il s'agit d'une peur destinée à démoraliser, à déstabiliser, à priver de tout sentiment de sécurité une population qui n'a rien [...] à voir avec le conflit. Selon la chambre de Première instance du TPIY, qui a analysé la problématique du crime de terrorisation de la population civile en période de guerre dans son jugement rendu dans l'affaire *Dragomir Milosevic* : « le crime de terrorisation recouvre uniquement les actes ou menaces de violence qui ont spécifiquement pour but de répandre la terreur parmi la population civile. Il faut démontrer que la terreur va au-delà de la peur qui est seulement l'effet accessoire des opérations menées par des forces armées au cours d'un conflit armé. Aussi faut-il toujours distinguer l'interdiction de répandre la terreur parmi la population civile et les effets que des actes de guerre licites peuvent avoir sur cette même population. La Chambre observe que dans la quasi-totalité des conflits armés, la population civile est exposée à un certain niveau de peur et d'intimidation, dont l'intensité augmente en fonction de la proximité du théâtre des opérations. Cela est particulièrement vrai lorsque le conflit se déroule dans un milieu urbain, où même des attaques licites contre des combattants peuvent provoquer une peur et une intimidation intenses au sein de la population civile ; cependant, l'intention de susciter la peur au-delà de ce niveau doit être

68 *Ibid.*, §137.

établie pour que le crime de terrorisation soit constitué. En conséquence, il convient de tenir compte des circonstances propres à chaque conflit armé pour déterminer si le crime de terrorisation a été commis ou si les auteurs avaient l'intention de (...) répandre la terreur parmi la population civile. »[69] Dans l'affaire *Galic*[70], la chambre d'appel du TPIY ajoute que le crime de terrorisation peut prendre la forme d'attaques, ou de menaces d'attaques, indiscriminées ou disproportionnées. Les premières regroupent les « attaques qui ne sont pas dirigées contre un objectif militaire déterminé ; [celles] dans lesquelles on utilise des méthodes ou moyens de combat qui ne peuvent pas être dirigés contre un objectif militaire déterminé ; ou [celles] dans lesquelles on utilise des méthodes ou moyens de combat dont les effets ne peuvent pas être limités (...) ; et qui sont, en conséquence, dans chacun de ces cas, propres à frapper indistinctement des objectifs militaires et des personnes civiles ou des biens de caractère civil »[71]. L'appui offensif ou les opérations de frappe ayant pour objet de répandre la terreur parmi la population civile, les bombardements aveugles et systématiques et les bombardements réguliers des villes, mais aussi les cas de violence, de viols, de sévices et de tortures de femmes et d'enfants et les massacres constituent des crimes de terrorisation.

Le crime de terrorisme relève donc du maintien de l'ordre (moyens de police judiciaire et de police administrative)[72]. En effet, l'attentat terroriste est un « acte isolé et sporadique de violence » pouvant être rattaché aux « tensions internes » ou aux « troubles intérieurs » dont le seuil de violence est, entre autres, insuffisant pour constituer un conflit armé susceptible de se voir appliquer le droit international humanitaire[73].

---

[69] TPIY, Jugement du 12 décembre 2007, *Le procureur c. Dragomir Milosevic, § 888*

[70] TPIY, Jugement du 05 décembre 2003, *Le Procureur c. Galic*, § 102

[71] Voir article 51, §4 du Protocole additionnel I,

[72] https ://dommagescivils.wordpress.com/ , consulté le 03 avril 2015

[73] *Ibid.* À ce titre, certains États, comme la France, ont émis des réserves excluant le crime de terrorisme, qu'il soit isolé ou collectif, des situations de conflit armé. Par contre, un acte terroriste d'une particulière gravité comme les attentats du 11 septembre 2001 constitue une agression armée susceptible de fonder une action en légitime

La difficulté en matière de terrorisme intervient au niveau de l'intervention judiciaire en matière d'arrestation et de détention des personnes soupçonnées d'appartenir à des réseaux terroristes[74]. Le droit protège en effet les personnes contre des détentions arbitraires. Une personne soupçonnée d'activités terroristes et placée en détention provisoire a donc droit au contrôle régulier de la légalité de sa détention par un tribunal. Durant cette détention, il doit être traité de façon spécifique.

II. Un traitement polémiqué

Le traitement réservé aux personnes soupçonnées d'être des terroristes, et arrêtées pendant la lutte contre ce phénomène provoque des débats acharnés dans la société internationale. Tandis que les organisations de protection des droits de l'homme dénoncent les exactions commises à leur égard, certains autres membres de la société considèrent que, compte tenu de la déshumanisation[75] qui caractérise le terrorisme, ceux qui sont arrêtés dans le cadre de cette lutte méritent un châtiment pire que celui administré par les autorités. En règle générale, toute mesure prise par les États pour lutter contre le terrorisme doit avoir une base juridique, puisqu'en droit pénal, le principe fondamental de la légalité des délits et des peines impose que la loi définisse de façon précise les comportements susceptibles de faire l'objet de sanctions pénales, de même que les

---

défense déclenchant un conflit armé à condition qu'on puisse le rattacher à un État (ce dernier point est contesté).

[74] À cet égard, la CEDH a eu à affirmer que : « La cour a déjà admis à plusieurs reprises par le passé que les enquêtes au sujet d'infractions terroristes confrontent indubitablement les autorités à des problèmes particuliers (Voir les arrêts *Brogan et autres c. Royaume-Uni* du 29 novembre 1988, *Murray c/ Royaume –Uni* du 28 octobre 1994, etc.). Cela ne signifie pas toutefois que celles-ci aient carte blanche, au regard de l'article 5, pour arrêter et placer en garde à vue des suspects, à l'abri de tout contrôle effectif par les tribunaux internes et, en dernière instance, par les organes de contrôle de la Convention, chaque fois qu'elles choisissent d'affirmer qu'il y a infraction terroriste (*Arrêt Murray*, p. 27, § 58).

[75] Lors d'une attaque commise le 4 février 2015 dans la ville de Fotokol, à ce jour la plus meurtrière en territoire camerounais, Boko Haram aurait tué de nombreuses personnes, incendié des églises et des mosquées, et utilisé des civils comme boucliers humains.

sanctions elles-mêmes. Ainsi, aux dénonciations de violations des droits de l'Homme (A), les États concernés ne peuvent que traiter les membres des groupes terroristes avec humanité (B).

A. L'exigence du traitement d'humanité

Quel que soit le statut juridique attribué ou reconnu à une personne détenue, il est exigé que celle-ci soit traitée avec humanité. Le paragraphe 6 de la résolution 1456 (2003) du Conseil de sécurité souligne que les États doivent veiller à ce que les mesures qu'ils prennent pour lutter contre le terrorisme soient conformes à toutes leurs obligations internationales et respectent les normes du droit international, en particulier les instruments relatifs aux droits de l'Homme, au droit des réfugiés et au droit humanitaire. C'est la raison pour laquelle des dénonciations de violations des droits de l'Homme à l'égard des membres des groupes terroristes sont faites.

1. L'interdiction de la torture et autres traitements cruels, inhumains et dégradants

Un ensemble de dispositions conventionnelles interdit la torture, et les traitements cruels, inhumains et dégradants à l'égard de toute personne, quelle que soit sa condition[76]. La torture et les autres peines ou traitements cruels, inhumains ou dégradants ont été reconnus partout dans le monde comme relevant des crimes les plus sérieux, et leur interdiction comme une norme fondamentale de la communauté internationale. L'article 75 du protocole I de 1977 indique que : « Dans la mesure où elles sont affectées par une situation visée à l'article premier du présent protocole, les personnes qui sont au pouvoir d'une Partie au conflit et qui ne bénéficient pas d'un traitement plus favorable en vertu des Conventions et du présent Protocole seront traitées avec humanité en toutes circonstances et bénéficieront au moins des protections prévues par le présent article sans aucune distinction de caractère défavorable fondée sur la race, la couleur, le sexe, la langue, la religion ou la croyance, les opinions politiques ou autres, l'origine nationale ou sociale, la

---

[76] Tribunal pénal international pour l'ex-Yougoslavie, *Le Procureur c. Anto Furundzija.*

fortune, la naissance ou une autre situation, ou tout autre critère analogue. Chacune des Parties respectera la personne, l'honneur, les convictions et les pratiques religieuses de toutes ces personnes ».

L'article 3 commun aux quatre conventions de Genève rappelle le droit de tout prisonnier à un procès équitable et interdit la torture, les actes cruels et les outrages à la dignité de la personne, en particulier les traitements humiliants et dégradants. Selon le projet d'article 14 du projet de convention générale sur le terrorisme, « Toute personne placée en détention ou contre laquelle toute autre mesure est prise ou une procédure est engagée en vertu de la présente Convention se voit garantir un traitement équitable et tous les droits et garanties conformes à la législation de l'État sur le territoire duquel elle se trouve et aux dispositions applicables du droit international, y compris le droit international des droits de l'homme et, en particulier, l'Ensemble de règles minima pour le traitement des détenus ». Peu importent donc la provenance du prisonnier et les circonstances dans lesquelles il a été arrêté, il doit bénéficier d'un traitement avec humanité. De nombreux autres textes internationaux prohibent la torture et les mauvais traitements[77]. L'article 2(2) de la convention contre la torture insiste sur le fait qu'« Aucune circonstance exceptionnelle, quelle qu'elle soit, qu'il s'agisse de l'état de guerre ou de menace de guerre, d'instabilité politique intérieure ou de tout autre état d'exception, ne peut être invoquée pour justifier la torture ». À cet égard, la CEDH a souligné que, « même dans des situations extrêmement difficiles, telles que la lutte contre le terrorisme et le crime organisé, la Convention prohibe en termes absolus la torture et les peines et traitements inhumains ou dégradants, quels que

---

[77] Il s'agit notamment de la Déclaration universelle des droits de l'homme, la Convention des Nations unies contre la torture et autres peines ou traitements cruels, inhumains ou dégradants et le Pacte international relatif aux droits civils et politiques. L'article 10 (1) du PIDCP dispose que : « Toute personne privée de sa liberté est traitée avec humanité et avec le respect de la dignité inhérente à la personne humaine. » L'article 7 précise en outre : « Nul ne sera soumis à la torture ni à des peines ou traitements cruels, inhumains ou dégradants. »

soient les agissements de la victime »[78]. Le droit international humanitaire interdit aussi spécifiquement les traitements cruels et la torture, ainsi que « les atteintes à la dignité des personnes, notamment les traitements humiliants et dégradants ». En ce qui concerne les droits des personnes détenues, il faut noter, de prime abord, que ces prisonniers particuliers doivent être traités avec humanité en tout temps, ce qui implique qu'ils ont droit, entre autres, à des soins médicaux[79], à une alimentation adéquate [80], à des installations conformes aux règles de l'hygiène[81], etc. Dans les cas où ils sont privés de ces considérations élémentaires d'humanité[82], des dénonciations sont faites par les ONG.

2. Des dénonciations de violation des droits de l'Homme

Il est difficile pour un État de ne pas se voir accusé de violer les droits de l'Homme dans le cadre de la détention des présumés terroristes. Face à un ennemi qui opère dans l'invisible et qui utilise des civils, la confusion est fréquente. Les soldats réguliers sont toujours sur leurs gardes et la moindre suspicion entraîne des arrestations et des tensions. Cette menace permanente crée des tensions et le respect scrupuleux des règles est très vite battu en brèche[83]. Si jusqu'à présent les États et les organisations internationales se sont abstenus d'intervenir sur cette question, les membres de la société civile ne s'en sont pas privés. Les organisations de la société civile dénoncent, dans des rapports périodiques ou à travers les médias, les abus commis sur les personnes détenues dans le cadre de la lutte contre le terrorisme[84]. Ces initiatives

[78] CEDH, 11 juill. 2006, n°54810/00, Jalloh c/ Allemagne, §99 ; JCP G 2007. I 106, obs. F. Sudre)

[79] Convention III de Genève, Article 30

[80] Ibid., article 26

[81] Ibid., article 29

[82] Pour reprendre son expression à la CIJ dans son 1er arrêt de 1949, *Détroit de Corfou.*

[83] A Haditha, en Irak, en novembre 2005, une unité de l'armée américaine a massacré 24 civils dont 7 femmes et 3 enfants, en représailles a la mort d'un de leurs camarades tué par l'explosion d'une charge artisanale.

[84] L'ONG Amnesty International a publié un rapport sur la situation des droits de l'Homme au Nigeria intitulé : « *Bienvenue en enfer. Torture et mauvais traitements au Nigeria* », qui fait ressortir le comportement des policiers et militaires nigérians qui ont

participent de l'alerte en temps de conflit sur l'urgence d'appliquer le droit humanitaire. À cet égard, dans une déclaration datée du 15 janvier 2015 et relayée par un communiqué de presse publié le 18 février 2015, le porte-parole du RHEDAC a fait état, sous forme de dénonciation, de graves exactions perpétrées sur les populations de l'extrême nord du Cameroun par nos forces de défense et de sécurité[85]. L'ONG « REDHAC » a prétendu la mise à mort de façon sommaire par les forces

---

couramment recours à la torture sur des hommes, des femmes et parfois des adolescents âgés de 12 ans au moyen de diverses techniques. Selon Amnesty, l'ampleur de la torture s'explique en partie par le fait que personne, y compris dans la hiérarchie des autorités nigérianes, n'est tenu de rendre compte de ses actes. Ces pratiques vont au-delà des tortures et des homicides dont sont victimes les membres présumés de la secte « Boko Haram », assure le rapport.

[85] Selon le gouvernement camerounais, « ...dans la nuit du 26 au 27 décembre 2014, afin de parer à une attaque planifiée de la part des agresseurs, dont faisaient état les renseignements militaires, une opération de ratissage a été organisée dans les villages de Magdeme et de Doublé. Ce bouclage, conduit par un détachement interarmées et de la sûreté nationale, a permis de procéder à l'interpellation de soixante-dix suspects, qui ont été transférés à la Légion de Gendarmerie de Maroua pour des besoins d'enquête approfondie. Le convoi transportant les suspects est arrivé à Maroua le 27 décembre 2014 aux environs de 22h30. Quatorze des personnes interpellées ont été conduites dans les cellules de la Brigade territoriale de Maroua, alors que les autres, soit cinquante-six, ont été gardés à vue dans un local aménagé pour la circonstance à la Légion de Gendarmerie, en raison du fait que toutes les cellules de Gendarmerie, ainsi que les locaux de la prison centrale de Maroua étaient saturés. Le tri devait être effectué le lendemain, afin éventuellement de remettre en liberté ceux des suspects mis hors de cause après examen de leur situation, et de déférer les autres devant les tribunaux compétents. Au petit matin du 28 décembre 2014, en ouvrant le local où avaient été enfermés les suspects la veille à la Légion de Gendarmerie, l'on a constaté que vingt-cinq de ces cinquante-six suspects avaient perdu la vie. Le médecin légiste requis a alors effectué des autopsies sur les dépouilles et a ordonné l'inhumation. Deux officiers supérieurs des services centraux de gendarmerie, dont un magistrat, ont été dépêchés sur le terrain pour mener des investigations approfondies et faire la lumière sur cette situation. La justice militaire s'est donc saisie de l'affaire. Elle continue ses investigations et se prononcera sur les responsabilités ». (« Allégations de torture et d'exécutions sommaires proférées par L'ONG REDHAC à l'encontre des forces de défense et de sécurité camerounaises dans le cadre de la lutte contre Boko Haram », *Conférence de presse, propos liminaire de s.e.m. Issa Tchiroma Bakary*, Ministre de la communication, *Yaoundé,* 13 mars 2015).

de défense et de sécurité camerounaises, de plusieurs dizaines de personnes soupçonnées d'appartenir ou d'être en intelligence avec Boko Haram. Il pointe de ce fait du doigt les interrogatoires qu'il estime musclés, menés par des militaires qui, sous le prétexte de recueillir des renseignements dans le cadre de la lutte contre Boko Haram, tétanisent et terrorisent les populations qu'elles sont censées protéger. Cette publication, relayée à l'international par plusieurs organisations de défense des droits de l'Homme et de nombreux médias a suscité une vive émotion au sein des populations[86]. Ces dénonciations ont amené le gouvernement camerounais à réagir pour contredire les allégations de cette ONG. Il ne s'agit là que d'un exemple en ce qui concerne le Cameroun, car des rapports d'ONG font état, presque chaque année, du mauvais traitement administré aux personnes soupçonnées d'être des terroristes à travers le monde. Ces préoccupations sont accentuées par la présence dans les rangs de Boko Haram d'enfants soldats et de nombreux hommes et garçons qui ont été recrutés de force comme combattants[87].

[86] Un journaliste camerounais a fait le commentaire suivant : « L'initiative du REDHAC a donné lieu à une interprétation subjective du travail de l'armée camerounaise sur le terrain, semant ici et là dans les esprits une grande confusion et jetant même sur les défenseurs des droits de l'homme une grande suspicion. Nous suivons l'agitation autour des supposées bavures de l'armée camerounaise. Je dois dire qu'à ma connaissance, il n'en est rien et je suis bien placé pour l'affirmer parce qu'ici à Fotokol, l'on a les réfugiés et les déplacés. C'est un melting-pot. Il ne faut donc pas nous distraire. Qui égorge nos femmes et nos enfants ? Qui nous égorge à la moindre occasion ? C'est Boko Haram. A présent, l'on fait comme si c'est l'armée qui nous égorge, qui nous tue… Sans elle, que serions-nous ? Ici à Fotokol, qui peut se plaindre d'une bavure ? Personne. Parce qu'il n'y en a pas. Que ceux qui veulent voir les bavures viennent ici me voir, je leur montre là où les miens ont été enterrés, égorgés par Boko Haram. Les gens ne doivent pas confondre le petit racket des forces de l'ordre qui existait déjà en temps de paix, et une politique mise sur pied pour maltraiter les populations », indique Mahamat Abakoura, un fonctionnaire à la retraite installé à Fotokol. Son voisin, Moussa Abdourahman, âgé d'une soixantaine d'années poursuit : «Est-ce que vous savez ce que les militaires nigérians font de l'autre côté de la frontière ? Allez discuter avec les réfugiés qui sont ici, allez-y, ils vont vous dire ce à quoi se livre une armée qui commet des bavures. » (Douwouré Ousmane, « Lutte contre Boko Haram : Polémiques autour des bavures de l'armée », *L'œil du Sahel).*

[87] Les forces de sécurité nigérianes suscitent des préoccupations toutes particulières. Dans le cadre de leur riposte à Boko Haram depuis 2009, elles ont eu recours à une

Selon Amnesty International, les policiers sont mal formés à la conduite des enquêtes. Ils s'appuient essentiellement sur les interrogatoires et les aveux pour résoudre les affaires, et ils procèdent régulièrement à des arrestations avant toute investigation. De même, les opérations militaires menées contre Boko Haram prennent souvent la forme d'opérations de « ratissage » et d'arrestations massives de personnes qui sont ensuite détenues pendant de longues périodes sans inculpation ni procès[88]. Ce serait au cours de ces procès qu'un statut spécifique pourrait surgir de la jurisprudence. En ce sens, l'article 5 du Protocole additionnel I précise qu'en cas de doute, le statut des détenus soit déterminé par un tribunal compétent. L'ancien secrétaire général des Nations unies, M. Koffi Annan, lors de son discours prononcé à la Commission des droits de l'homme le 12 avril 2002 déclarait que : " M. le Président, je soutiens, encore une fois, que le droit international, y compris le droit international humanitaire, doit être respecté partout où l'on a recours à la force -que ce soit par un État ou un mouvement de résistance. En particulier, nous devons veiller au respect des quatre Conventions de Genève. Leur objectif est très clair et leur formulation est assez large pour s'appliquer à tous les conflits armés, peu importent les circonstances. Il n'y a pas lieu de les réinterpréter. Elles doivent absolument être respectées dès à présent ".

3. L'effort pour assurer un traitement avec humanité aux détenus

Chaque État engagé dans une lutte antiterroriste cherche à montrer qu'il tient compte de l'humanité qui réside en chaque prisonnier, quel qu'il soit. Les mesures de traitement sont d'ordre purement interne. En effet, alors que les diverses conventions internationales contiennent des

---

force excessive, ont incendié des habitations et des villages, et ont torturé et détenu des milliers de suspects dans des conditions inhumaines. De nombreuses personnes qu'elles ont arrêtées sont mortes en détention ou ont été tuées. (Cf. Human Rights Watch, Afrique de l'Ouest : Offensive régionale contre Boko Haram 11 février 2015 http ://www.hrw.org/fr/news/2015/02/11/afrique-de-l-ouest-offensive-regionale-contre-boko-haram consulté le 23 mars 2015).

[88] « *Bienvenue en enfer. Torture et mauvais traitements au Nigeria* », Rapport de Amnesty international, Amnesty International – septembre 2014, p. 7.

dispositions relatives au traitement des personnes détenues, elles n'établissent pas clairement de mécanisme spécifique de contrôle pour vérifier que ces mesures sont effectives. Comme l'a observé le Haut-commissaire des Nations unies aux droits de l'homme, Mary Robinson : "Actuellement il n'y a aucun organe international doté d'un mandat clair pour évaluer si les mesures prises et justifiées par un État, comme étant nécessaires afin de combattre le terrorisme, sont en violation de leurs obligations en matière de droits de l'homme, ou requièrent une dérogation. Malheureusement, le Comité contre le terrorisme, établi par le Conseil de Sécurité, ne considère pas que cela relève de ses fonctions"[89]. À cet égard, le ministre camerounais de la Communication a eu à signaler que : « ... plusieurs centaines de terroristes de Boko Haram, faits prisonniers par nos forces de défense, sont actuellement détenus dans nos pénitenciers, sans qu'aucune exaction ni aucun acte de torture ne soient commis à leur préjudice. Beaucoup ont pourtant été pris les armes à la main. Certains avaient des téléphones portables sur lesquels on pouvait les voir se livrer à des égorgements. Ils n'ont pourtant pas été exécutés sommairement. Ils ont été emprisonnés et seront jugés conformément aux lois de la République. Des moyens financiers importants dont nous avons besoin par ailleurs sont consacrés à leur surveillance, à leur alimentation et leur entretien ; ce, pendant que leurs comparses criminels encore en liberté ne manquent aucune occasion de faire subir les pires atrocités à nos concitoyens, et de piller leurs biens, mettant ainsi à mal en partie des pans de notre économie dans ces zones. Sur ce point aussi, à savoir celui du respect des droits des humains par nos forces de défense et de sécurité dans leur combat quotidien

---

[89] Mary Robinson, United Nations Commissioner for Human Rights, *Human Rights in the Shadow of 11 September*, Fifth Commonwealth Lecture, London, 6 June 2002, [traduction du texte d'origine qui suit : "*there is currently no international institution with a clear mandate to assess whether measures taken and justified by a State as necessary to combat terrorism are in violations of human rights standards which it has accepted, or which would require that a derogation be made. And it is, indeed, unfortunate that the Counter-terrorism Committee established by the Security Council does not believe this to be part of its mandate.*"], disponible en anglais à :
http ://www.thecommonwealth.org/Templates/Internal.asp ?NodeID=37475.

contre Boko Haram, le Cameroun n'a donc rien à se reprocher »[90]. Dans le même ordre d'idées, malgré le refus catégorique de considérer les détenus de Guantanamo comme des prisonniers de guerre, l'ancien vice-président américain, Dick Cheney, à la suite de sa visite sur la base militaire de Guantanamo Bay en 2005, donnait un bref aperçu des conditions de détention des prisonniers en ces termes : « Ils sont très bien traités là-bas. Ils vivent sous les tropiques. Ils sont bien nourris. Ils ont tout ce qu'ils pourraient désirer »[91]. Cette déclaration faisait suite aux nombreuses alertes provenant d'Organisations internationales de défense des droits humains comme Amnesty International ou le Comité international de la croix-rouge, dénonçant le véritable trou noir dans lequel se trouvaient les prisonniers transférés sur cette partie de l'île cubaine. Ces dénonciations faisaient non seulement écho aux témoignages d'ex- détenus, mais aussi et surtout aux contenus de certains documents officiels faisant état de pratiques assimilables à des actes de torture perpétrés à l'encontre des prisonniers. Bien que ne reconnaissant pas aux détenus de Guantanamo le statut de prisonnier de guerre pour pouvoir bénéficier de la protection offerte par les conventions de Genève, le président George Bush avait annoncé que les États-Unis s'engageaient à en respecter les dispositions essentielles.

Pour administrer un traitement d'humanité aux détenus de Guantanamo, le président George Bush a signé en juillet 2007 un décret (*executive order*) autorisant la CIA à reprendre son programme d'interrogatoires dans des lieux de détention tenus secrets. Il y réaffirme sa décision de considérer les membres d'Al-Qaida et les talibans comme des "ennemis combattants illégaux" n'ayant pas droit à la protection des conventions de Genève. Il rappelle aussi que la loi de 2006 créant des commissions militaires pour juger les détenus de Guantanamo lui a

---

[90] « Allégations de torture et d'exécutions sommaires proférées par L'ONG REDHAC à l'encontre des forces de défense et de sécurité camerounaises dans le cadre de la lutte contre Boko Haram », *Conférence de presse, propos liminaire de Mr. Issa Tchiroma Bakary*, Ministre de la communication, Yaoundé, 13 mars 2015.

[91] Amnesty International, Communiqué Public, « Guantanamo, accès refusé. Non à la torture et aux mauvais traitements dans la « *guerre contre le terrorisme* » », décembre 2005.

donné autorité pour préciser le "flou" de l'article 3 des conventions de Genève. Sont également spécifiquement mentionnés par le décret le meurtre, la torture et la mutilation, ainsi que les mauvais traitements destinés "à humilier ou à avilir l'individu".

B. Le doit à un procès équitable

Les personnes arrêtées dans le cadre de la lutte contre le terrorisme ne sauraient être maintenues éternellement en détention provisoire. Cette situation, souvent décriée par les organismes de défense des droits de l'Homme serait préjudiciable pour l'image de l'État, quelles que soient les raisons avancées[92]. Ces dénonciations trouvent leur fondement juridique dans l'article 14 du PIDC qui dispose clairement que : « Toute personne a droit à ce que sa cause soit entendue équitablement et publiquement par un tribunal compétent, indépendant et impartial, établi par la loi, qui décidera soit du bien-fondé de toute accusation en matière pénale dirigée contre elle, soit des contestations sur ses droits et obligations de caractère civil... ». Allant dans le même sens, la résolution 1356 (2003) du Conseil de sécurité exige que : « Les États doivent traduire en justice ceux qui financent, planifient, appuient ou commettent des actes de terrorisme ou donnent asile à leurs auteurs, conformément au droit international, en particulier en appliquant le principe « extrader ou juger ».

[92] Conformément à la stratégie antiterroriste mondiale et au plan d'action correspondant, les États s'engagent « à tout faire pour mettre en place et maintenir un appareil national de justice pénale efficace et reposant sur la primauté du droit, qui garantisse, suivant les obligations qui nous incombent en vertu du droit international, que quiconque participe au financement, à l'organisation, à la préparation ou à la perpétration d'actes de terrorisme ou qui y apporte un appui soit traduit en justice, sur la base du principe *aut dedere aut judicare*, dans le respect des droits de l'homme et des libertés fondamentales ». Les États ont l'obligation de veiller à ce que les garanties de procédure régulière soient respectées quand des personnes soupçonnées d'avoir commis des infractions liées au terrorisme sont arrêtées, inculpées, détenues et poursuivies. L'observation d'une procédure régulière, notamment pour les personnes soupçonnées d'activité terroriste, est cruciale pour garantir que les mesures de lutte antiterroriste sont efficaces, conformes à la légalité et considérées comme équitables.

Seulement, les personnes arrêtées dans le cadre de la lutte contre un mouvement terroriste sont une catégorie particulière de délinquants, qui ne sauraient connaître le même sort que les délinquants ordinaires. D'ailleurs, ces personnes rentrent difficilement dans les catégories de délinquants prévues par le code pénal d'un État, en particulier lorsqu'il s'agit des étrangers capturés sur le champ des conflits. La détention secrète, d'une durée indéterminée et sans contact avec l'extérieur de personnes soupçonnées de terrorisme sans accès à un tribunal et en dehors de toute procédure régulière suscite habituellement de vives inquiétudes et de soupçons de tortures et autres formes de mauvais traitement. Il semble essentiel qu'un individu détenu, indépendamment du contexte de son arrestation, ait droit à une procédure régulière, un examen judiciaire et la reconnaissance devant la loi. Ces garanties ne sont pas automatiques et requièrent de l'État des efforts et des moyens appropriés, car « Les droits des suspects sont susceptibles d'être facilement sacrifiés à l'autel de la protection de l'intérêt général s'ils ne sont pas suffisamment encadrés dans la phase préparatoire du procès pénal »[93]. En ce sens, il s'agit, pour les États, de concilier lutte efficace contre le terrorisme et respect des garanties procédurales, voir de garantir aux présumés terroristes, le droit à un procès équitable. Le terrorisme et le crime organisé transnational sont en effet des délits graves qui doivent être passibles de lourdes peines et qui mettent en péril la sauvegarde de l'intérêt général. Tous les signataires de la convention sur la prévention du crime transnational organisé sont tenus de définir ces crimes particuliers dans leur dispositif pénal national. Les États sont responsables de juger ou d'extrader toute personne accusée d'avoir participé à des actions de terrorisme ou de crime organisé et ne peuvent se donner la prérogative de priver le prévenu d'un jugement. C'est la raison pour laquelle des législations spécifiques sur le terrorisme sont adoptées dans divers pays[94].

---

[93] J.C. MEBU NCHIMI, «

[94] Il s'agit en fait d'une obligation qui découle directement des conventions internationales relatives au terrorisme. À cet égard, l'article 2 de la convention de l'UA sur la prévention et la répression du terrorisme dispose que les États parties s'engagent à

La lutte efficace contre le terrorisme impose cependant une interprétation souple de certaines garanties du procès équitable. Il n'y a que des mécanismes compensatoires qui pourraient permettre d'éviter que les mesures prises en matière de lutte contre le terrorisme ne vident de sa substance le droit au procès équitable.

1. La détermination de la juridiction compétente

Plusieurs pays ont procédé à une modification significative de leur organisation judiciaire pour attribuer compétence à certains tribunaux spécifiques, la compétence de connaître des infractions terroristes ou liées au terrorisme. Certains États ont créé des juridictions spéciales[95], ou des chambres spéciales ou spécialisées au sein des tribunaux ordinaires, et d'autres ont créé des tribunaux spéciaux pour l'examen des cas relatifs au terrorisme. La conception des juridictions appelées à connaître des affaires terroristes est fortement divergente d'un État à un autre[96]. En

---

« ...réviser leur législation nationale et à établir comme crimes les actes terroristes tels que définis dans la présente Convention et pénaliser ses actes en tenant compte de leur gravité ». (...) « mettre en application les actions requises notamment légiférer en vue de la pénalisation de ces actes en tenant compte de leur gravité conformément aux instruments internationaux visés au paragraphe (b) et que ces États ont ratifiés ou auxquels ils ont adhéré ».

La France s'est dotée de plusieurs lois tendant à renforcer le dispositif de prévention et de répression des attaques terroristes. Ainsi a-t-elle adopté en novembre 2014 une nouvelle loi contre le terrorisme (loi n°2014-1353 du 13 novembre 2014), qui s'inscrivait directement dans un contexte général de renforcement des outils de surveillance. Ces outils sont destinés à lutter contre la criminalité organisée et trouvent une application dans la lutte contre le terrorisme telle que la loi sur la géolocalisation (loi n°2014-372 du 28 mars 2014) ou celle relative à la programmation militaire (loi n°2013-1168 du 18 décembre 2013) qui renforce le dispositif étatique en matière de cyber défense et de surveillance des traces numériques et dont un décret (n°2014-1576 du 24 décembre 2014) relatif à l'accès administratif aux données de connexion, entré en vigueur au 1er janvier 2015, prévoit un accès très vaste des services de l'État aux télécommunications (téléphone, SMS, Internet, etc.).

[95] L'Irlande dispose par exemple d'une juridiction spéciale qui a vocation à connaître des actes de terrorisme et autres (*special criminal court*) et non d'une juridiction spécialisée en matière de terrorisme.

[96] En France, l'article 706-16 du code de procédure pénale prévoit que les infractions définies aux articles 421-1 à 421-4 du code pénal ainsi que le délit d'association de

France par exemple, les articles du code pénal qui définissent les actes de terrorisme se contentent donc d'énumérer des infractions de droit commun qui, lorsqu'elles sont "en relation avec une entreprise individuelle ou collective ayant pour but de troubler gravement l'ordre public par l'intimidation ou la terreur", selon les dispositions de la loi de 1986, seront jugées par la Cour d'assises de Paris composée de juges professionnels. Cette juridiction ne connaît que des actes de terrorisme puisqu'elle a été conçue pour prévoir l'intervention de juges professionnels, spécialement pour connaître des infractions terroristes prévues par le code pénal, même si la composition de cette cour d'assises spécialisée est la même que la juridiction chargée de connaître des crimes militaires en temps de paix.

Au Cameroun, le crime de terrorisme relève de la compétence exclusive des juridictions militaires, tel que le prévoit l'article 1er alinéa 3 de la loi sur le terrorisme. Les articles 2 et suivants de la loi sur le terrorisme indiquent les condamnations prononcées à l'encontre des auteurs et coauteurs d'actes terroristes. Ces dispositions laissent présager un procès au cours duquel il serait envisagé l'observation d'une série de droits exigés en matière de procédure. Il s'agit entre autres du principe de l'égalité de toutes les personnes devant la justice, de la présomption d'innocence, du droit à être entendu dans une procédure contradictoire, et du droit à être jugé dans des délais raisonnables par un tribunal

---

malfaiteurs de l'article 450-1, lorsqu'il a pour but la préparation de ces infractions seront jugées par la Cour d'assises de Paris (706-17) composée comme prévu à l'article 698-6 (Art. 706-25). Si la loi française de 1986 a été déférée par les députés au Conseil constitutionnel, en partie parce qu'ils estimaient que la définition des actes de terrorisme n'était pas suffisamment claire et précise et ne répondait pas aux exigences de la Déclaration des droits de l'homme et du citoyen pour le critère de légalité de l'article 8. Le Conseil constitutionnel français, dans sa décision du 3 septembre 1986 relative à la loi du 9 septembre 86, a rejeté la requête des députés portant sur le critère légal des actes de terrorisme en estimant que : « La première condition fixée par la loi, qui renvoie à des infractions qui sont elles-mêmes définies par le code pénal ou par les lois spéciales en termes suffisamment clairs et précis, satisfait aux exigences du principe constitutionnel de la légalité des délits et des peines ; que de même, la seconde condition est énoncée en des termes d'une précision suffisante pour qu'il n'y ait pas méconnaissance de ce principe ».

compétent, indépendant et impartial, et du droit à un recours contre la condamnation et la peine en instance. Ces droits sont prévus par l'article 10 de la Déclaration universelle des droits de l'homme et l'article 14 du Pacte international relatif aux droits civils et politiques. Ces articles énoncent des normes fondamentales applicables dans tous les procès, qu'il s'agisse ou non de terroristes présumés. L'avantage d'un système judiciaire spécialisé permet de confier à une cour spécialisée le jugement des affaires qui ne peuvent être connues par les juridictions ordinaires, sans mettre en cause l'administration de la justice. Il est vrai que l'inconvénient principal ici réside dans les risques de dérives des pouvoirs de ces tribunaux spéciaux.

2. Les garanties procédurales

L'une des plus grandes difficultés ici concerne les garanties procédurales qui, en principe, devraient être assurées depuis l'arrestation de ces personnes jusqu'à leur jugement[97]. Les garanties procédurales relatives aux preuves sont davantage relatives[98]. Habituellement, les dénonciations sur l'obtention des aveux sous torture sont faites par les ONG[99]. La question centrale dans ces procès est très souvent liée à celle de l'admissibilité de la preuve, admissibilité qui s'avère particulièrement

---

[97] En Europe par exemple, depuis l'arrêt du 24 novembre 1993 *Imbriosca c. Suisse*, il est acquis que le droit au procès équitable s'étend aux « phases qui se déroulent avant la procédure de jugement », à commencer par la garde à vue. L'arrêt *Salduz c. Turquie du 27 novembre 2008* impose ensuite la présence de l'avocat dès le début de la garde à vue. On sait que cette décision est directement à l'origine de la condamnation de la France par la décision *Brusco c. France* du 14 octobre 2010, condamnation qui a suscité une évolution radicale du droit de la garde à vue.

[98] Voir sur l'importance du rôle du juge face aux mesures antiterroristes intrusives, Avis n°8 (2006) du Conseil consultatif de juges européens à l'attention du comité des ministres du Conseil de l'Europe, *Le rôle des juges dans la protection de l'État de droit et des droits de l'homme dans le contexte du terrorisme*, 8-10/11/2006.

[99] Dans son dialogue d'André Destouche à Siam, publié en 1766, Voltaire, à travers une ironie décrivant le système pénal français, fait dire à Croutef : « ... Comme il y a des demi-preuves, c'est-à-dire des demi-vérités, il est clair qu'il y a des demi-innocents et des demi-coupables. Nous commençons donc par leur donner une demi-mort, après quoi nous allons déjeuner ; ensuite vient la mort tout entière, ce qui donne dans le monde une grande considération, qui est le revenu du prix de nos charges ».

problématique lorsque la preuve est obtenue en violation des dispositions conventionnelles relatives à la protection des droits de l'homme[100]. La question centrale en la matière, et de manière générale en droit pénal, est celle de l'obtention de la preuve, puisque seule la preuve d'agissements répréhensibles permettra l'arrestation puis le jugement du suspect. En dehors de l'hypothèse de torture, l'exclusion de telles preuves obtenues par un traitement inhumain ou dégradant n'est pas automatique[101].

La garantie procédurale qui peut être requise ici se trouve essentiellement dans les divers codes de procédure pénale des États engagés dans la lutte contre le terrorisme. Disposant déjà d'une telle législation en matière de procédure pénale en général, on voit mal les États se doter d'une législation spécifique sur la procédure judiciaire en matière de terrorisme. Le code de procédure pénal camerounais est à cet égard un instrument relativement récent, qui tient compte de l'évolution des exigences d'État de droit et de la démocratie. Ainsi pose-t-il l'assistance de l'avocat dès les premières heures de l'interpellation du suspect[102] et réglemente la procédure d'*habeas corpus*[103]. En matière de répression des présumés terroristes, il serait difficile de se passer de ces dispositions. Le problème qui pourrait se poser cependant est celui relatif à l'assistance judiciaire, question liée au souci du respect des droits de la défense. Le droit à l'assistance d'un avocat est garanti, pour les accusations en matière pénale par les conventions internationales ratifiées par les États engagés dans la lutte contre Boko Haram[104] et par la

---

[100] Voir CEDH, arrêt *Ibrahim c/ Royaume-Uni* du 16 décembre 2014.

[101] En l'état de sa jurisprudence, pour déterminer si les preuves matérielles obtenues par un traitement inhumain ou dégradant doivent ou non être exclues du procès, la Cour vérifie tout d'abord si ces éléments ont influé sur l'issue de la procédure. Elle vérifie ensuite si les droits de la défense ont été respectés et, en particulier, le droit de ne pas contribuer à sa propre incrimination qui « présuppose que, dans une affaire pénale, l'accusation cherche à fonder son argumentation sans recourir à des éléments de preuve obtenus par la contrainte ou les pressions au mépris de la volonté de l'accusé » (CEDH, *Jalloh c/ Allemagne, 11 juill. 2006,* §100 ; JCP G 2007. I 106, obs. F. Sudre).

[102] S. YAWAGA, « La garde à vue » in J.M. TCHAKOUA (Dir.), *Les tendances de la nouvelle procédure pénale camerounaise*, P.U.A. 2007, p. 55 et s.

[103] Procédure organisée par les articles 584 et s. du C.P.P. du Cameroun.

[104] Il s'agit notamment de

législation camerounaise. C'est un droit qui, pourtant, dans la situation et le contexte particulier de la lutte contre Boko Haram, pourrait connaître de nombreuses exceptions. L'État peut ainsi démontrer, à la lumière des circonstances particulières de l'espèce, qu'il existe des raisons impérieuses de restreindre ce droit[105]. Ainsi que l'a fait savoir la CEDH dans l'arrêt *Salduz*[106], « même lorsque des raisons impérieuses peuvent exceptionnellement justifier le refus de l'accès à un avocat, pareille restriction – quelle que soit sa justification – ne doit pas indûment préjudicier aux droits découlant pour l'accusé de l'article 6. Il est en principe porté une atteinte irrémédiable aux droits de la défense lorsque des déclarations incriminantes faites lors d'un interrogatoire de police subi sans l'assistance possible d'un avocat sont utilisées pour fonder une condamnation ». Les droits de la défense dans la phase pré-juridictionnelle doivent donc être respectés, étant entendu qu'un accusé se trouve « dans une situation particulièrement vulnérable à ce stade de la procédure (…) notamment en ce qui concerne les règles régissant la collecte et l'utilisation des preuves. Dans la plupart des cas, cette vulnérabilité particulière ne peut être compensée de manière adéquate que par l'assistance d'un avocat, dont la tâche consiste notamment à faire en sorte que soit respecté le droit de tout accusé de ne pas s'incriminer lui-même »[107]. L'accès à un avocat fait donc partie des garanties procédurales exigées aux États en matière de traitement des présumés terroristes. Comme l'a relevé d'ailleurs la CEDH, "ces principes revêtent une importance particulière dans le cas des infractions graves, car c'est face aux peines les plus lourdes que le droit à un procès équitable doit être assuré au plus haut degré possible par les sociétés démocratiques »[108]. C'est un problème qui requiert des ressources humaines et financières

[105] Dans l'arrêt *Salduz*, la CEDH a ouvert une brèche de dérogation à cette exigence aux États si deux conditions sont réunies. D'une part, l'État doit démontrer qu'il a des *« raisons impérieuses »* de restreindre ce droit. D'autre part, l'admission comme preuve des déclarations faites dans ces conditions à la police ne doit pas avoir porté une atteinte effective au droit au procès équitable.

[106]CEDH, *Salduz c/ Turquie, 27 novembre 2008* ; *GACEDH* n°37, § 56.

[107] *Ibid.*, § 54.

[108] *Ibid.*

considérables. Paradoxalement, la liste des garanties à assurer aux présumés terroristes ne cesse de s'allonger.

Sur le plan international, les mécanismes spécifiques de répression du crime de terrorisme tardent à prendre corps. Si le droit humanitaire et le droit des conflits armés prévoient des incriminations pouvant à première vue correspondre aux actes à caractère terroriste, comme celles de crime de guerre, de crime contre l'humanité, de crime de génocide et de crime d'agression figurant dans le Statut de Rome, force est de constater leur inapplicabilité à la réalité des situations de terrorisme en raison notamment de l'exclusion de cette menace du domaine de compétence de la Cour pénale internationale. L'inapplicabilité des normes internationales aux actes de terrorisme, et l'absence d'incrimination spécifique qui en découle nuisent non seulement à la répression des auteurs des actes terroristes, mais permettent le développement d'un système d'impunité dans une société résolue à mettre fin à l'impunité. En effet, en l'absence de crime de terrorisme défini par un texte, il n'est pas possible de prononcer des mesures coercitives pour punir cette action. Par conséquent, sans incrimination applicable aux attaques de la nébuleuse Boko Haram, il est difficile de sanctionner les crimes commis par ses membres au niveau international. Ce vide juridique est actuellement extrêmement pénalisant et dangereux pour la sécurité juridique internationale puisqu'il laisse impunis les auteurs d'actes à caractère terroriste, ou les sanctionne sur le fondement de textes et d'incriminations inadaptés. Il apparaît donc plus que jamais nécessaire, au vu de l'inflation des crimes terroristes et de l'envergure croissante de telles actions, d'œuvrer à la mise en place d'une juridiction internationale spécialisée en la matière. L'absence d'organe juridiquement compétent, au niveau international, pour réprimer les attaques terroristes renforce davantage le vide juridique résultant de l'absence d'incrimination correspondant aux crimes terroristes à proprement parler.

Le terrorisme étant un crime aux particularités très marquées l'empêchant de tomber sous le coup des incriminations déjà existantes, la création d'une juridiction spécialisée expressément compétente dans ce domaine apparaît comme une mesure plus que salutaire pour la sécurité internationale. Dans tous les cas, la mise sur pied des tribunaux spéciaux pour connaître des crimes liés aux actes de terrorisme nécessite des coûts importants, insupportables par les pays touchés. Aux dépenses effectuées pour combattre ces mouvements, il faudrait encore prévoir des dépenses supplémentaires nécessaires au procès des membres des mouvements terroristes. Ce serait trop demander à ces États aux économies fragiles, dont la situation économique est aggravée par la lutte contre le terrorisme. C'est la raison pour laquelle sans assistance de la communauté internationale, une garantie du procès équitable aux détenus terroristes, fût-elle promise par les membres des gouvernements engagés dans la lutte contre Boko Haram, ne saurait être assurée. Au-delà des coûts de procédure, il faudrait encore des coûts liés à la détention, même après la condamnation. Des mécanismes judiciaires spécifiques de répression devraient rapidement être mis sur pied. Il serait possible d'envisager des tribunaux *ad hoc* régionaux chargés de juger les présumés terroristes, et rattachés à la CPI par le biais d'une convention spécifique ou même créés par le Conseil de sécurité. Il s'agit d'une aspiration qui découle directement de la montée en puissance des mouvements terroristes à travers le monde. Le droit ne saurait rester longtemps indifférent face à cette situation qu'il tente depuis des années de cerner.

LE CONTRÔLE PARLEMENTAIRE RÉNOVÉ DES FINANCES PUBLIQUES DANS LE NOUVEAU RÉGIME FINANCIER DE L'ÉTAT DU CAMEROUN

Samuel Eric KOUA*

Résumé

Le Nouveau régime financier de l'État du Cameroun, a rénové le contrôle parlementaire des finances publiques. Il a institué de nouveaux mécanismes de contrôle parlementaire, renforcé certaines techniques traditionnelles en la matière et enrichi l'information financière à destination du Parlement. Seulement, ce contrôle demeure perfectible.

INTRODUCTION GÉNÉRALE

La reddition des comptes prend, de nos jours, une place de plus en plus importante au point de devenir un enjeu majeur de toutes les politiques publiques[1]. Ce principe est affirmé par la Déclaration française des droits de l'homme et du citoyen (DDHC)[2] : « *la société a le droit de demander des comptes à tout agent public de son administration* »[3]. Dans la République, la reddition des comptes et la gestion de la chose publique sont consubstantielles. Bien entendu, le Parlement, en raison de sa légitimité démocratique, est l'instance républicaine la plus habilitée à recevoir la reddition des comptes des gestionnaires de la chose publique[4].

---

*Doctorant en droit public / Université de Douala, ex-cadre des services du Contrôle supérieur de l'État et diplômé de l'ENAM (magistrature administrative). Contact : kouaerics@vahoo.fr ; tel : 675169856.

[1] F. LAFARGE, *Rendre des comptes-rendre compte*, Projet de colloque ENA et *Revue française d'administration publique*, p. 1.

[2] *Ibid.*

[3] Art. 8, DDHC.

[4] Issue du Latin*res publica,*la chose publique renvoie à la fortune publique, c'est-à-dire (au sens large), à l'ensemble des biens meubles et immeubles gérés par les personnes publiques selon des règles spéciales et destinés à la satisfaction de l'intérêt général.

Sous ce rapport, l'article 14 de la Constitution camerounaise du 18 janvier 1996 prévoit : «*le parlement légifère et contrôle l'action du gouvernement* ».

La notion de contrôle est assez subtile. Elle n'a pas encore été explicitée en droit administratif[5]. Ici, le diptyque généralement admis est celui qui oppose le contrôle hiérarchique au contrôle de tutelle[6]. En droit des finances publiques, le contrôle, selon Jacques FABRE, renvoie à « *l'idée de vérification, c'est-à-dire le fait de s'assurer qu'une chose est bien telle qu'on l'a déclarée ou telle qu'elle doit être par rapport à une norme donnée* »[7]. À la vérité, cette définition est restrictive puisqu'elle ne vise que le contrôle de régularité. En effet, du point de vue organique, le contrôle peut être juridictionnel, administratif et politique. C'est dans ce dernier registre qu'est rangé le contrôle parlementaire des finances publiques. Du point de vue matériel, on a le contrôle de régularité (ou de conformité)[8] et le contrôle de performance[9]. Quant aux finances publiques, ce sont les ressources financières appartenant à une personne publique[10] et/ou confiées à une personne privée, gérées selon des règles spéciales et destinées à la satisfaction de l'intérêt général. De ce qui précède, il ressort que les critères les plus déterminants, pour délimiter la notion de finance publique sont : le critère finaliste[11] et le critère fonctionnel[12].

---

[5] C. TOURE, « Le système de contrôle des finances publiques au Mali », *Afrilex* N°4, décembre 2004, p. 152.

[6] *Ibid.*

[7] J. FABRE, *Le contrôle des finances publiques,* Paris, PUF, 1968, p. 9.

[8] C'est celui qui vérifie la conformité d'un acte au droit en vigueur.

[9] Dont l'objet est de s'assurer de la compatibilité d'une gestion donnée avec les trois E (économie, efficacité et efficience).

[10] De nos jours, l'expression finances publiques recouvre les fonds de ce type, appartenant à l'État (finances publiques nationales), aux établissements publics administratifs, aux collectivités territoriales décentralisées (finances publiques locales) et aux entités communautaires (CEMAC, CEDEAO, UE...).

[11] L'affection à la satisfaction des besoins d'intérêt général.

[12] La gestion des finances publiques est régie par les règles de droit public. Ce qui permet de conclure que les fonds des sociétés d'État, gérés selon les règles du droit OHADA, ne constituent pas des finances publiques.

Signe des temps, les différentes modalités de contrôle des finances publiques précitées ont été consacrées par le Nouveau régime financier de l'État (NRFE). Le NRFE procède de la loi n°2007/006 du 26 décembre 2007. Celle-ci a abrogé le premier régime financier du Cameroun indépendant : l'ordonnance n°62/07/4 du 04 février 1962 réglant le mode de présentation, les conditions d'exécution du budget de la République fédérale du Cameroun, de ses recettes, de ses dépenses et de toutes les opérations s'y rattachant[13]. Les innovations notables induites par cette ordonnance furent la création de la Cour des comptes et l'érection du ministre des Finances en ordonnateur principal du budget de l'État.

L'adoption du NRFE a été dictée par quatre soucis : la poursuite de la rénovation administrative, financière et institutionnelle du Cameroun à travers un nouveau texte qui doit être un puissant vecteur de développement[14] ; la recherche de la transparence dans la gestion financière publique, la nécessité d'arrimer le régime budgétaire et comptable camerounais aux exigences internationales et la modernisation de la gestion budgétaire nationale pour tenir compte des exigences de bonne gouvernance. De ce point de vue, le passage au NRFE s'explique par l'obsolescence de l'ordonnance du 07 février 1962. La rupture saisissante existant entre ces deux textes réside principalement dans le passage du budget de moyens au budget-programme[15]. En consacrant le

---

[13] Pour adapter cette ordonnance à l'évolution de l'administration publique camerounaise, elle fut modifiée par le décret n°67/0F/211 du 16 mai 1967 portant aménagement de la législation financière de la République fédérale du Cameroun, assorti d'une instruction sur la comptabilité de l'État.

[14] D. MBARGA NYATTE, « Vers une maîtrise des finances publiques au Cameroun », *Revue Africaine des Sciences Juridiques (RASJ)*, Vol.6, N° 1, 2009, p. 337.

[15] Voir art. 18 al. 3 et 43 al. 5, NRFE. Le budget programme est un outil de gestion des finances publiques consistant à élaborer, présenter et exécuter la loi de finances sur la base des programmes. Ses principales caractéristiques sont : la structuration par programme, la fixation des résultats, la pluri annualité et la mesure de performance. Ses origines remontent au Rapport de la "Commission Hoover, lequel, en 1949 aux États-Unis, à la suite d'un constat d'une déficience du système de gestion des administrations publiques, avait recommandé des mesures de réforme administrative et financière. Ses premières applications ont eu lieu au ministère de la Défense des USA qui introduit en

budget-programme, le NRFE a sonné le glas du budget de moyens institué par l'ordonnance du 07 février 1962.

Le passage au budget programme se justifie en grande partie par les limites de la logique du budget des moyens : la faible articulation entre le budget et les priorités nationales, la prise en compte insuffisante des besoins des populations à la base, la limitation des engagements budgétaires sur l'année, la difficulté de percevoir les finalités de dépense dans le budget, l'absence d'exigence de performance, le manque de prévisibilité à long terme, la reconduction automatique des moyens d'une année à l'autre, etc. Compte tenu de ces différentes limites et mutations socioéconomiques, le budget des moyens s'avérait caduc, et le budget programme s'imposait. Les principaux apports de ce dernier sont : l'allocation des ressources publiques en fonction des besoins prioritaires des citoyens, l'incitation des administrations à promouvoir la qualité de la dépense, le renforcement de la viabilité et de la stabilité macroéconomique et budgétaire, etc.

Le NRFE fait partie des instruments de promotion du renouveau budgétaire et financier national[16]. En dehors du passage au budget programme, ses principales innovations sont : l'instauration des principes de sincérité et de réalisme budgétaires, la création de plusieurs catégories d'ordonnateurs, l'extension des inflexions au principe de l'annualité, la rénovation du contrôle parlementaire des finances publiques, etc.

La plupart des innovations précitées sont contenues dans la loi organique relative aux lois de finances (LOLF) de la France. La LOLF

1960 le « *planning, programtning and budgeting System* ». Il est introduit en France en 1970 avec la rationalisation des choix budgétaires, et institutionnalisé avec l'adoption de la LOLF. De 1980 à 2000, il est diffusé dans d'autres pays de l'OCDE. Sa diffusion en Europe de l'Est, Amérique latine et Afrique a lieu à partir de 2000. Pour ce qui est de l'Afrique, le fait accélérateur de cette diffusion est la mise en place des stratégies de lutte contre la pauvreté.

[16] D. MBARGA NYATTE, « Vers la maîtrise des finances publiques au Cameroun », *op. cit.*, p. 324.

qui date de 2001 aurait donc influencé le NRFE[17] entré en vigueur en 2007, soit avant les directives CEMAC relatives aux lois de finances[18].

Dès lors, la rénovation précitée augure-t-elle une renaissance du contrôle parlementaire des finances publiques au Cameroun?

Pour y répondre, il sied de s'appesantir sur l'articulation de la rénovation dudit contrôle (I) et la limitation persistante de ce dernier, nonobstant cette rénovation (II).

I/ L'articulation de la rénovation dudit contrôle

La tendance contemporaine est de donner sens et portée au contrôle parlementaire des finances publiques[19]. Le NRFE s'inscrit dans cette mouvance à travers la reconfiguration des moyens de contrôle parlementaire des finances publiques (A) et l'extension de l'information financière à destination du Parlement (B).

A- La reconfiguration des moyens de contrôle du Parlement

Le NRFE a procédé à la dynamisation de certains moyens de contrôle parlementaire classiques (1) et à l'instauration de nouveaux (2).

1. La dynamisation de certains moyens de contrôle parlementaire classique

Cette dynamisation tient à la renaissance de la loi de règlement (a) et à la dynamisation des commissions d'enquête parlementaire (b).

---

[17] Pourrait-on alors parler de l'autonomie du droit budgétaire des États francophones d'Afrique ? Le doyen Magloire ONDOA, viscéralement attaché à l'idée de l'autonomie du droit des États précités, aura, certainement, matière à réflexion à la suite de cette question.

[18] La directive 2008-01 relative aux lois de finances des pays membres de la CEMAC et la directive 2011 relative aux lois des finances au sein de la CEMAC. La seconde citée, est venue corriger les imperfections de la première.

[19] G. PROTIERE, *Parlement et dépenses publiques,* Communication orale, prononcée lors des *Xe Rencontres juridiques,* organisées par la faculté de droit et sciences politiques (université Lyon II), le 1er décembre 2006, à l'hôtel du Département du Rhône, p. 1.

a. **La renaissance de la loi de règlement**

L'origine de la loi de règlement remonte à la loi française du 15 mai 1818 qui avait confié au Parlement un pouvoir de contrôle *a posteriori* sur l'exécution du budget[20]. Sous l'empire de l'Ancien régime financier de l'État du Cameroun, l'on observait un certain désintérêt des parlementaires à l'égard de cette loi dénommée alors règlement de l'exercice[21]. Ce désintérêt s'expliquait en grande partie, par son adoption des années après l'exercice budgétaire auquel elle se rapportait. Cette renaissance tient à l'autonomie et à la précision du délai de dépôt du projet de loi de règlement (a-1) et à l'extension de l'objet de ce dernier (a-2).

a-1. L'autonomie et la précision du délai de dépôt du projet de loi de règlement

Dans l'ordonnance de 1962, le projet de loi de règlement (PLR) relevait des documents qui accompagnaient le projet de la loi de finances de l'année[22] (PLFA), et déposés à la même date que ce dernier. Le PLR était une pièce annexe au PLFA[23]. Avec le NRFE, la loi de règlement cesse d'être dans l'antichambre de celle-ci[24]. Le PLR et le PLFA ne sont plus déposés au même moment. En effet, d'après l'article 21 du NRFE, le projet de loi de règlement et ses annexes doivent être déposés au Parlement au plus tard le 30 septembre de l'année suivant celle de l'exercice budgétaire auquel elle se rapporte. Le PLFA quant à lui doit être déposé au plus tard 15 jours avant le début de la session budgétaire[25].

Le décalage entre la date de dépôt du PLFA et le PLR permet aux parlementaires de bien s'imprégner du résultat de l'exécution du budget

---

[20] O. TOGOLO, « A propos de la loi de règlement du budget », *Miroir du Droit*, n°l/2011, janvier-février-mars 2011, p.101.

[21] Voir chapitre II, Ordonnance n°62-OF-4 du 7 février 1962 réglant le mode de présentation, les conditions d'exécution du budget de la République fédérale du Cameroun, de ses recettes, de ses dépenses et de toutes les opérations s'y rattachant.

[22] Art. 50 et 52, Ordonnance du 07 février 1962.

[23] *Ibid.*

[24] *O.* TOGOLO, « A propos de la loi de règlement », *op. cit.* (*supra*, note n° 20), p. 101.

[25] Art. 33 al. 1, NRFE.

de l'année N-l, avant de voter celui de l'année N+l. Ce décalage permettrait aux parlementaires d'être éclairés sur les données prospectives du projet de loi de finances grâce aux enseignements tirés de l'exécution du budget du dernier exercice budgétaire clos[26].

La précision du délai de dépôt du projet de la loi de règlement et la pratique par les parlementaires camerounais depuis la session budgétaire 2008, de la technique du chaînage vertueux[27], alors que celle-ci n'est prévue dans aucun texte au Cameroun, laissent penser que l'époque où la loi de règlement était adoptée deux, trois ans, voire plus, après l'exercice budgétaire auquel elle se rapportait, est désormais révolue[28]. La nouvelle génération des parlementaires camerounais, depuis la session budgétaire précitée, vote la loi de règlement avant la loi de finances de l'année, comme si le vote de la première conditionne celui de la seconde[29]. Qu'en est-il de l'extension de l'objet de la loi de règlement ?

a-2. L'extension de l'objet de la loi de règlement

Sous l'empire de l'ordonnance de 1962, le rôle du Parlement était fondamentalement passif lors de l'adoption de la loi de règlement. La loi de règlement se bornait alors à arrêter les comptes[30]. Ce qui confortait la thèse selon laquelle le Parlement est une boîte d'enregistrement en matière budgétaire. Dans la nouvelle donne," l'objet de cette loi est assez étendu. Ainsi, outre les missions précitées, cette loi ratifie les modifications apportées par décrets d'avance aux crédits ouverts par la dernière loi de finances, arrête le montant définitif des ressources et charges de trésorerie ayant concouru à la réalisation de l'équilibre

---

[26] Voir, F. CHOUVEL, *Finances publiques,* 14e édition, Gualino, 2011, p. 221.

[27] D'après cette technique, le vote de la loi de finances est toujours précédé de celui de la loi de règlement.

[28] À titre d'exemple, voir la loi n°2008/010 du 29 décembre 2008, portant loi de règlement de l'exercice budgétaire 2007, la loi de règlement de l'exercice budgétaire n°2010/014 du 21 décembre 2010 portant règlement de l'exercice 2009.

[29] Or, « *Le vote de l'une de ces lois ne conditionne pas celui de l'autre* » (voir art. 43 al.2, NRFE).

[30] C'est-à-dire arrêter le montant définitif des recettes et des dépenses, et à constater les résultats financiers du dernier exercice budgétaire clos.

financier de l'année concernée, affecte le résultat comptable de l'exercice, arrête les soldes des comptes spéciaux non reportés à l'exercice suivant[31], etc.

Compte tenu du caractère pluriel de l'objet de la loi de règlement, l'on peut, en théorie et *a priori,* dire que dorénavant, son adoption permet aux parlementaires de passer au crible l'action financière gouvernementale du dernier exercice budgétaire clos, avant de voter le budget de l'année N +1. Le vote de loi de règlement est devenu un moment très attendu lors de la session budgétaire. Il n'est pas à exclure qu'au cours d'une session budgétaire, les parlementaires, sur la base des irrégularités qu'ils ont relevées pendant l'examen du PLR, refusent d'accorder tel ou tel crédit au gouvernement. L'époque où la loi de règlement était votée dans l'indifférence totale des parlementaires nous semble révolue. Les débats houleux auxquels donne lieu son adoption depuis 2008, attestent amplement cette idée. Qu'en est-il de la dynamisation des commissions d'enquête en matière de finances publiques ?

b) La dynamisation des commissions d'enquête parlementaire en matière des finances publiques

Dans le NRFE, la dynamisation des commissions d'enquête parlementaire en matière de finances publiques tient à deux éléments au moins : la flexibilité dans leur déploiement (b-1) et l'accroissement de leurs pouvoirs (b-2).

b-1. La flexibilité dans le déploiement des commissions d'enquête parlementaire sur les sujets intéressant les finances publiques

Avant 2007, la commission d'enquête ne pouvait être instituée que pour une durée non renouvelable, n'excédant pas quatre (04) mois. Elle ne pouvait être constituée de nouveau pour le même objet avant l'expiration d'un délai de douze mois à compter de la fin de leur

[31] Art. 20 al. 2, NRFE.

mission[32]. On le voit bien, sous l'ordonnance de 1962, la marge de manœuvre du Parlement en matière de déploiement des commissions d'enquête parlementaire était limitée. S'inscrivant résolument dans la logique de valorisation des pouvoirs financiers du Parlement, le NRFE a rectifié le tir en prévoyant en son article 71 al. 1 que : « *Le parlement peut désigner des commissions d'enquête sur un sujet intéressant les finances publiques, pour une durée n'excédant pas six mois. Cette durée est renouvelable en tant que de besoin* ».

b-2. L'accroissement des pouvoirs desdites commissions

Dans la nouvelle donne, les commissions d'enquête parlementaire en matière de finances publiques disposent de pouvoirs étendus. Ainsi, elles peuvent se faire assister par des personnes de leur choix, auditionner toute personne utile à l'exception du chef de l'État[33]. Cette exception qui place le président de la République hors de portée de la sphère d'influence du Parlement confirme la nature présidentialiste du régime politique camerounais.

Il faut noter que, toute personne qui entrave l'action de la commission d'enquête s'expose à des poursuites judiciaires pour entrave à l'exécution d'une mission de service public. Et c'est là l'innovation la plus saisissante, la commission peut transmettre aux autorités judiciaires tout fait susceptible de constituer une infraction. Une telle transmission vaut plainte au nom de l'État. Autre fait nouveau notable, la commission d'enquête peut transmettre au Conseil de discipline budgétaire et financière (CDBF), tout fait apparaissant comme une faute de gestion. Bien plus, sous réserve du secret-défense, de l'instruction et médical, tout document requis par la commission lors du contrôle sur place et sur pièce doit lui être fourni. Quoi qu'on en dise, le Parlement, à travers le renforcement des commissions d'enquête parlementaire sur les sujets intéressant les finances publiques, se trouve véritablement impliqué dans

---

32 Voir art. 67, loi N°2002/005 du 2 décembre 2002 portant règlement intérieur de l'Assemblée Nationale.

33 Art. 71, al. 2, NRFE.

le contrôle du budget. Il en est de même avec l'instauration de deux nouveaux moyens de contrôle parlementaire des finances publiques.

2. L'instauration de deux nouveaux moyens de contrôle parlementaire des finances publiques : le rapporteur général et les rapporteurs spéciaux

Le rapporteur général et les rapporteurs spéciaux ne doivent pas être confondus avec le traditionnel rapporteur budgétaire. Ce dernier est chargé de faire la synthèse des débats qui se déroulent au niveau de la commission des finances et d'en présenter le rapport à l'assemblée plénière de la chambre concernée. S'il y a un point commun entre les deux premiers rapporteurs cités et le rapporteur budgétaire traditionnel, c'est la désignation de tous par la commission des finances. En effet, selon l'article 69 du NRFE : « *La commission chargée des finances désigne chaque année, à l'ouverture de la première session ordinaire de l'année législative, un rapporteur général pour les recettes et des rapporteurs spéciaux chargés des dépenses publiques et du contrôle de l'usage des fonds publics, y compris les fonds de développement publics* ». Ils ont un mandat d'une année renouvelable et sont tous membres de la commission des finances. C'est le 26 mars 2015 que le tout premier rapporteur général et les tout premiers rapporteurs spéciaux de l'histoire parlementaire du Cameroun ont pris fonction au cours d'une cérémonie très courue, présidée par le président de l'Assemblée nationale (PAN) et à laquelle l'on notait la présence du président de la Chambre des comptes de la Cour suprême.

Le rapporteur général contrôle les recettes alors que chaque rapporteur spécial, dans sa sphère de compétence, contrôle la gestion des dépenses et l'usage des fonds y compris les fonds de développement publics[34]. Les rapporteurs ont vocation à jouer un rôle primordial dans la protection de la fortune publique au Cameroun[35]. À cet égard, la loi leur accorde d'énormes pouvoirs à la mesure de leur mission. Ainsi, ils disposent d'un

---

[34] Art. 69, NRFE.

[35] À propos de cette dernière, lire S. E. KOUA, *La protection de la fortune publique au Cameroun,* Éditions Magolo Makélé, 2014, 282 p.

pouvoir de contrôle sur pièce et sur place[36]. Aucun document ne peut leur être refusé, réserve faite des sujets touchant à défense nationale, au secret de l'instruction et au secret médical[37]. Répartis par champ de compétences en fonction des différents groupes de ministère, ils effectueront des contrôles réguliers dans les grands projets en cours de réalisation au Cameroun. Les rapporteurs et les personnels appelés à les appuyer dans leurs activités de contrôle devraient être suffisamment outillés en matière de finances publiques, de compatibilité, de marchés publics. L'on comprend donc pourquoi au mois de juin 2015, cinq personnels devant assister les rapporteurs étaient en formation au Canada. Quoi qu'on en dise, avec l'existence des rapporteurs, le Parlement n'aura plus besoin d'attendre que le Gouvernement lui fournisse l'information financière. Il ira lui-même à la quête de celle-ci, par l'entremise des diligences effectuées par les rapporteurs.

B- L'extension de l'information financière destinée aux parlementaires

Le NRFE a accru du point de vue quantitatif (1) et du point de vue qualitatif (2), la dose d'informations financières que le Gouvernement doit mettre à la disposition du Parlement.

1. L'extension quantitative de l'information financière fournie au Parlement par le Gouvernement

En règle générale, les parlementaires, pour avoir l'information, recourent à la procédure des questions (écrites ou orales). Ils peuvent aussi l'acquérir à travers l'examen des différents projets de lois de finances et la lecture du rapport annuel de la Chambre des comptes. L'augmentation quantitative de la fourchette d'information financière à mettre à la disposition du Parlement par le Gouvernement tient à l'augmentation des documents joints aux différents projets de lois de finances (a) et à la multiplication des procédures de délivrance de l'information financière du Parlement (b).

---

[36] Art. 70, NRFE.

[37] *Ibid.*

a) La multiplication des documents joints aux projets de lois de finances

Pour que le Parlement prenne en connaissance de cause les décisions .financières cruciales, les articles 19, 20 et 36 du NRFE prévoient qu'un certain nombre de documents doit être joint aux différents projets de lois de finances (de l'année, rectificative et de règlement). Pour ne prendre que cet exemple, dans l'ordonnance de 1962, le projet de loi de finances de l'année était accompagné de neuf (09) documents. Avec le NRFE, dix (10) documents plus riches en informations que ceux prévus par l'ordonnance de 1962, l'accompagnent. Ces documents sont :

- un rapport sur la situation et les perspectives économiques, sociales et financières de la Nation. Il comprend notamment la présentation des hypothèses de la loi de finances et des projections y afférentes ;

- une annexe présentant les perspectives d'évolution sur trois (3) ans, des dépenses publiques, en tenant compte des projections des équilibres budgétaires ;

- une annexe détaillant les prévisions de recettes budgétaires selon la nomenclature budgétaire des recettes, la liste et l'évaluation par catégorie de bénéficiaires des impôts et taxes affectés à des personnes morales autres que l'État ;

- une annexe explicative développant pour chaque chapitre les dépenses d'investissement et les dépenses courantes pour les deux années précédant l'année en cours et l'année considérée, par programme au sein des sections fonctionnelles et, pour chacune d'elles, l'état de consommation des autorisations d'engagement depuis l'origine de chaque programme et les prévisions de consommation de crédit pour l'année en cours et l'année considérée par article budgétaire ;

- une annexe présentant les dépenses des administrations par chapitre, par section et détaillée par article et paragraphe, pour l'année en cours et l'année considérée ;

- une annexe détaillant le montant et l'utilisation des comptes spéciaux au cours des années précédentes, pour l'année en cours et les années à venir ;

- une annexe détaillant les projets d'investissement ;

- un état des opérations financières ;

- une annexe présentant les concours financiers de l'État aux entreprises ;

- une annexe présentant par ministère les informations relatives à l'évolution de la masse salariale.

En prescrivant l'accompagnement du PLFA, du PLR[38] et du projet de loi de finances rectificative par une panoplie de documents, le NRFE voudrait au maximum réduire les zones d'incertitudes dans le processus décisionnel du Parlement en matière budgétaire. L'enrichissement de l'information financière à destination du Parlement participe, sans aucun doute, du souci de permettre à ce dernier de jouer pleinement le rôle qui est le sien dans le système camerounais de contrôle des finances publiques. Seulement, une exploitation judicieuse de cette information par les parlementaires requiert de ceux-ci une certaine gymnastique intellectuelle.

b) La multiplication des procédures de délivrance de l'information financière du Parlement

Sous le règne de l'ordonnance de 1962, le Parlement n'exploitait pas l'intégralité des moyens légaux de contrôle et d'acquisition de l'information financière. Il n'avait jamais fait recours aux commissions d'enquête parlementaire et à la loi de finances rectificative[39]. Les parlementaires ne pouvaient accéder à l'information financière que lors de la session budgétaire à travers l'examen du projet de loi de finances et les questions posées aux membres du gouvernement. L'information financière du Parlement était donc limitée.

S'écartant de la logique de sous-information financière du Parlement qui caractérisait l'ordonnance de 1962, le NRFE a multiplié les

[38] Le projet de loi de règlement est accompagné de six (06) documents budgétaires énumérés par l'article 22 du NRFE.

[39] Depuis l'accession du Cameroun à l'indépendance, le Parlement camerounais n'a jamais fait recours à la LFR.

procédures de délivrance de l'information financière aux parlementaires par le Gouvernement. Ainsi, outre les procédures précitées : le NRFE prévoit que : «*l'exécution à mi-parcours du budget de l'État fait l'objet d'une information écrite fournie au parlement par le Gouvernement au plus tard le 30 septembre de l'année courante*»[40]. De même, en vue de l'examen du PLFA, chaque rapporteur peut adresser au mois de septembre, un questionnaire sur les dépenses qui entrent dans le cadre de sa compétence[41]. Les réponses à son questionnaire doivent être fournies par l'autorité destinataire huit (08) jours avant le dépôt du projet de loi de finances de l'année. L'on peut regretter que le rapporteur, confronté à un refus de réponse d'une autorité destinataire du questionnaire, n'ait aucun moyen de contrainte à son encontre. En effet, l'autorité qui refuse de répondre au questionnaire du rapporteur peut juste faire l'objet d'observation de la part de l'Assemblée à laquelle appartient ce dernier[42]. Le législateur aurait dû offrir au rapporteur confronté à un tel refus, la faculté de le signaler au chef de l'État, compte tenu de l'influence de ce dernier à l'égard des autorités soumise au questionnaire précité.

L'extension de l'information financière du Parlement procède aussi de ce que le Gouvernement est tenu de transmettre à la représentation nationale pour information, tout décret d'annulation de crédits[43]. Le NRFE n'a pas conféré au Parlement le pouvoir d'apprécier la sincérité des annulations de crédits et de s'opposer aux annulations de crédits non sincères, le cas échéant. Cela est regrettable, car derrière l'annulation d'un crédit peut se profiler l'insincérité budgétaire.

2. L'extension qualitative de l'information financière destinée au Parlement : l'exigence d'une information sincère

Si l'on en croit Anne GRUSZKA, «*personne, peut-être, n'a jamais été sincère pour définir la sincérité*»[44]. Si cette affirmation est en partie

[40] Art. 35. al. 2, NRFE.

[41] Art. 37, NRFE.

[42] *Ibid.*

[43] Voir art. 55 al. 2, NRFE.

[44] A. GRUSZKA, *L'effectivité du principe de sincérité dans les finances publiques de l'Etat,* Mémoire Master II, Droit public, Panthéon ALSAS Paris 2, 2009-2010, p. 4.

fondée, il n'en demeure pas moins que, la sincérité, c'est ce qui est vrai ou reflète la réalité. En matière budgétaire, est empreinte de sincérité, toute information qui reflète de façon fidèle (*sans omission ou exagération*) la situation financière ou comptable de l'État.

Seulement, en règle générale, les gouvernants ont une propension à rendre publique l'information financière, de façon orientée. Conscient de cet état de fait, le NRFE prescrit au gouvernement la mise à la disposition du Parlement d'une information financière sincère. Cette obligation se déduit de la lecture combinée des articles 3 et 60 du NRFE. L'article 3 dispose que *«La loi de finances présente de façon sincère l'ensemble des ressources et charges de l'État. Ce principe implique que les informations fournies soient claires, précises et complètes, au regard des données disponibles, au plan national et international, au moment de l'élaboration des prévisions»*. L'article 60 pour sa part prévoit que« *Les comptes de l'État doivent être réguliers, sincères et donner une image fidèle de son patrimoine et de sa situation financière*»[45]. Le principe de sincérité astreint le Gouvernement à une triple obligation de moyen, de résultat et de comportement[46].

La sincérité de l'information fournie aux parlementaires par le Gouvernement permet au Parlement de prendre la bonne décision financière et d'allouer les crédits en connaissance de cause. À cet égard, en consacrant le droit d'accès à l'information financière (sincère) de la représentation nationale, le législateur financier du 27 décembre 2007 instaure une nouvelle dynamique visant la valorisation des pouvoirs financiers du Parlement[47] et de la démocratie. Le droit d'accès du Parlement à l'information financière étant l'un des piliers de la démocratie participative[48].

---

[45] Il faut noter que cette information, à sa conception, peut être sincère, mais ne plus l'être à destination à cause des aléas d'ordre économique et des évolutions survenues de sa conception à sa mise à la disposition des parlementaires. Dans cette situation, l'insincérité sera de bonne foi.

[46] Pour approfondir, lire A. S. BESSALA, A. G. BESSALA, « Le principe de sincérité en droit public financier camerounais », *RASJ*, N° 2, 2013, p. 247-253.

[47] *Ibid*, p. 221.

[48] *Ibid.*

Le NRFE ne dit pas ce qui adviendrait, si jamais les parlementaires avaient des doutes sur la sincérité des documents qui accompagnent un projet de loi de finances. Peuvent-ils déférer au Conseil constitutionnel les griefs d'insincérité desdits documents ? Si cela est possible en droit français, compte tenu de la valeur constitutionnelle du principe de sincérité budgétaire en France[49], au Cameroun où ledit principe a encore une valeur législative, un tel scénario est peu probable[50]. Sauf à penser que le juge constitutionnel camerounais accepte d'ériger la sincérité au rang des principes de valeur constitutionnelle. Si tel est le cas, il prononcera *ipso facto,* en cas d'insincérité, l'annulation des PLF et de leurs documents annexes.

S'il est vrai que le NRFE a revalorisé le contrôle parlementaire des finances publiques, il n'en demeure pas moins que ledit contrôle demeure perfectible.

II/ La limitation persistante du contrôle, nonobstant sa rénovation dans le NRFE

Pour mieux cerner cette perfectibilité, il sied d'étudier les facteurs limitant l'efficacité du contrôle parlementaire des finances publiques dans le NRFE (A) et de décliner quelques solutions pour l'améliorer (B).

A. Les facteurs limitant l'efficacité du contrôle parlementaire dans le NRFE

Malgré sa rénovation dans le NRFE, la portée du contrôle parlementaire des finances publiques au Cameroun demeure limitée par des facteurs sociopolitiques (1) et d'ordre juridique (2).

[49] En fait, Le Conseil constitutionnel français a accepté, depuis le début des années quatre-vingt-dix, de répondre au grief d'insincérité des lois de finances. L'accessoire suivant le principal, il est à penser que si le juge constitutionnel français retient sa compétence pour apprécier la sincérité des projets de lois de finances, il peut aussi valablement examiner celle des documents annexés aux dits projets.

[50] Contrairement à la France où la LOLF qui consacre le principe de sincérité relève du bloc de constitutionnalité, au Cameroun, le texte portant régime financier de l'État qui en est le principal fondement juridique, n'en fait pas partie.

1. Les facteurs sociopolitiques

Il s'agit des liens sociopolitiques (a) et du désintérêt des parlementaires à l'égard de certains moyens de contrôle prévus dans le NRFE (b).

a- Les liens sociopolitiques divers

Dans le microcosme sociopolitique camerounais, tout le monde connaît tout le monde. Confronté à un contrôle susceptible d'entraîner des sanctions à leur égard, certains contrôlés n'hésitent pas à solliciter l'intervention d'une connaissance haut placée, à l'effet de paralyser la procédure. Et comme l'a relevé Cheick na TOURE, « *les liens sociaux et familiaux sont tels que leur enchevêtrement permet toujours à un agent ou un politique en voie d'être sanctionné d'invoquer le parapluie de telle ou telle personne haut placée* »[51]. Cet état de fait semble culturellement légitime en Afrique. Et comme le fait remarquer Philippe DECRAENE, « *il est resté (...) plus déshonorant, pour un Africain conséquent avec lui-même, de ne pas secourir un des membres de sa parenté que de voler au secours de quelqu'un qui est étranger à cette dernière* »[52]. Le rapporteur général et les rapporteurs spéciaux pourraient, à l'occasion de leur mission, être confrontés à cette triste réalité.

Le fait majoritaire peut aussi compromettre l'objectivité du contrôle parlementaire des finances publiques. Le fait majoritaire est une situation politique dans laquelle la majorité présidentielle et/ou gouvernementale est identique à la majorité parlementaire. En droit constitutionnel français, elle s'oppose à la cohabitation. Le fait majoritaire pourrait assouplir la rigueur des députés de la majorité lors du contrôle de la gestion financière des membres du gouvernement. À cause du fait majoritaire, certains parlementaires pourraient fermer les yeux sur les indélicatesses financières des membres du gouvernement camarades du parti. Dans tous les cas, l'on constate d'une manière générale que les réponses des ministres aux députés ne participent pas véritablement à la

---

[51] C. TOURE, « Le système de contrôle des finances publiques au Mali », *op.cit.*, p.160.
[52] PH. DECRAENE, « La corruption en Afrique », *Pouvoir,* n° 31, p. 95.

finalité de tout contrôle, à savoir la sanction en cas d'irrégularité dûment établie[53].

En outre, plusieurs parlementaires demeurent imprégnés de la logique politique selon laquelle leur rôle est de défendre, au détriment de l'intérêt national parfois, les intérêts de la circonscription où ils ont été élus. Ils tendent à tolérer les indélicatesses managériales des ministres qui ont inscrit dans le programme économique de la nation, des projets à réaliser dans leurs circonscriptions d'élection. Cette mansuétude s'explique par le concours de certains des projets précités, à la réalisation des promesses électorales des parlementaires.

b. Le désintérêt des parlementaires vis-à-vis de certains moyens de contrôle prévus par le NRFE

Ce désintérêt se justifie par le sentiment de l'inapplication des sanctions aux irrégularités qu'ils ont eu à relever antérieurement, et l'absence de prise en compte des améliorations proposées par eux, pour une gestion des finances publiques plus saine. Ce désintérêt résulterait aussi de la complexité des questions de finances publiques. Les finances publiques sont d'une technicité avérée qui rebute les citoyens et même les élus du peuple[54]. À dire vrai, le contrôle parlementaire des finances publiques dans le monde en général, et en Afrique en particulier, a succombé sous le poids de la technocratie financière qui entoure l'élaboration et l'exécution de la loi de finances[55].

En règle générale, le désintérêt des parlementaires pour le contrôle des finances publiques se traduit par le non-recours à certains moyens d'information et de contrôle. À titre d'illustration, depuis l'accession du Cameroun à l'indépendance, le Parlement camerounais n'a jamais suscité une commission d'enquête ni adopté une loi de finances rectificative. Or, cette dernière permet aux parlementaires de corriger les prévisions

---

[53] S.T.BATOUM- BA- NGOUE, «Démocratisation et processus budgétaire dans les Etats de la Commission économique et monétaire de l'Afrique Centrale (CEMAC) : cas du Cameroun », *Afrilex* n°4, décembre 2004, p. 24.

[54] *Ibid., p. 20.*

[55] *Ibid., p. 24.*

budgétaires initiales qui se sont avérées inefficaces, de procéder aux ajustements que le Gouvernement n'est pas habilité à opérer lui-même[56] ; et de prendre en compte les évolutions conjoncturelles[57]. Ce désintérêt se manifeste aussi par l'absence de certains députés aux sessions parlementaires[58].

2. Les facteurs d'ordre juridique

L'analyse va s'appesantir sur le parlementarisme rationalisé (a) et la mansuétude du NRFE à l'égard des dépenses parlementaires (b).

a. Le parlementarisme rationalisé

Le parlementarisme rationalisé renvoie à l'ensemble des mécanismes juridiques et sociopolitiques qui accroissent la marge de manœuvre de l'exécutif à l'égard du Parlement et restreignent celle de ce dernier à l'encontre du premier cité. L'analyse va porter sur deux aspects du parlementarisme rationalisé : le rétrécissement des délais de l'action financière du Parlement (a. l) et les restrictions au pouvoir d'autorisation budgétaire de ce dernier (a.2).

a-1. Le rétrécissement des délais de l'action financière du Parlement

Le Parlement a 20 jours[59] pour adopter la loi de finances[60]. Ce délai peut être ramené par le Gouvernement à 8 jours en cas d'urgence. La brièveté du délai d'adoption de la loi de finances et le traditionnel dépôt tardif du PLFA ne garantissent pas aux parlementaires un temps matériel suffisant pour jauger profondément la pertinence des demandes de crédits présentées par le Gouvernement. Les parlementaires s'empresseraient d'adopter la loi de finances dans les délais, sous peine du

---

[56] *Ibid,* p. 163.
[57] *Ibid,* p. 163.
[58] Le président de l'Assemblée nationale a, dans son allocution de l'ouverture de la session parlementaire de mars 2015, dénoncé l'absentéisme de certains parlementaires à l'hémicycle.
[59] Or, en France, le Parlement dispose d'un délai de 70 jours pour adopter la loi de finances (voir art. 47, LOLF).
[60] Art. 39 al. 2, NRFE.

douzième provisoire[61]. Selon un parlementaire qui a sollicité l'anonymat : « *la tonne de documents qui accompagne le projet de loi de finances ne sert rien compte tenu de son dépôt tardif* ». À cet égard, l'on ne saurait parler d'un véritable contrôle parlementaire des finances publiques lors de l'examen du PLF.

a-2. Les restrictions au pouvoir d'autorisation budgétaire du Parlement

À l'observation, il semble interdit aux parlementaires de perturber le Gouvernement en modifiant la configuration initiale des ressources et des charges[62]. En d'autres termes, il est presque impossible aux parlementaires de corriger, par des amendements, les irrégularités qu'ils ont eu à relever lors de l'examen du PLFA. Pour être recevables, les propositions d'amendement doivent respecter certaines conditions. En effet, « *Aucune proposition d'amendement à une loi de finances ne peut être présentée par un parlementaire si elle a pour effet, soit une diminution des ressources publiques, soit l'aggravation des charges publiques sans réduction à due concurrence d'autres dépenses ou création de recettes nouvelles d'égale importance* »[63]. L'attachement du NRFE et de la Constitution camerounaise [64] à l'équilibre budgétaire reflète le lien de filiation existant entre ces deux textes et les programmes d'ajustement structurel qu'a connus le Cameroun par le passé. Cet attachement illustre parfaitement, l'hostilité du législateur financier national à l'égard de la politique budgétaire expansionniste. Celle-ci consiste à adopter un budget déséquilibré en faveur des dépenses à l'effet d'intensifier l'investissement public, avec en filigrane l'objectif d'obtenir l'équilibre budgétaire à moyen ou à long terme (à la fin d'un cycle de 2 à 5ans). Le NRFE est

---

[61] Cette procédure est prévue par l'article 16 de la constitution et 42 du NRFE. Le douzième provisoire qui est l'une des sanctions de l'inertie parlementaire en matière budgétaire, constitue par ailleurs une limite au principe de l'annualité de l'impôt, en ce qu'il permet aux crédits de l'exercice budgétaire précédent d'être utilisés pour le compte de l'exercice N+l jusqu'à l'adoption du nouveau budget par le Parlement.

[62] E.C. LEKENE DONFACK, *Finances publiques camerounaises,* Paris, Berger Levrault, 1987, p. 142.

[63] Voir art. 44, NRFE.

[64] Voir articles 18 et 23 de la Constitution du 18 janvier 1996.

marqué du sceau de l'idéologie libérale réfractaire à la politique budgétaire expansionniste[65].

Quoi qu'on en dise, la rationalisation du travail parlementaire empêche au Parlement d'user pleinement de ses prérogatives de contrôle de l'action financière gouvernementale. Elle participe de ce fait de l'éviction des pouvoirs de contrôle du Parlement en droit interne[66],

b. **La mansuétude du NRFE à l'égard des dépenses parlementaires**

Si l'on en croit Odile TOGOLO, *«A l'observation, la conformité des actes du parlement à la légalité semble être le dernier souci des députés »*[67]. Le NRFE, œuvre du Parlement, permet aux assemblées parlementaires de fonctionner dans l'opacité quand elles agissent comme autorité dépensière. Est-ce là une influence de la LOLF sur le NRFE ? Toujours est-il que : « *si la LOLF permet au parlement (français) de mieux cerner son contrôle sur les dépenses publiques étatiques, les assemblées restent extrêmement opaques quand elles agissent en qualité de pouvoir dépensier* »[68]. À titre illustratif, la gestion des fonds alloués aux microprojets demeure un véritable mystère au Cameroun. Le NRFE ne comporte aucune prescription tendant à un véritable contrôle des fonds alloués aux parlementaires pour les microprojets. Comment expliquer le silence et l'escamotage sibyllins de la question des microprojets parlementaires par le NRFE. Le NRFE a-t-il eu peur de mettre le pied dans la fourmilière ? Ou est-ce simplement une manifestation de l'adage « *La bouche qui mange ne parle pas* » ? Or, des voix s'élèvent de plus en plus au niveau de la presse et des électeurs pour dénoncer l'usage à titre personnel des microprojets par des députés.

---

[65] En matière de configuration du budget, les libéraux soutiennent l'équilibre budgétaire. Pour eux, il est gage de la discipline budgétaire en ce qu'il permet aux personnes publiques d'éviter la gabegie financière et de s'endetter.

[66] O. TOGOLO, « Le contrôle politique des finances publiques au Cameroun », *RASJ*, Vol. 1, N°3, 2003, p. 125- 127, (spéc. p. 125).

[67] *Ibid.*, p. 129.

[68] G.PROTIERE, *Parlement et dépenses publiques*, *op.cit.*, p. 12.

Par ailleurs, les microprojets dont la base légale est douteuse[69] sont frappés d'une double inconstitutionnalité. D'une part, ils participent d'une logique contraire à la séparation des pouvoirs[70]. Ils font intervenir le parlementaire dans une sphère de compétence qui, selon la séparation des pouvoirs, relève du rayon d'action de l'exécutif. D'autre part, la philosophie qui les sous-tend est incompatible avec la Constitution qui interdit le mandat impératif[71]. Derrière les microprojets parlementaires, se profile une logique qui laisse penser que le député représente au Parlement ses électeurs. Or, il y représente la nation camerounaise[72].

B/ Solutions souhaitables pour plus d'efficacité dans le contrôle parlementaire des finances publiques au Cameroun

Pour améliorer l'efficacité dudit contrôle, il faut assortir l'exigence de sincérité de sanctions (1), étendre la marge de manœuvre du Parlement en matière d'annulation des crédits (2), opérer certaines précisions terminologiques (3), la quête du savoir par le Parlement assortie de son érection en évaluateur des politiques publiques (4) et intensifier la collaboration entre le Parlement et d'autres structures du système camerounais de contrôle des finances publiques (5).

1. Assortir l'exigence de sincérité de sanctions

La sincérité est une notion orpheline d'un régime de sanction spécifique [73] en droit public financier camerounais. D'une manière générale, le NRFE ne permet pas au Parlement de déférer de façon systématique à la justice les états financiers non sincères présentés à lui par le Gouvernement. Ce qui limite considérablement la portée du contrôle parlementaire des finances publiques. Seule l'insincérité financière décelée par une commission d'enquête parlementaire peut

---

[69] TOGOLO, « Le contrôle politique des finances publiques au Cameroun », *op.cit.* {*supra*, n° 66), p. 129.
[70] *Ibid., p.* 128.
[71] Art. 15 al. 3, Constitution « *Tout mandat impératif est nul* ».
[72] Voir Art. 15 al. 2, Constitution camerounaise.
[73] Voir A. S. BESSALA, *op.cit.*, p. 252.

donner lieu à des poursuites pénales enclenchées par le Parlement[74]. De même, s'il est vrai que la commission d'enquête parlementaire peut saisir [75] le Conseil de discipline budgétaire et financière (CDBF), il ne peut le faire à l'effet d'y engager la responsabilité disciplinaire (financière) du ministre qui a produit des informations non sincères à la représentation nationale. Le NRFE a consacré l'immunité des ministres sur le plan de la discipline budgétaire et financière. Cette immunité se déduit de la lecture combinée des articles 23 et 25 de ce texte. L'immunité des ministres sur le plan de la discipline budgétaire et financière n'est pas une spécificité camerounaise[76]. Le droit comparé l'illustre parfaitement. Si le législateur n'assortit pas la sincérité budgétaire d'un régime de sanction spécifique, elle demeurera un propos incantatoire sans substance.

Toutefois, l'inexistence d'un régime de sanction spécifique à la sincérité budgétaire n'en fait pas moins une obligation. D'après les naturalistes, il peut exister des règles de droit sans sanctions organisées.

2. Étendre la marge de manœuvre du Parlement en matière d'annulation des crédits

Le Gouvernement est tenu de transmettre au Parlement les décrets d'annulation de crédits à titre d'information uniquement. Pour plus de transparence dans la gestion financière publique, il est souhaitable de réviser le NRFE et d'y prévoir un délai d'examen rapide par le Parlement de la sincérité des annulations de crédits, assorti de la possibilité pour les parlementaires de saisir le juge administratif, en cas de soupçon d'insincérité. Par une telle procédure, l'insincérité entrera, allègrement, dans le bloc des motifs d'illégalité [77] des actes administratifs. Cette procédure pourrait s'appeler le référé administratif parlementaire ou référé budgétaire. Pour que cette procédure ne paralyse pas la continuité du service public, il faudrait assigner au juge administratif un délai raisonnable pour décider, soit huit (08) jours.

---

[74] Voir Art. 71 al. 3, NRFE.

[75] Art. 71 al. 3, NRFE.

[76] C'est aussi le cas en France où les ministres et les autorités locales sont irresponsables devant la Cour de discipline budgétaire et financière.

[77] Il relèvera des motifs d'illégalité de fond.

3. Les nécessités de précision terminologique : cas de la notion de secret- défense

L'ordre public et le secret-défense font partie des notions les plus imprécises du droit public d'inspiration française en vigueur dans les États d'Afrique noire francophone. Le secret est ce qui n'est pas connu, ou qui est connu par un nombre limité de personnes. C'est aussi ce qui est ou doit être caché au public. De ce point de vue, le secret-défense est l'ensemble des connaissances concernant strictement la sécurité de l'État et connues uniquement par des personnes y habilitées. Ces informations ne doivent pas être révélées au public.

Le secret-défense fait échec à toute forme de contrôle. Seulement, pour que cette notion ne soit pas un fourre-tout de nature à mettre hors de portée du contrôle politique ou juridictionnel une part importante de l'activité financière gouvernementale, il serait souhaitable que le législateur ou le juge fixe les critères de ce qui en tient lieu.

4. La quête du savoir par le Parlement, assortie de son érection en évaluateur des politiques publiques

Les finances publiques, par essence, sont réputées complexes. La complexité des finances publiques explique en grande partie le désintérêt des parlementaires à contrôler la gestion financière gouvernementale. Dans un contexte de quête de l'émergence, il est impératif que les parlementaires s'outillent profondément en matière de finances publiques, d'économie et de comptabilité publique. En outre, les parlementaires doivent aller à la quête du nouveau savoir relatif au budget programme. Le budget programme a un vocabulaire spécifique[78] dont la maîtrise est un préalable incontournable pour bien contrôler son exécution.

Une fois que la représentation nationale aura maîtrisé les prérequis relatifs au budget programme, il lui restera de passer du simple contrôleur de régularité à un évaluateur. L'évaluation qui ne doit pas trop

[78] Les termes qui meublent ce vocabulaire sont : efficience, efficacité, économie, résultat, indicateur, objectif, mission, etc.

vite être assimilée au simple contrôle[79], est inséparable du budget programme. Comment le Parlement pourrait-il apprécier la performance du gouvernement dans l'exécution d'un programme, sans au préalable devenir un évaluateur des politiques publiques ?

5. **Intensifier la collaboration entre le Parlement et d'autres structures clés du système camerounais de contrôle des finances publiques**

Il est urgent qu'une collaboration entre le Parlement et le Contrôle supérieur de l'État (CONSUPE) soit engagée. Ainsi, les rapports de mission du CONSUPE pourraient être transmis à la fois au chef de l'État et aux présidents des assemblées parlementaires. L'institution d'une plate-forme d'échange d'informations entre le CONSUPE et le Parlement est souhaitable. Une telle plate-forme permettrait aux parlementaires d'être suffisamment édifiés sur la gestion des membres du gouvernement appelés à subir l'épreuve des questions écrites et orales, et de bien ficeler celles-ci. Il serait aussi important que la commission des finances puisse solliciter en tant que de besoin, à l'occasion de ses travaux, l'expertise de l'Agence de régulation des marchés publics (ARMP), de la Commission nationale anti-corruption (CONAC), des commissaires aux comptes officiant au niveau des sociétés d'État et des inspecteurs d'État du CONSUPE. Une forte collaboration entre le Parlement et les comités locaux de contrôle de l'exécution du Budget d'investissement public (BIP) s'avère aussi nécessaire. Elle favorisera l'émergence d'un contrôle parlementaire plus averti en matière d'exécution des projets sur l'étendue du territoire national. Une collaboration entre le Parlement et le CDBF est aussi souhaitable. Inconnu hier, le CDBF occupe le devant de la scène en raison de certaines décisions qu'il a rendues dans le cadre de l' »Opération Épervier ». La collaboration entre le CDBF et le Parlement permettra des échanges d'informations entre les deux structures.

---

[79] Voir N. MEDE, « L'expérience des budgets de programme au Bénin », *Afrilex* n°4, 2004, p. 76.

CONCLUSION

En définitive, nonobstant la rénovation du contrôle parlementaire des finances publiques par le NRFE, il demeure perfectible à plusieurs égards. La transposition des directives CEMAC[80] sur les finances publiques contribuera à renforcer substantiellement ce contrôle.

[80] Notamment la directive n°06/ll-UEAC-190-CM-22 relative au code de transparence et de bonne gouvernance dans la gestion des finances publiques des États membres de la CEMAC et la directive n°01/11-UEAC-190-CM- 22 relative aux lois de finances. Cette dernière précise que le Gouvernement, avant le 1er août de chaque année, transmet au Parlement des documents financiers. Sur la base de ceux-ci, le Parlement organise un débat d'orientation budgétaire (art.9). Elle prévoit aussi des modalités d'association du Parlement à la préparation du budget, le renforcement de l'assistance du juge des comptes aux parlementaires et l'élargissement de l'information fournie aux parlementaires grâce aux articles 44, 45 et 48(PLFI).

PROTOCOLE DE RÉDACTION DES ARTICLES

L'envoi des articles au Comité éditorial se fait exclusivement par courrier électronique à l'adresse suivante : rasj.soa@gmail.com. La Revue n'endosse aucune responsabilité pour tout article envoyé à une autre adresse.

Le comité éditorial de la revue attache un prix particulier au respect des normes et standards ci-dessous indiqués :

1. La taille des contributions ne doit pas excéder 20 pages au format de la revue pour les articles proprement dits et 15 pages pour toute autre contribution.

2. Tout article soumis pour publication doit être envoyé sous le format Word, interligne simple, police d'écriture Times New Roman, taille de police 12, paragraphe aligné, marges de 2,5 cm.

3. Les articles sont accompagnés d'une biographie succincte de l'auteur, incluant sa qualité (grade, responsabilité académique, ou statut professionnel), son adresse e-mail dans une première note de bas de page, et d'un résumé de dix lignes maximum en français et en anglais avec quatre à six mots-clés.

4. Les citations dans le corps du texte doivent être transcrites entre guillemets doubles, avec le même type et la même taille de la lettre du texte.

5. L'appel de note est continu et se place après le mot ou le groupe de mots auquel il se rapporte, séparé par un espace insécable.

6. Les références bibliographiques des articles sont citées comme suit :

a) Pour les articles des revues : Nom (intégral)et Prénom (initial) de l'auteur, Titre de l'article entre guillemets doubles, *Titre de la revue en italique*, Numéro du volume, Numéro du fascicule, Année de la publication, Pages initiale et finale de l'article ou Page (s) exacte (s) de la citation.

Exemple : LECA J., « Pour une analyse comparative des systèmes politiques méditerranéens », *Revue française de science politique ou RFSP*, vol. 27, n° 4, 1977, p. 557-581.

b) Pour les livres : Nom (intégral) et Prénom (initial) de l'auteur, *Titre du livre en italique,* Lieu de publication, Maison d'édition, Année de publication, Pages initiale et finale de l'article ou Page (s) exacte (s) de la citation.

Exemple : MBAYE K., *Les droits de l'homme en Afrique*, Paris, Pedone, 2002, p. 180.

c) Pour les ouvrages collectifs : Nom (intégral) et Prénom (initial) de l'auteur, Titre de l'article entre guillemets doubles, Mention « in » en italique, Nom du directeur de l'ouvrage, nom de l'ouvrage en italique, Lieu d'édition, Maison d'édition, Année d'édition, Pages initiale et finale de l'article ou Page (s) exacte (s) de la citation.

Exemple : MAZERES J.-A., « Qu'est-ce que la puissance publique ? », *in* Raimbault P. (dir.), *La puissance publique à l'heure européenne*, Paris, Dalloz, 2006, p. 9 à 20.

N.B. Les articles expertisés (selon le principe de *Peer Review)*, retenus et publiés dans la *RASJ* deviennent la propriété de celle-ci. Leur reproduction partielle ou intégrale est soumise à l'autorisation expresse de la direction de la Revue.

PROTOCOL FOR SUBMITTING ARTICLES

Contributions can only be submitted through electronic mailing to the following address : rasj.soa@gmail.com. The editorial board of AJL shall not be liable for any contribution which is not sent to above address. The editorial policy of the Journal requires strict adherence to the following guidelines and standards :

1. Articles must not exceed 20 pages and other contributions (Case Law, Legislation and Bibliographic Surveys) 15 pages.

2. All contributions must be sent in Word format (.doc or .docx), single line spacing, Times New Roman font, size - 12, aligned paragraphs, and margins of 2.5 cm.

3. All contributions must include a brief biography of the author in an opening footnote, their academic or professional status, email address and, for articles, a short abstract written in French and English of not more than 200 words each followed by four to six key words ;

4. Citations in the body of the paper should be in single smart quotes, with the same font as the text but smaller in size (10).

5. Footnoting should be continuous and must appear after the relevant word or group of words, separated by normal spacing.

6. Bibliographic references of articles should be quoted as follows :

a) For articles of a Journal : Author's name and surname, Title of the article in inverted commas, *Title of the Journal in italics*, Volume Number, Fascicle Number, Year of publication, first and last pages of the article or exact page(s) of the quotation.

Example : Flemming P., "The Justiciability of Socio-Economic Rights in Africa", *International Human Rights Law Review* or *IHLR*, vol.vol. 27, n° 4, 1977, pp. 557-581.

b) For books : Author's name and surname, *Title of the book in italics*, Place of publication, Publishing house, Year of publication, First and last pages of the article or Exact page(s) of the quotation.

Example : Raz J., *Authority of the Law*, London, Stevens, 2002, p.180.

c) For collective works : Author's name and surname, Title of the article in inverted commas, *"in"* in italics, Name of the director of the book, *Title of the book in italics*, Place of publication, Publishing house, Year of publication, First and last pages of the article or Exact page(s) of the quotation.

Example : IngelmanJ. "Foreign Direct Investments in Africa ?" *in* Craig P.(Ed.), *Foreign Capital Flows in Developing Countries : Incidence on Development*, Cincinnati, Butterworths, 2006, pp. 9 - 20.

N. B. Articles reviewed (following the Peer Review principle), validated and published by the AJOL become the property of the Journal. Any partial or complete reproduction is subject to the prior authorisation from the Editors of the Journal.

Questions juridiques aux éditions L'Harmattan

Dernières parutions

DIVORCE (LE) DU CHEF D'ENTREPRISE
Artiste, libéral, artisan, commerçant, actionnaire – Se marier, payer, divorcer
Rond Patrice
Patrice Rond, expert financier auprès des tribunaux, donne dans cet ouvrage les clés incontournables qui permettent à un entrepreneur, quel qu'il soit, d'anticiper sur ses droits et ses risques en cas de divorce. Prendre les bonnes décisions de protection de son patrimoine en choisissant les bons contrats de mariage, savoir changer de régime matrimonial quand il s'avère inadapté est tout à fait possible et souhaitable.
(16.50 euros, 158 p.)
ISBN : 978-2-343-05282-3, ISBN EBOOK : 978-2-336-36540-4

L'EXPERTISE NON JUDICIAIRE À L'AUNE DES DROITS FONDAMENTAUX
Goujon-Bethan Thibault
L'expertise déjudiciarisée est en plein essor, d'une part parce que l'avis d'experts se révèle indispensable dans un nombre croissant de matières juridiques irriguées par la technique (construction, dommage corporel), et d'autre part, car la recherche d'une efficacité économique conduit à minimiser le recours au juge. Cet ouvrage est conçu comme un mode d'emploi pour aider à la décision.
(Coll. Droit privé et sciences criminelles, 21.00 euros, 196 p.)
ISBN : 978-2-343-05335-6, ISBN EBOOK : 978-2-336-36778-1

TRANSPARENCE (LA) FINANCIÈRE DES ÉLUS POLITIQUES FRANÇAIS
Les conséquences des mesures législatives de 2013
Cael Céline - Préface de Sébastien Jakubowski ; postface de Pierre-Yves Néron
Cet ouvrage veut étudier les apports des lois et dispositifs mis en œuvre pour lutter contre la corruption depuis l'affaire Cahuzac, avec notamment la mise en place d'une haute Autorité pour la Transparence de la Vie Publique, le durcissement des conditions d'éligibilité, l'encadrement du *lobbying*, la naissance d'un procureur financier,... L'auteur analyse les conséquences de ces mesures et rend compte à l'aide d'entretiens d'élus politiques, des résistances de ces derniers à une publicité financière envers les citoyens.
(Coll. Logiques sociales, 21.00 euros, 214 p.)
ISBN : 978-2-343-05013-3, ISBN EBOOK : 978-2-336-36817-7

QUI A PEUR DE LA NOUVELLE PEINE SANS PRISON ?
Ajouter du «lien» et non du «rang» pour réussir la contrainte pénale et en finir avec la récidive
Delamotte Danielle
La contrainte pénale, nouvelle peine sans prison, fait peur. Car, ce qu'on retient d'elle, c'est qu'elle évite la prison. Le sujet est pourtant plus complexe et plus nuancé. Les psychologues et les criminologues s'accordent à dire que la délinquance est la maladie du lien. Pour soigner cette maladie, il faut s'intéresser à la personne et la placer au centre de la réflexion pour envisager la «contrainte pénale» sous un autre angle.
(11.50 euros, 86 p.)
ISBN : 978-2-343-04717-1, ISBN EBOOK : 978-2-336-36487-2

JUSTICE (LA) PÉNALE INTERNATIONALE EN AFRIQUE
Aspects juridiques, défis et perspectives
Diakité Kémoko - Préface du professeur Alioune Sall
Cet ouvrage met en exergue le contexte de création ainsi que les aspects juridiques et judiciaires des juridictions pénales internationales en Afrique, notamment le TPIR (Tribunal Pénal International pour le Rwanda), la CPI (Cour Pénale Internationale)... Il montre également les défis et les perspectives de la Justice pénale internationale en Afrique.
(23.00 euros, 234 p.)
ISBN : 978-2-343-05050-8, ISBN EBOOK : 978-2-336-36705-7

GOUVERNANCE, ENJEUX ET MONDIALISATION
Recherche sur les politiques environnementales de zonage maritime
Le challenge maritime de la France de Méditerranée et d'Outre-mer
Sous la direction de François Féral et Bernard Salvat
Dans le Pacifique et l'Océan Indien, la France ne participe pas très activement au mouvement de création d'aires marines protégées géantes alors que les possibilités y sont grandes. En métropole et Outre-mer, la mise en place des parcs naturels marins apparaît laborieuse. Le programme Gouvernance des Grandes Aires Marines Protégées a donné l'occasion à deux équipes de se pencher sur ce phénomène institutionnel majeur dans la conduite globale des politiques de protection des mers et des océans.
(23.00 euros, 218 p.)
ISBN : 978-2-343-04160-5, ISBN EBOOK : 978-2-336-36489-6

COLLECTIVITÉS TERRITORIALES ET ORGANISATIONS RÉGIONALES
De l'indifférence à l'interaction
Sous la direction de Danielle Perrot
Cet ouvrage traite des modes d'insertion des collectivités territoriales dans des organisations internationales conçues par leurs États de rattachement dans diverses régions du monde. Ces collectivités, ou «entités infra-étatiques» selon le droit international, sont souvent oubliées lors des débuts de ces constructions régionales. Elles tentent d'obtenir d'être représentées, et leur participation peut générer une interaction moins inégalitaire.
(Coll. Grale, 47.00 euros, 488 p.)
ISBN : 978-2-343-05111-6, ISBN EBOOK : 978-2-336-36639-5

ÉTHIQUE (L') DE L'AVOCAT PÉNALISTE
Rude-Antoine Edwige - Préface de Jean Danet
L'avocat est représenté, dans la fiction, sous les traits d'un être ambigu, sans cesse sur le fil... ce livre tente d'en approcher la réalité, qui est tout autre. Quelles relations d'ordre éthique l'avocat entretient-il avec lui-même mais aussi avec l'autre : son client, qu'il soit prévenu ou accusé, les jurés, les magistrats ? Peut-on parler du rapport de l'avocat à la vérité ? Comment peut-il construire des lignes de défense tout en restant partenaire de justice ?
(Coll. Éthique en contextes, 21.00 euros, 208 p.)
ISBN : 978-2-343-05222-9, ISBN EBOOK : 978-2-336-36460-5

NAISSANCE DE L'OBSERVATOIRE DE LA RÉCIDIVE ET DE LA DÉSISTANCE
Un long processus inachevé
Tournier Pierre V.
L'analyse de la récidive aurait logiquement dû relever de la compétence de l'Observatoire national de la délinquance et des réponses pénales placé sous l'autorité du Premier ministre. Mais sous l'impulsion de Christiane Taubira le choix s'est porté sur la création d'un observatoire *ad hoc* de plus, dépendant du ministère de la Justice : l'Observatoire de la récidive et de la désistance (août 2014). Ne s'est-on pas ainsi privé des outils d'une évaluation indépendante de la loi du 15 août 2014 sur la contrainte pénale et la libération sous contrainte ?
(Coll. Criminologie, 19.00 euros, 184 p.)
ISBN : 978-2-343-05118-5, ISBN EBOOK : 978-2-336-36387-5

ÉLÉMENTS DE PRÉVENTION DU CRIME
Lemaître André
Cet ouvrage montre la diversité des modèles de prévention de la délinquance, leur spécificité mais aussi leur nécessaire complémentarité. Il insiste également sur l'obligation de veiller aux aspects éthiques des politiques de prévention mises en place. En effet, l'utopie d'une société débarrassée de toute forme de criminalité contient la disparition de toute liberté.
(Coll. Sciences criminelles, série Controverses, 15.50 euros, 160 p.)
ISBN : 978-2-343-04666-2, ISBN EBOOK : 978-2-336-36324-0

SEXUALITÉ (LA) À L'ÉPREUVE DU COUPLE
Les révélations d'une avocate
Dalbin Agnès
Dans la majorité des divorces, les difficultés d'ordre sexuel sont souvent pointées du doigt comme une cause majeure de la rupture. S'appuyant sur les confidences recueillies lors de ses entretiens avec les couples qui divorcent, l'avocate Agnès Dalbin tente d'apporter son éclairage personnel sur cette problématique. Ce livre évolue comme une véritable histoire humaine, du mariage au divorce, en passant par la parentalité et l'après-divorce.
(Coll. La justice au quotidien, 13.50 euros, 118 p.)
ISBN : 978-2-343-04938-0, ISBN EBOOK : 978-2-336-36399-8

DROIT (LE) DU HANDICAP ET LA GESTION DU PATRIMOINE CULTUREL
Vers un modèle européen ?
B. Degros Eric
La rencontre entre le droit du handicap et le droit du patrimoine peut conduire à une confrontation d'intérêts contradictoires, nécessitant de trouver un équilibre entre le principe de l'accessibilité et le respect de l'authenticité, en faveur d'une conservation durable du patrimoine culturel. Il apparaît essentiel de trouver un équilibre entre «le droit des gens» et celui «des pierres».
(40.00 euros, 424 p.)
ISBN : 978-2-343-04418-7, ISBN EBOOK : 978-2-336-36269-4

DROIT BANCAIRE ISLAMIQUE
Notions, mécanismes et protections pénales
Jafari Amin
Conçu comme un manuel de droit, l'ouvrage étudie trois thèmes principaux : la notion de finance islamique et son fonctionnement, les instruments bancaires islamiques et enfin la protection du système bancaire dans l'ensemble de ses instruments et fonctionnements. La 3e partie propose un regard classique de droit pénal des affaires en matière de droit bancaire de finance islamique. Les branches chiite et sunnite de la finance islamique ont été distinguées dès le départ, permettant ainsi une comparaison tout au long du livre.
(Coll. Sciences criminelles, 33.00 euros, 326 p.)
ISBN : 978-2-343-04637-2, ISBN EBOOK : 978-2-336-36380-6

DROIT (LE) INTERNATIONAL. ASPECTS POLITIQUES (Volume 1)
Sous la direction de Jacques Bouineau – Textes réunis par Burt Kasparian
Ces contributions invitent à réfléchir sur la recomposition contemporaine de l'espace méditerranéen et sur le droit international qui s'y applique, à partir d'exemples tirés des plus grandes civilisations méditerranéennes aux époques antique et médiévale. Elles invitent le lecteur à s'interroger sur les piliers de la Méditerranée dans le jeu des relations entre les hommes et les institutions, et à découvrir l'essence des réponses juridiques et politiques.
(Coll. Méditerranées, 16.50 euros, 158 p.)
ISBN : 978-2-343-04661-7, ISBN EBOOK : 978-2-336-36366-0

DROIT (LE) INTERNATIONAL. ASPECTS POLITIQUES (Volume 2)
Sous la direction de Jacques Bouineau – Textes réunis par Burt Kasparian
Ce volume offre une réflexion sur la recomposition de l'espace méditerranéen contemporain à partir de l'histoire ou de l'actualité. L'histoire est traitée de la période qui s'étend de la Renaissance

à la fin du XIXe siècle. En ce qui concerne l'actualité, le jeu des emprunts et des modèles juridiques transparaît aussi bien dans la fiscalité internationale actuelle que dans les transpositions constitutionnelles du droit français en Égypte ou dans l'observation du fonctionnement de l'Europe.
(Coll. Méditerranées, 19.00 euros, 184 p.)
ISBN : 978-2-336-30904-0, ISBN EBOOK : 978-2-336-36367-7

SECRETS (LES) DU DROIT
Secret, droit et cinéma
Sous la direction de Stéphane Boiron, Nathalie Goedert et Ninon Maillard
Notre société du visible, pour savoir, exige de tout voir et tout montrer, sans délai, au risque de confondre espaces privés et espaces publics. Parce qu'on l'accusait de dissimuler les abus, de servir l'arbitraire, de diviser les hommes entre initiés et profanes, le secret a été condamné comme contraire au pacte démocratique. Pourtant, c'est aussi au nom de la liberté que, face à une transparence érigée en dogme, certains osent faire l'éloge du secret. C'est pourquoi, il appartient au droit d'orchestrer l'équilibre et de distinguer le bon du mauvais secret.
(Coll. Presses Universitaires de Sceaux, 24.00 euros, 248 p.)
ISBN : 978-2-343-04670-9, ISBN EBOOK : 978-2-336-36326-4

TABLES (LES) DE LA LOI : DE L'ARGILE AU NUMÉRIQUE
La diffusion de la règle de droit à travers les âges
Evrard Sébastien
On parle aujourd'hui de «culture digitale» ou culture numérique et de diminution du papier. Est-ce un bien ou un mal ? Comment les textes, la jurisprudence et toutes les normes juridiques sont-ils diffusés aujourd'hui ? Enfin, quelles sont les spécificités de l'édition dite juridique par rapport à l'édition générale ? Répondre à ces questions nécessite d'envisager l'histoire de la connaissance puis de la diffusion de la règle de droit, ce qui fait l'objet de ce livre.
(Coll. Logiques Juridiques, 13.00 euros, 122 p.)
ISBN : 978-2-343-04478-1, ISBN EBOOK : 978-2-336-36201-4

ARTICULATION (L') DES VOIES DE DROIT DANS LE CONTENTIEUX DE LA COMMANDE PUBLIQUE À L'INITIATIVE DES TIERS AU CONTRAT
Tallet-Preud'homme Laura - Préface de Paul Cassia
Parallèlement à la formation progressive d'un «droit de la commande publique», le contentieux à l'initiative des tiers au contrat a muté, à tel point que le changement de paradigme opéré tend à faire émerger un «contentieux de la commande publique». Diverses voies de droit ont été instituées, engendrant «l'embarras du choix» voire «l'embarras tout court» du tiers concurrent évincé. La complexité de ce contentieux est telle qu'il faut détruire pour reconstruire ce paysage contentieux.
(Coll. Logiques Juridiques, 49.50 euros, 536 p.)
ISBN : 978-2-343-04827-7, ISBN EBOOK : 978-2-336-36265-6

APPRÉHENSION (L') DES PRATIQUES RESTRICTIVES PAR LES AUTORITÉS FRANÇAISES ET EUROPÉENNES DE LA CONCURRENCE
Analyse des pratiques contractuelles abusives entre professionnels à l'épreuve du droit des pratiques anticoncurrentielles
Mallen Guillaume - Préface de Linda Arcelin-Lécuyer
Définies au sens de l'étude comme des comportements contractuels unilatéraux et abusifs dans les rapports commerciaux entre professionnels, les « pratiques restrictives » peuvent être réprimées au titre du droit des pratiques anticoncurrentielles (abus de domination et entente). L'ouvrage permet d'exposer l'office des autorités de concurrence lorsqu'elles sont confrontées à ces pratiques contractuelles abusives et d'envisager des solutions concrètes en vue de perfectionner le droit positif actuel.
(Coll. Logiques Juridiques, 65.00 euros, 874 p.)
ISBN : 978-2-343-04739-3, ISBN EBOOK : 978-2-336-36189-5

L'HARMATTAN ITALIA
Via Degli Artisti 15; 10124 Torino
harmattan.italia@gmail.com

L'HARMATTAN HONGRIE
Könyvesbolt ; Kossuth L. u. 14-16
1053 Budapest

L'HARMATTAN KINSHASA
185, avenue Nyangwe
Commune de Lingwala
Kinshasa, R.D. Congo
(00243) 998697603 ou (00243) 999229662

L'HARMATTAN CONGO
67, av. E. P. Lumumba
Bât. – Congo Pharmacie (Bib. Nat.)
BP2874 Brazzaville
harmattan.congo@yahoo.fr

L'HARMATTAN GUINÉE
Almamya Rue KA 028, en face
du restaurant Le Cèdre
OKB agency BP 3470 Conakry
(00224) 657 20 85 08 / 664 28 91 96
harmattanguinee@yahoo.fr

L'HARMATTAN MALI
Rue 73, Porte 536, Niamakoro,
Cité Unicef, Bamako
Tél. 00 (223) 20205724 / +(223) 76378082
poudiougopaul@yahoo.fr
pp.harmattan@gmail.com

L'HARMATTAN CAMEROUN
BP 11486
Face à la SNI, immeuble Don Bosco
Yaoundé
(00237) 99 76 61 66
harmattancam@yahoo.fr

L'HARMATTAN CÔTE D'IVOIRE
Résidence Karl / cité des arts
Abidjan-Cocody 03 BP 1588 Abidjan 03
(00225) 05 77 87 31
etien_nda@yahoo.fr

L'HARMATTAN BURKINA
Penou Achille Some
Ouagadougou
(+226) 70 26 88 27

L'HARMATTAN SÉNÉGAL
10 VDN en face Mermoz, après le pont de Fann
BP 45034 Dakar Fann
33 825 98 58 / 33 860 9858
senharmattan@gmail.com / senlibraire@gmail.com
www.harmattansenegal.com

L'HARMATTAN BÉNIN
ISOR-BENIN
01 BP 359 COTONOU-RP
Quartier Gbèdjromèdé,
Rue Agbélenco, Lot 1247 I
Tél : 00 229 21 32 53 79
christian_dablaka123@yahoo.fr

Achevé d'imprimer par Corlet Numérique - 14110 Condé-sur-Noireau
N° d'Imprimeur : 124768 - Dépôt légal : décembre 2015 - *Imprimé en France*